The Mastmakers' Daughters

By Jack van Ommen

Translated from the original Dutch version
"De Mastmakersdochters"
by Jack van Ommen

Author: Jack van Ommen
Cover Design: MV LevievanderMeer, Amsterdam
Title ID: 4077181
ISBN-13: 978-1481129275
Copyright © Jack van Ommen 2013
Published January 2013
Revised: August 17th., 2022

1. Preface

Mother told us at times about her growing up above the mastmaker shop in De Lemmer, a small seaport town on the Zuiderzee. She was born in the first year of the twentieth century and passed away in 1993.

Occasionally, the Lemster Courant, the local newspaper, would publish stories she sent in about her years living in De Lemmer. When she was close to eighty, I asked her to write down for us her memories of growing up in De Lemmer. She did.

Her memoirs cover the period from her very first recollections until her marriage in 1933. I have used her writing as much as possible and added details that would not be obvious to readers other than her close relatives. The years from her marriage until her death have been reconstructed from several sources; especially the Second World War years. I could use several short stories she wrote about the years after 1933 and a journal I discovered, scribbled in handwriting and cryptography interpretable only by her most intimates. Another source was our father's diary he kept from the date he was imprisoned, in April '44 up until our mother returned from German captivity. I found answers to many questions but it also generated new ones. I invite your comment if you can help me with additional information on the book's web site: www.TheMastmakersDaughters.us . On the web site are more more links, color photographs relating to the story, that would otherwise have made this print version considerably more expensive. Though this story qualifies as an autobiography and it has been written by Mother in the first person, I have at times let Mother write my own discoveries and imaginations that surrounded her life's story.

In the process of writing this I have come to know Mother better and I have gained an even greater admiration for her. This alone was worth the many hours of research and translation. It is also my hope that my children, grandchildren and great grandchildren in reading the book will come to a greater appreciation of their heritage. More importantly, I wish to fulfill my mother's wishes that more people will come to share the joy and strength she received from her faith in God.

How to read this story:

Part One ends before the start of the Second World War and is the story of Rennie de Vries growing up in De Lemmer. This was a time before the Zuiderzee became a freshwater lake, before electricity, before running water and before women's suffrage.

Because you might become overwhelmed with all the names and dates in the beginning of this story, I have added a graph detailing the relationships of the five mastmakers generations. There is no need to try and remember all the names other than the two Rennies and their parents. Throughout this book, the European sequence for married women names is used: Married Name-Maiden Name. Example: Rennie van Ommen (her husband's family name) –de Vries (her maiden name)

Part Two takes place, for the most part, in the Second World War and can be considered a separate story. It details the tragic and often moving account of how the first Mastmakers' Daughter along with her group of 193 Dutch women managed to survive three German concentration camps. And how ironically, simultaneously, the second Mastmakers' Daughter, also named Rennie de Vries, marched to a completely different drummer under the Nazi swastika.

To avoid confusing the two Rennies I have written the second Mastmakers' Daughter, *Rennie* the Nazi, in *cursive* throughout this book. I have also included parts of Father's diary he wrote during the fourteen months from his imprisonment until Mother's return from captivity.

Like so many survivors, Mother seldom discussed her prison experiences with us.

The story continues being told in the first person the way Rennie van Ommen would have experienced her thirteen months in three concentration camps. The parts, where she bears witness of her Faith and she recounts the religious interactions, come directly from her written accounts. The rest of the story I have reconstructed using parts of her companion prisoners accounts.

One source are the memoirs of Tiny (pronounced Teenee) Boosman. I happened to find her story under the most unusual circumstances. I was crossing the Atlantic Ocean on my sailboat in July of 2009. At that time, I was on my way from the Azores to France. Every evening I checked in on the short-wave radio with Herb Hilgenberger in Toronto to get his weather forecast. One evening a new voice checked in with the group of sailors who were somewhere in the same part of the Atlantic Ocean. He turned out to be a young Dutchman who was returning from Newport, R.I. to Holland. He had participated in the Single Handed OSTAR Race and done well. His name was Bart Boosman. I was intrigued and wanted to know more about him. I talked to him on the short-wave radio and we exchanged e-mail addresses.

We met in Amsterdam in the Six-Harbor, on his return, in late August. He read on my blog that I was planning to attend the 65th anniversary commemoration of the evacuation of all the prisoners from Camp Vught in early September 1944. Bart then sent me an e-mail that his grandmother, Tiny Boosman, had been a part of that evacuation with our mother.

I sent him a picture of a reunion that took place after the war of the survivors of that group of women. His grandmother was in the picture with our mother. Then I received a phone call from his aunt, Bep Boosman, who is of my generation and after the introduction she mentioned that her mother had worked for Henk Dienske.

I had been searching for years for others who might have worked with Mother for Henk Dienske the leader of the regional Resistance organization.

But after all was said and done, it turned out that Tiny Boosman and my mother never had anything to do with each other in their work for Henk Dienske. And it is also most likely that they never found out that they had a leader in common, because that was strictly taboo to discuss even with your most trusted prisoner friends.

I gained access to a wealth of information about the road our mother travelled in those thirteen months, because Tiny Boosman wrote very detailed memoirs of her journey.

Tiny was arrested shortly after our mother and Henk Dienske, together with two other young women Tiny worked with.

Bep Boosman, her older brother Paul, and his wife Ineke, took me to meet one of the last survivors of the women of the concentration camps; Lies Bueninck, she remembered my mother well, she was 99 at that time. Lies passed away at age 100, the last day of 2009.

The other source I have used are the 128 typed pages of Kiky Heinsius[1]. Her story starts in Vught and ends with their liberation by the U.S. Army. Her story is more personal where as Tiny's work gives more details and historical facts. Between the two an excellent picture developed of the road these women travelled.

Part Three is a piece of history that resulted from many hours of research; it gives a clearer picture of the Resistance our mother was involved in. It also sheds more light on the NAZI persecution of the Resistance, the Jews, and the role of the Dutch traitors.

Part Two and Part Three are historical in that they contain a wealth of information about the Resistance group of Henk Dienske and of the, so called, "AGFA Kommando" that has, till now, never been published.

For those readers who are in particular interested in the details on how the Resistance and the German counter forces worked, it might be advisable to read Part Three before Part Two.

---

[1] Kiky Heinsius memoir in possession of her husband P. Gerritsen

Part One: From Cradle till the Second World War

By Rennie van Ommen-de Vries, as told to her son Jack van Ommen

Rennie de Vries at 18 years

2. Twice in my life

Twice in my life when the evening fell the day ended in disappointment.

The first was in 1923. My fiancée, Henk, and I had broken up again, but I missed him very much and I was hoping all day long that he would come back.

The second time was in the late spring of 1944, in prison, I was hoping that I would be released that day, but by 5 o'clock, I knew that nothing more would happen on that day. Days later, when my name was finally called out, it turned out to be for a transfer to the Vught concentration camp.

The days pass by quickly, especially on these dark winter days. When the curtains are drawn here, in the rest home, I ask myself: "Another day gone, what all did I do today?" Honestly, that is not that important to me any longer.

Polderdijk around 1905 The Rien where we worked and lived, last building is the sail loft of M.F. de Vries (no relation)

3. Growing up in De Lemmer

What did we do as children during the day? And in the evenings?

I played with the neighbor girls outside on the Polderdijk[2], or if it got dark early and it was too cold to play outside, I would play with my cousins Rens and Hanna in the shop where the masts were made. The workers had gone home by then; they would leave a lantern burning for us. Rens was one year older and Hanna a year younger. Their parents sailed a large Tjalk, "de Onderneming" ("The Enterprise"), on the European waterways and only occasionally would they have a cargo that brought them home into De Lemmer. My cousins lived next to us above the mastmaker shop with Opoe[3] and my Pa's[4] unmarried sister, Aunt Trijn.

What fun we had playing hide and seek, there were so many hiding places; behind the big band saw, the planer, the rigger's work bench, under the stairs going up to the loft and behind piles of wood. Slabs of wood that had been cut from the butts of mast spars served as our chairs and square pieces that were trimmed from the foot of a mast made our table. And everywhere hung the sweet smell of the pitch from the Pitch Pine[5] that was used to make the masts and spars. Yes, we had the biggest play ground a child could wish for. Life was good on the Polderdijk.

The waterway that runs along the Polderdijk, "The Rien", was at that time a very busy route from the Zuiderzee, via Groningen to the North Sea on the border with Germany. Tjalks, Klippers, Skûtsjes and all sorts of sailing barges passed by and an occasional skipper would moor alongside our quay for a while and we would get to know the children aboard who were still too young to have to stay ashore to go to school. There was something intriguing and mysterious in trying to figure out where these ships came from, their home ports painted on their stern, names we had never heard of and maybe we would never see again.

---

[2] Polder: Reclaimed land below sea level. Dijk: (you guessed it) dike
[3] grandmother
[4] father
[5] Long Leaf Yellow Pine

The Mastmaker shop, photo taken in recent time. Little has changed since Rennie played here over a century ago.

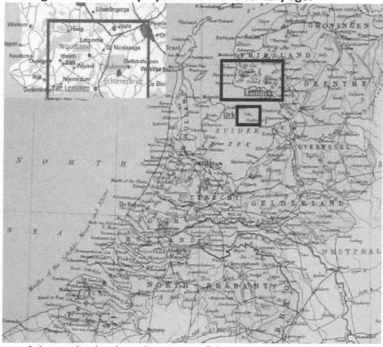

Old map of the Netherlands and an inset of the area where this story takes place

My youngest sister, Rientje[6], put her recollections of the Polderdijk in a poem:

The approximate translation:
"The Polder Dike"

smell of the soil
horses that toil
slip sliding boats
white swans afloat
bare feet on soft moss
and I......oh, I was!

clouds silver lining
milk cans shining
ships slowly sailing
sea gulls loud wailing
surf salting the air
and I.......I was there!

clip clapping clogs
hop scotching frogs
flowering trees
songs of the seas
dreams running wild
and I...... I was child!

De Polderdijk"

geurende aarde
glanzende paarden
wondere slootjes
glijdende bootjes
bloemen in't gras
en ik......o, ik was!

heggen vol mussen
heldere bussen
Zeilende schepen
wolken met strepen
stemmen zo klaar
en ik...... ik was daar!

kleppende klompen
piepende pompen
bloeiende bomen
tijd om te dromen
water en wind
en ik....ik was kind!

---

[6] Rientje van den Boogaard- de Vries

11

Home with adjoining mastmakershop on the Langestreek, then and as photographed in 2010

Polderdijk in 1911 L.R.: Opoe, me, Moe and Pa with Ina on shoulder, blacksmith then M.F. de Vries sailmaker and family, etc.

4. It all began in 1805

Now I will tell you how we ended up here on the Polderdijk. My great-great-grandfather Sybolt Ottes de Vries started as mast and block maker in Woudsend in 1805. Woudsend is situated on one of the Frisian lakes and at that time enjoyed a thriving trade from its fresh water fishing, particularly the export of smoked eel to England. Jan Sybolts de Vries, the second oldest son of Sybolt Ottes, my great grandfather, saw a better future in the saltwater port of De Lemmer, on the Zuiderzee. He purchased an existing mastmaker shop on the Korte Streek in 1840. Jan Sybolts married Gerbrigje Jentjes Tromp in 1842.

Gerbrigje grew up on a large farm in Woudsend and missed her garden where they lived on the Lijnbaan (Ropewalk). Her father, a well to do farmer, related to the ship building and trading ships owners, the Tromp family in adjoining Ypecolsga, wanted to please the young family and bought for them a larger shop with adjoining home on the Lange Streek in 1847. Gerbrigje got her patch of ground behind the home where she could garden to her heart's desire.

My grandfather, Siebold Jan de Vries, third generation, born in 1843 took over the business and until this date the company name still carries his initials, S.J. in the company name. His younger brother Jentje Michiel chose to take over his grandfather's farm in Woudsend, which his mother Gerbrigje inherited as their only child. My grandfather married Rinsje Tjeerd Ages in 1867. My father, Jan Siebold, was born in 1876, their first son after two daughters. His brother Jentje was next in line and then two more sisters.

The modest home on the Lange Streek was starting to become a bit crowded

5. Drafted to fight for Napoleon

Napoleon invaded Holland in the winter of 1795-1796 and added the Netherlands to his empire. One of many changes the French instituted was the requirement for everyone to be registered and to have a surname. Sybolt Ottes was the first to use the name **de Vries**, which he registered in the town hall of Woudsend on December 18, 1811.

My Aunt Gepke, wrote about Sybolt Ottes, who was born in 1769 and married in 1805:

"Their marriage was blessed with ten children, but after the fourth child was born Sybolt Ottes was conscripted to fight with Napoleon, to everyone's regret, but when this expedition was over, he returned safely after having endured many hardships".

Their fourth child, Poite, was born in 1811 and it is most likely that Sybolt Ottes de Vries was part of the 25,000 Dutch troops that were drafted to fight the Russians in the ill-fated expedition to Moscow in 1812. Only ten percent of Napoleon's 600,000 soldiers returned from this battle.

More than one million people died in total including those casualties of the "Grande Armée". Most of these soldiers and civilians alike died not only in the fighting, but also from starvation, exhaustion, and the sub-freezing cold of the 1812-1813 Winter. Typhus killed more of Napoleon's troops than those who died at the hands of Russian defenders.

Gepke also wrote about the military accomplishments of Sybolt Ottes' son, my great grandfather, Jan Sybolts de Vries: "….and he also was drafted in the war with Belgium. He was garrisoned in Waalwijk from where he returned safely after earning the Antwerp Citadel Medal. The Dutch regent, Willem van Oranje Nassau, who had returned from exile in England, after Napoleon had been defeated at Waterloo in 1815 and banned to St. Helena, declared himself King William the First of the Netherlands as well as Belgium and Luxemburg. In 1830 the Belgians, demanded their independence, which prompted the Dutch king to march his troops against his southern subjects who had challenged the Dutch from their fortified position in the Citadel of Antwerp.

The Belgians, who had received the help of French and British forces, defeated the Dutch.

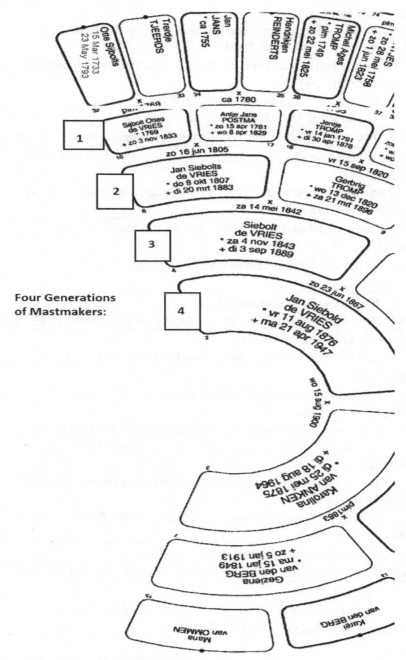

Four Generations of Mastmakers:

Family tree from early 18th century

15

3rd Generation: Siebold de Vries 1843-1889 Married 1867 with Rinsje Tjeerds Ages 1843-1925

4th Generation: Gerbrigje (Gepke) de Vries 1868-1948 + 1893 with Age Tjalma 1863-1919

Jansje (Jantje) de Vries 1870-1956 + 1897 with Reinder van der Meer 1868-1943

Hantjen (Hanna) de Vries 1872-1887

Jan de Vries 1874-1874

The parents of the two Mastmakers' Daughters:

1) **Jan Siebold de Vries** 1876-1947 + 1900 met Karolien van Anken 1875-1964
2) **Jentje Siebold de Vries** 1878-1954 + Gerarda Hermina (Grada) Boot 1879-1951

Dirkje (Dukke) de Vries 1880-1934 + Hermanus Marius (Manus) Boot 1881-1938

Trijn de Vries 1884-1964

5th Generation:

Mastmakers' Daughters #1:

Rinsje (Rennie) de Vries 1901-1993 + 1933 Dick van Ommen 1898-1956

Her brothers and sisters:

Jan Siebold de Vries 1903-1980 + 1927-Hinke Visser 1902-1993

Gezina Jantina (Ina) de Vries 1905-1950 + 1931 Jan Hartkamp 1907-1984

Siebold de Vries 1908-1998 + 1932 Saakje Schirm 1906-1985

Maria (Mieke) de Vries 1911-2002 + 1948 Jan Buddingh 1912-1969

Jentje (Jan) de Vries 1912-1998 + 1940 Rika Johanna (Riek) de Rijk 1915-2005

Rientje Carolina de Vries 1915-2005 + Willem (Wim) van den Boogaard 1913-2007

Mastmakers' Daughters #2:

Rinsje (*Rennie*) de Vries 1904-1990 + 1927 August Arendt 1898-????

Her sister:

Adriana Anna (Adri) de Vries 1908-1943 + 1938 Cornelis (Kees) Bakker 1913- 1942

6. Iceskating

I never knew my grandfather Siebolt Jans de Vries. He passed away at the age of 45 in 1889 from complications sustained in a long battle with pneumonia. He was on his way at the end of the winter that year on ice skates. He was pushing a sled with a load of rigging blocks for the shipyard of Jan Jans Bos in Echternebrug, about ten miles from De Lemmer. He had smooth skating on the Rien where the water is shallow and the ice was strong enough, but when he had to cross the deeper shipping channel on the Tjeukemeer Lake, the ice started to crack, and he broke through the ice. He managed to hold on to the large wooden sled which gave him enough flotation to climb back on the ice. He had to leave the sled and its valuable cargo of the blocks behind. He skated home soaked to the bone. Opoe[7] helped her shivering husband out of his frozen clothes. His oldest daughter, my Aunt Gepke, had already started to bring up the heat on the peat fire in the wood stove. And with the aid of a couple of shots of brandy the mastmaker started to get some feeling back. But he developed a fever during the night and his temperature did not come down for the next several days. At times, he was in delirium. Opoe sent Pa[8] for the doctor, who already had heard what had happened. He diagnosed that Pake[9] had developed pneumonia. After a couple weeks, he felt better but he never completely recovered and five months later he passed away.

On his death-bed he motioned Opoe to his side and told her: "jow my nou mar in tútsje" (Frisian for "Come and give me a kiss now").

But this sad ending has never heldd us back from getting on our skates. When it started to get dark after a day of ice skating on the river and canals, you'd see the towns' people flock on the ice with kettles of boiling water to pour on the cracks in the ice so that the skating fun could resume the next day.

---

[7] Grandmother
[8] Father
[9] Grandfather

17

My great-uncle, Jentje Michiel de Vries, the farmer in Ypecolsga, once told the story that Moe[10] suggested to Pa that she'd like to visit the family in Ypecolsga. In his words, because Pa only spoke Dutch with Moe, he replied: "Sawn sturen mei 't boatsje en in heal pon allerhande, nee we dogge it mar net" (translated from Frisian: "Seven nickels for the boat fare and a half pound of *allerhande*[11]", no we'd better not do that.) They waited until the canals and lakes were frozen over and made their way on skates to their family in Ypecolsga.

My father's second oldest sister, Jantje, was a very competitive skater. She won the national championship, one year, on the 460-foot short track. Her mother-in-law, Antje Siebes van der Meer- Visser won the very first skating competition for women, organized by the "IJsvereniging Lemmer" in 1871.

Opoe sold ice skates in our chandlery[12]. On December 15, 1899, she purchased 50 pairs of skates for 1.60 guilders per pair from Sybolt Okkes de Vries in IJlst. S.O. de Vries was my grandfather's cousin whose father had started a mast and block making business in IJlst.

In 1947 at age 71, Moe skated from Amsterdam to Ouderkerk on the Amstel River and back, about twelve miles. My brother Siebold and his oldest son Jan helped her on each end of a flagpole with Moe in the middle.

My oldest brother, Jan, completed six "Eleven Cities Tours" (Elf Steden Tochten). This 200 km/122 miles tour is the most coveted accomplishment for a Dutch skater. In my younger years, it was held nearly every winter but the winters have turned much milder and it has only been held fifteen times since its inception in 1909.

---

[10] Mother

[11] *allerhande* literally means "something of everything". This was the name given to an assortment of cookies from the better bakeries.

[12] Chandlery: store for nautical gear

18

7. Opoe lets the wood chips fly

Did my grandfather have a premonition of his early death?

He had paid a visit to notary Frans Schaafsma less than a year before his skating accident. The two men knew each other well judging from the mastmaker's ledger where Schaafsma had an outstanding personal loan of 1000 guilder. This was not the reason for his visit. Pake came to have his last will and testament drawn up.

He arranged that his wife, Gerbrigje, would enjoy the earnings of his estate for the rest of her life unless she remarried. The children were to have their shares of his estate but she would retain the earnings until her death. Opoe Rinsje had her will drawn up on the same day in Schaafsma's office. Pake died on September 3rd, 1889 and was buried three days later. The costs for the funerals are recorded as 110 guilders. The widow was left with six children, all minors.

She did not waste any time arranging for the transition into her new role as single mother and owner of a thriving chandlery, mast and block making business. A woman in those years still had very few privileges. Women's suffrage did not become a reality in the Netherlands until 1922; the year when I turned twenty-one.

The first item on her agenda was to find a guardian for the children. She appointed Jan Jans Bos, the shipbuilder in Echternerbrug, the destination for the ill-fated delivery on skates, on October 24. Jan Bos was a very good customer of the mastmaker. Bos was known far and wide for building fast sailing ships. He built at least 21 skûtsjes between 1895 and 1910 of which several are still winning the annual Sneek Week regatta prize. Bos was the very first boat builder to build iron sailing barges, as well as the traditional wood construction. His Lemster Aaks[13] were known for their excellent performance under sail. His daughter Trijntje van der Veer-Bos was the mother in law of my cousin Wiebren Tjalma.

The young widow called for the notary Schaafsma once more, on November 21.

---

[13] Lemster Aak, was a common design for the Zuiderzee fishing boats. Similar to a Botter.

In the presence of guardian, Jan Jans Bos, expert local gold and silversmith, Nicolaas Koopmans de Jong, and two more witnesses, she listed the value of her estate.

Everything was painstakingly recorded in an impressive handwritten document.

When I had a chance to read this document there were a few items that gave me some insight in the man my grandfather must have been. First it showed that Jan Bos, the guardian, owed the mastmaker the most money; nearly 60% of the outstanding loans; 11,000 guilders, a small fortune in those days. There was also a debt of 775 guilders from a Rentske Aantjes Post and another three widows in Moddergat with a 4% rate of interest. The books also showed similar outstanding collections on the island of Urk. All together these added up to 1,950 guilders. Opoe reclassified these as doubtful receivables.

Six years prior, on March 6th, the fishing fleet out of Moddergat[14] was caught in a violent storm with wind force nine to ten (40/55 mile an hour) on the Wadden Zee near the island of Borkum. Seven of the twenty-two ships fleet sunk and 83 fishermen drowned.

The rest of the Dutch fishing fleet also suffered heavy losses that day, 121 fishermen, Including the 83 from Moddergat lost their lives and left 80 widows and 200 minor children behind. It looks as if Pake converted the debts into low interest-bearing loans and Opoe subsequently wrote them off.

Pa was only thirteen years old when Pake died. His two older sisters were a big help to their mother.

Gerbrigje[15], who now preferred to be called Gepke, the oldest, was twenty-one. She got married two years later. Then it was Jante, her sister's, turn who was 21 when Gepke left home. Pa finished grade school a year before his father died and was then put to work in the mastmaker shop. One of my aunts told me once that the shop foreman proposed to the 46-year old widow.

---

[14] Moddergat, literally Mud Hole, is a small fishing community on the very far north shore of Friesland, on the Waddenzee.

[15] Gerbrigje/Gepke, in case you have lost the thread, was my aunt who wrote about the Napoleon period.

That was good thinking on his part to try to get on board a thriving business, but Opoe would not have any of it. She gave him his wages and showed him the door to the Lange Streek.

Before the crocuses had stopped blooming on the grave of her mother-in-law, who passed away in March of 1896, my Opoe was once again in the office of the notary. Her brother-in-law, Jentje Michiel the farmer and the only other heir, was also present to witness the appraisals of the estate of her mother-in-law, Gerbrigje Jentje de Vries.

Jantje, Pa's second oldest sister married in 1897 with Reinder van der Meer, a barge skipper, and moved aboard the "de Onderneming". This opened up a little more room in the cramped quarters on the Lange Streek. Dirkje (later called Dukke) took over the task from Jantje in assisting Opoe. Dirkje was then seventeen and Pa was twenty-one.

In the eight years since Pake died, Pa had taken a crash course to assist his mother, and to eventually take the reigns over from her. He was frequently out of town to visit customers and suppliers.

The fishermen on the island of Urk were an important part of the mastmaker's customers. There were no mast or block makers on the small island, and in 1900 the Urker fishing fleet counted 119 botters alone. The Urker fishermen were accustomed to buying on credit and paying their bills when their catch was sold. The only time Pa could find them in port was between their arrival on Saturdays and departure on Monday mornings. The catch on the botters could be kept alive in large holding tanks, called "buns". These tanks were open to the sea with holes through the hull below the water line. The catch was usually sold to fast sailing fish buying vessels out at sea who resold it in the larger metropolitan areas such as Amsterdam.

On their return to Urk, on Saturday, the wives and mothers of the fishermen would peel off their baggy costumes and many layers of flannel then scrub them down in the wooden tubs filled with hot water heated on the wood stoves.

There were no hotels then on the island. Pa had a room in a kind of bed and breakfast with "Marretje of Willem of Wouter". Sunday mornings, Pa went to church not only to have his debts forgiven but also to collect the debts the Urkers owed him.

He was easily noticed in church because of his striking red hair, and because he was one of the few not wearing the traditional Urker costume.

If there happened to be a special collection that day, or if it was announced for a later date, then Pa would be second in line because the debts to the Lord always had priority over the mastmakers bills. On one of those trips to Urk, four years before the turn of the century, Pa's eye was caught by one of the lovely daughters of the Reformed Pastor on Urk.

Marretje (of Willem of Wouter), his hostess, could not help but see him staring through the curtains and encouraged him in the island's dialect with:*"Ja die Karolien, da's een goeien iene"*. (Yes, this Karolien, she's a good one). And that's what started it all. It was the best catch Pa ever made.

Occasionally, when there had been an exceptionally good catch, Pa would come home with a sack of money and a stack of new orders for the shop. The anchovy season ran from May until July and could be very lucrative depending on the strength of the run and the prices paid. Many a fisherman, in a good season, could afford to trade in his botter for a new one and have money left over to buy a new home.

Jan Jans Bos, the shipbuilder from Echternerbrug and guardian for the minors in the de Vries clan, also made the same journey to Urk, in order to receive payment for the botters he had built for the Urkers. Bos sailed to Urk on his own sailing yacht, and Pa used to catch a ride with him, instead of taking the twice-weekly sailing service from Lemmer to Urk.

However, Bos was not a churchgoing man. One Monday morning, when the pious Urkers considered his methods of bill collecting a bit too bold, a few of his customers carried him by his arms and legs to the edge of the West Harbor and threatened to dump him in.

Opoe purchased an English Pilot Cutter in 1906 from Jan Oost[16] in Enkhuizen. From then on, the "Top" became Pa's preferred mode of travel to Urk. She was also used to make deliveries to destinations for which there was no commercial delivery service available by water. Our rigger, Huite Zijlstra, as skipper, together with another helper in the shop would crew the company flagship. Huite had made many trips on "Paling Aken" (The sailing ship that transported smoked eel from the smoke houses on the Frisian lakes and seaports) to London. On one of these trips, Huite had an anchor tattooed on his hand.

Pa was not a very good sailor. When my sister in law, Hinke, once told me this, I was taken aback. But I also knew she was right. She came from a commercial barge skipper's family, and she knew the difference. Pa was always so happy being on the water.

I can still picture him there with a white sailor's cap (he burnt easily with his red hair and fair complexion) a pipe between his teeth and a big smile on his face with his hand on the helm. I remember sailing trips to Urk and Kampen to visit family. I never learned to swim and did not share the love of sailing that Pa and my siblings had. When I was fourteen years old, I was aboard "Top" when we ran into a bad storm. The experience stayed with me for the rest of my life.

Opoe was not very pleased with her oldest son's choice for several reasons. First of all, preachers' daughters did not bring any money into the family and secondly, because her son switched from the Dutch Reformed to the Reformed Church, his wife's affiliation. She would have preferred a daughter-in-law from a farmer or a merchant family who would have brought some money with her.

Opoe and Pa decided to branch out with the opening of another mast and block making shop in Heeg on a busy shipping route about twenty miles north west of De Lemmer. She purchased the existing business from Dirk Molenaar in March 1900.

---

[16] Jan Jan Oost (1866) his mother was Hielkje Harmens de Boer (1844), a Lemster. He married Jannetje Post from Urk

My parents were married on Urk August 15, 1900

1) Jan Siebold de Vries 2) Karolina de Vries-van Anken

3) Rinsje de Vries-Ages (Opoe, groom's mother)

4) Gezina van Anken- van den Berg 5) Jan Fokkes van
Anken, bride's parents

6) Jantje van de Meer-de Vries with daughter Rinsje

7) Reinder van der Meer

8) Jentje de Vries

9) Grada deVries- Boot (parents of *Rennie* and Adri de Vries)

10) Maria Sijbesma-van Anken with Gezina 13/03/1900 13)
Jan Sijbesma

11) Dirkje (Dukke) de Vries 12) Karel van Anken

14) Age Tjalma? 15) Gerbrige (Gepke) Tjalma- de Vries?

16) Fokke van Anken 17) ? and 18) ?

19) Jan van Anken 20) Rientje van Anken?

21) Trijntje (Tine) van Anken

22) Trijntje de Vries

8. Born in Heeg

My parents moved into the house with the mastmaker shop in Heeg right after their marriage. I was born there on August 30, 1901, a Friday evening. My grandmother Gezina van Anken was with us to help her daughter and she had quietly hoped that I would be named after her. But on Monday evening, when Pa returned from De Lemmer, Moe was told that I had been registered in Sneek as Rinsje, on the specific directions of Pa's mother.

Pa's older sister had named her second daughter Rinsje a year earlier and the first born of Pa's brother obediently followed the strong-willed grandmother's directions. My three aunts did not have daughters. None of her grandchildren named their daughters after Rinsje but there are lots of Siebolds and Jans among my siblings' sons and grandsons.

That same Monday after I was born my parents received a notice from the Reformed Church in Heeg demanding an explanation why I had not been baptized the Sunday before. Pa explained that he had promised his wife that she'd be present at the christening, whereupon he was told that Moe was not allowed to respond to the question as to the responsibilities of the parents.

My parents reluctantly went along with this. But shortly afterwards their doctor, de Wit, forced the issue before the church commission when his wife was due to have her baby. As a result, they relented this local abuse.

At the same time, when I was being christened, there was a baby whose father was committed to a mental institution and in order to prevent Moe from opening her mouth, when she might feel prompted, they rephrased the question for the parents: "And what is the answer from the one who is holding the child for baptism?" In any event, Moe has never neglected her obligations to raise us as Christians. Her way of teaching us religion was in singing her repertoire of hymns and psalms.

We did not stay in Heeg for more than a couple years. The three of us moved back to De Lemmer in 1902. A new manager took over, Jelle Rijpkema. Later when I was a young girl I stayed at their house on several occasions. Moe told me once that during the winter of 1901-1902 she and Pa skated to Lemmer and back.

On the way home, it had already turned dark and in several spots on the Brekken, a long narrow lake, the ice would suddenly crack with a loud noise in the still of the cold winter's night. It was during the week before Saint Nicholas and Moe splurged and brought back a Marzipan letter for 35 cents.

Our first home, back in De Lemmer, was on the market above the chandlery shop. My brother Jan was born in this house on the first day of 1903.

The story is told that in the summer, Pa was called down stairs to help a customer. He had just poured himself a beer and had put it in the middle of the table. When he came back upstairs the glass was empty. Now, I can't remember any of this but apparently, I managed to pull the tablecloth far enough to get within reach of the glass....

We did not stay here very long either because I can remember that Pop, our maid, started work on the Polderdijk before Ina was born and that was in 1905. Pop said: "What do you want me to do, Madam?" and Moe answered: "Why don't you first of all shine the children's shoes". We liked her right away, because she'd bring us the cookie that the baker gave her when she bought our bread there. Popkje was with us for five years. For us children, that was quite a long time. She also deserves some of the credit for raising us.

The Polderdijk around 1920   credit Lammert Sloothaak

9. The Polderdijk

Now I will describe to you what our home and the business on the Polderdijk looked like. The business and different parts of Opoe's clan moved in stages from the Lange Streek to the Polderdijk. The mast and block-making activities first moved into an existing building on the Polderdijk. The chandlery remained where we lived on the Markt and was run from there.

The new location had a large shop on the ground floor, and the living quarters were above it with windows facing the dike. Above the living quarters, there was a large attic with one larger dormer offering a view over the Zuiderzee. Next, Opoe contracted to build an adjoining structure, also with our living quarters above it and a similar attic and large dormer, where we had our bedrooms. Next to our addition, she had a blacksmith shop built. Both were finished in early 1904. The four of us and the whole chandlery were moved from the Markt to the Polderdijk.

The next page shows the picture of the two different structures and the blacksmith shop. From left to right, first the door to the stairs to the living area on the second floor, next a window into the mast shop, then a double door, these were always open during the working hours, unless it was unusually cold. The floor of the shop was covered with old ships wooden leeboards. Next was another window, this is where Huite Zijlstra had his rigger's workbench.

Then the addition had two display windows for the chandlery, a door and then the door for the stairs to the second floor of our living area. The blacksmith shop next to us was below the street level of the dike, whereas the chandlery floor was even with the street surface. The properties were pie shaped due to the curve in the Rien, the waterway on which our properties faced.

Our neighbor, Marten Folkert de Vries, the sailmaker, had built his rooms and even the bedsteads[17] as parallelograms to accommodate the odd dimensions.

---

[17] Bedstead for Dutch "Bedstede or Bedstee" were common in this period. They are a kind of closet set in the walls of a living room or kitchen. With single or double beds. Their doors were closed at night.

Young children often slept at the foot of their parent's bed. And a baby was kept in their crib on a shelf above the parents inside the bedstead. Bedrooms were usually only found in homes of the wealthy.

Photo taken around 1915. A new mast is stepped on an Urker Botter. Pa, with his hands on his hips at the mast step. The Urker fisherman forward with his black lambskin hat.

Pa was surprised to discover that the neighbor children grew up straight after all. Sailmakers, unlike a mastmaker, are quite used to working with parallelograms. We loved to watch the fires and the clouds of sparks in the blacksmith shop, on a cold winter's late afternoon, after dark had set in. There were three separate fires in the black smith shop; a brown film of rust floated always on the water in the cooling basins. Occasionally the workers would let us pull the bellows. The foreman had his anvil in the front of the shop. We only forged for our own use.

My clearest memory is when the iron hoops were forged for the masts. When they were still red hot they would be quickly carried with a pair of long tongs, next door, to the mastmaker to be pushed down from the top of the mast to where the stays would be attached to support the mast.

They would push them as far as possible and then two workers, with sledge hammers, would hammer it further in place down the taper of the mast. Next, they would pour a bucket of cold water over the ring; shrinking it in place with a cloud of steam and a loud hissing sound. No need for fasteners, those rings would never budge. The iron hooks on the boat hooks were also made in the blacksmith shop.

Nowadays that is all mass produced. How did the other mastmaker further down the road manage without a blacksmith shop? I'll have to ask my brother Siebold.

There are still so many questions I would have liked to ask my parents, my oldest brother or my cousin Piet (Wybren) Tjalma who was older and knew much more about our family, just like his mother Gepke.

Along the west side of the chandlery stood a long counter and beside it along the wall were shelves on which everything a skipper would ever need was set out. All along the east wall were at least 100 deep wooden drawers with labels or a sample of the contents on the front of each drawer. All sizes and types of fasteners, hardware, turnbuckles, thimbles, oar locks, and you name it also special hardware used by the fishermen. The store stocked every kind of paint and lacquer and all the ingredients and pigments to make paint with, such as yellow ochre, linseed oil, turpentine, zinc white, colcothar, magenta and so on. Wood preservatives, Stockholm Tar[18], etc., all had their distinctive smells that gave the store its distinctive atmosphere.

Many of the commonly used boat hardware items are known by peculiar names: frogs for cleats, cat's head for a particular block, grape for the knob on the end of a boat hook. The hoop or ring around the top of the mast, I wrote about earlier, is called a "krans" which translates to wreath.

The yearly inventory was done on New Year's Eve. One time after our bookkeeper, Siebren Lighthart, had been carefully recording the items on his clipboard, Pa felt like testing his sense of humor, when he called out to Siebren: "One box of pig nose rings". Lighthart hesitated for a moment, he then wrote it on the inventory as Pa had called it out but entered the value as $f.$ 0.00.

---

[18] Pine resin used as a preservative on cordage and in the shipyards as a wood preservative.

10. Early childhood memories

The very first memory I have is of my second birthday. Now don't tell me: "That's impossible" for a two-year old. But I have proof of it and that's why there is no doubt in my mind. That is when I received a doll from my aunts on the island of Urk a doll they had dressed in the traditional colorful Urker costume.

My Urker doll

To prove that I did remember this, I told Moe years later: "I still remember how the doll was packaged, it came in a long, tall box with a wire handle through a wooden tube". Moe replied: "That is possible, that would have been a box in which Opa[19] received his Gouda clay pipes". I can recall Pa smoking his white clay Gouda pipes.

---

[19] Grandfather

One Sunday morning before church, Pa was dressed in his Sunday suit, when Pa took a brand-new Gouda pipe and put a finger over the mouth end of the long shaft then poured the leftover tea from the pot into the bowl of the pipe and walked with the pipe over to the potted flowers on the window sill. Then he released his finger from the mouthpiece and a nice thin stream poured into the flowerpots. This was a way of seasoning the clay. I was not quite three years old yet when this took place in the home above the chandlery on the Markt because we were already living on the Polderdijk in early 1904. We inherited Opa van Anken's pipe stand. It was a round mahogany bowl with a tall stand in the center with egg shaped holes from which the pipes were hung.

When the church elders would meet at my grandfather's parsonage, they would each have a spot in the rack for their pipes so they would not need to carry these fragile objects home with them. Their names were written on the pipes' bowls. Occasionally, we accidentally bumped into Pa while he was smoking his clay pipe, while we were roughhousing with each other, and he dropped the pipe. Of course, this did not go unpunished but we got to use the stem pieces to blow soap bubbles.

Moe told us how in the parsonage. Instead of receiving their compensation in cash, Pastors were often paid in kind from the farmers or fishermen. When Opa led a congregation on the main land he would receive a butchered pig in the fall. The pig was then displayed, hung on a ladder, and the entire church council with their respective spouses would accompany the Pastor to inspect the gift. This called for coffee and pastry and, for the men of course, a shot of brandy. The drawback to this custom was that when a Pastor did not make the grade with the donors, he would have to support his family on just his meager stipend. Likewise, farmers who were able to, could offer the fruits of their harvest to the church tended to want to swing their weight around in the church council. On Urk, instead of a whole pig, the donation was made in fish. And a generation later, my brother -in-law Jan Hartkamp, received cheese from his congregation in Alphen a/d Rijn. Later when the Hartkamp family had moved to Den Helder, a sea port, there was a standing arrangement between the church council and a fish wholesaler for a weekly meal of fish to feed their family of nine.

Jan and I were sitting on the kitchen table. We each had a pencil and a sheet of paper and were busy drawing. I can still see his chicken scratches.

31

"De Onderneming" Pavilion Tjalk built in 1897 for my Uncle Reinder van der Meer. Now used for passenger charters, home port De Lemmer. Picture: www.zeilonderneming.nl

Pa and Ma had visitors, up front in the living room, Oate[20] and Pake van der Meer, the grandparents of my cousins Jantje and Rinsje van der Meer who were boarding next door with Opoe and Aunt Trijn. All of a sudden my three year old brother announced: "I am going swimming!" He dove off the table and broke his arm. The doctor came and put a splint on his arm but he thought it might be advisable for my brother to be checked out in a hospital in Amsterdam.

Our Uncle Jentje accompanied the swimmer to Amsterdam. Pa could not leave the house because Moe was due any day and Ina was born only days later on July 15, 1905. Pa went to get Jan from the Burger Hospital but the little guy did not want to get into the tram. He was deadly afraid it would take him to another hospital. Therefore, they walked all the way from the Linnaeusstraat to the Prins Hendrikkade, about three miles from where the overnight ferryboat to De Lemmer departed. It was just before sunrise when they arrived back in De Lemmer; it was a warm summer morning and the bedroom window was open.

---

[20] Oate= grandmother in local Lemster (Frisian) dialect. Frisian for grandmother is Beppe

Before Jan passed Freeke's house, nearly a block away, we could hear his excited call: "Mom, I'm home again!" I slept in the bedroom with Pa and Moe. Jan showed the treasures he had brought back in a cardboard box; gifts that the nurses had given him. His brothers and sisters making fun of his swimming adventure, teased Jan, for many years. There was little I could have done to keep him from drowning because I never learned to swim.

Two Siebolds have been born in our home. The first was born in 1907; he died four months later of pneumonia. It was on Saint Nicholas Eve. He lay in the cradle, lined with red satin and lace sash. The cradle stood in the parlor when Pa took Jan and me to show us our brother. We stayed with Aunt Dukke and Uncle Manus, next door, till after the funeral.

When the doctor made house calls on the Polderdijk Moe would always have a basin with water and a clean towel ready for him so that he could wash his hands afterward. Running water was still years away. I thought that this was chic: "My mother comes from a good upbringing". We probably felt ourselves to be a little better than the average family around us. This had, in part, to do with the fact that Opa was a preacher and that in our home Dutch was spoken, instead of Frisian.

But I do not think that Moe was a snob. In fact, she had not aspired to end up between the four walls of a parsonage. Her oldest sister had married a preacher. I never figured out if this had to do with her fear of living in a parsonage's fish bowl or if she was afraid of the poverty that came with the call to serve the Lord.

At any rate my parents had a very good marriage. When I grew older, I sometimes wondered about the reason why Pa would always get a larger piece of meat than the rest of us. It was not egotism; it was just the custom in those days. But if we happened to have to scrimp a bit you had to make sure that the maid did get enough. Otherwise this could quickly hurt our good name around town.

August 28 1902. Wedding Wouter Boot (1) with Wilhelmina van Geer (2). Gerarda (Grada) Boot (3), sister of the groom, married on 20 Aug 1903 with my Uncle Jentje de Vries (4), Dirkje (Dukke) de Vries (5) married on 12 Jan 1904 with Manus Boot (6) brother of the groom, Adriana Anna Boot-Kop 7) mother of the groom, Izaak van Geer (8) father of bride, Johanna van Geer-van den Boon (9) Gerrigje Kop- van Wijk (11) aunt of the groom, Hermanus Kop (12) uncle of the groom. Number (10) looks like a de Vries, possibly Trijntje. Compare this photo with the earlier one of my parents wedding in 1900, you'll see some of the same guests in the same outfits.

11. The mastmaker goes multinational

My Uncle Jentje married Grada Boot on August 20th, 1903. They had moved in above the mastmaker shop on the Polderdijk just before the four us moved in next door. Grada Boot was the sister of Wouter Adrianus Boot, a ship builder in Woubrugge, which is near Gouda in the central western part of Holland. There were a couple striking similarities in the families of the bride and the groom. Both their mothers had lost their husbands prematurely in work related accidents and both widows decided to run the businesses until their oldest sons were ready to take over. Grada's father drowned in 1897 at age 43, together with his foreman, in a shipyard accident. Their oldest son, Wouter Adrianus was nineteen and had to quit his studies at the Polytechnic School in Delft, to assist his mother.

The two widows did business with each other and this is how my uncle met Aunt Grada. Pa's younger sister, Dukke, married the younger brother of Grada. She married Manus Boot in December 1904. This couple also moved in on the Polderdijk.

Wouter Boot married one year after my parents married. That makes four marriages within a four-year period. When you look at their wedding pictures, you can see the same hats and dresses in a number of the pictures.

My cousin and namesake, *Rennie* de Vries, was born on August 15, 1904. Little did anyone then suspect that she and I would end up following two very different drummers.

By now the clan on the Polderdijk had grown to: Opoe, with her two sons, two daughters-in-law and two daughters, one son-in-law; adding up to eight adults and five grandchildren between age five and infant.

Pa and Uncle Jentje often got into each other's way in the business. So, when Opoe heard from her customers that there was a need for a mastmaker and chandlery on the recently completed Kaiser Wilhelm Canal she decided to set up shop in Holtenau at the East end of the canal, right next to Kiel. This was going to be Uncle Jentje's new challenge. He opened shop in 1907. The canal cuts through the Schleswig-Holstein peninsula and connects the North Sea with the Baltic Sea; reducing the old route around Danish Jutland peninsula by about 300 miles.

The Kaiser Wilhelm Canal or Kiel Canal

The new store in Holtenau

Taeke Bijlsma, one of our most experienced mast and block makers, helped for a year or so to train local workers in the art of the trade. The canal was renamed North-East Sea Canal in 1948.

Opoe released the reins gradually to Pa and in 1906 she turned all her responsibilities over to her oldest son.

First day of school in Holtenau for the *second* Mastmakers' Daughter

12. Schoolmaster Funcke

My first day of school! Pa took me. I wore a brown velvet coat with a matching beret, lined with blue flannel. Moe had sewed it herself, of course. We stopped on our way to pick up my neighbor friend, Boukje, at the home and blacksmith shop of van Putten. Her dad gave my Pa a note to bring to school. I learned later that this was a so called "small pox notice".

Van Putten was in my eyes, a genius. He had so many skills. He could have become a very rich man. He could play the organ and tune it as well. He was the only photographer in town. He did not have a studio, so he took the pictures in his back yard, on the lawn. He'd hang a screen on which some Pastoral scene was depicted as a backdrop. There was a table and chairs where the subjects sat and where they would lay their hands on the table and then van Putten would memorialize his subjects with the click of the shutter. He also had the very first taxi service in town. Pa had to go with van Putten to buy his first automobile in Arnhem. He helped with the purchase negotiation and Pa put up the money.

Boukje and her father in front of the blacksmith shop and retail shop, in 1916. (Picture courtesy of John de Vries great-grandson of Cornelis Tjepke van Putten).

Van Putten was the first to have a radio in our town. Boukje became one of my closest friends. She had an older brother who would lend us his color crayons.

Drawing with crayons was our passion. Boukje's aunt, who lived with them, had a subscription to "De Gracieuse" a fashion magazine. The pictures fascinated us and we attempted to draw these figures from a magical world so far away from the Polderdijk.

Jan and Pa had been to Amsterdam but Kampen, Urk and Heeg were as far as I had ever ventured.

Boukje's grandfather and another aunt shared the two rooms with the van Putten family behind his black smith shop. My friendship with Boukje, was also shared at times with another girl and lasted for a long time. Boukje developed diphtheria, but the family did not want a doctor because then a notice would be posted on their door: "Contagious disease...." and that would scare potential customers away. At that same time, we had scarlet fever and diphtheria in our clan. The doctor restricted us to a salt free diet because otherwise we could develop kidney problems. Boukje died, at age twenty-eight, of a kidney infection.

Mr. Funcke taught us French in the fifth and sixth grade before the regular school hours from 7:45 until 8:45 a.m.

I was always in a rush to get ready for school. Moe braided my hair while I was eating breakfast or still studying my French vocabulary. Usually, I would catch a ride on the back of the bicycle from the butcher's delivery boy.

For the most, part I did not like school, except for singing, language and especially writing essays.

My one-year older cousin, Rinsje, one grade higher, knew everything better. She'd have her homework done when I was still playing outside. I sometimes wonder if Opoe played favorites between my cousin and me. She did not like the fact that her oldest son switched churches for Moe and the fact that she had wanted Pa to marry a woman from a family with money. The five classrooms all had their own entrance doors. Each entrance had a small half round vestibule with a second door into the classroom. Our music teacher would go and stand in the vestibule to check and listen to us when we sang harmony. We placed our wooden shoes under our coats on the back wall.

In the winter time the snow would stick to the soles of the wooden shoes and then melt, making a mess.

There was no custodian in our school; the teachers came early to fire up the wood stove in the wintertime. We discovered that, Mr. Funcke, the principal, also had to get on his knees to start the stove for our early French classes.

There were nine grades and in the ninth grade there were a few tables added for students who were prepped for a higher education, like teaching. Wil de Vries[21] and later Fedde Schurer[22] and Sientje Ylst received their teaching certificates in this school.

Behind our school were a couple outhouses and an unenclosed urinal for the boys. There was always a bad smell. There was no running water yet. In the same spot, behind the school, stood a pail of water, which was refilled from the rain barrel at the principal's home. A half of a coconut shell floated in the pail to take a drink. When it got really hot, our teacher would bring a pail of water into the classroom. Everyone took their turn. In our class was a girl whose mother did not practice basic hygiene; our classmate and her sisters often had head sores so that they wore hats in class. The poor girl was ashamed and knew that we tried to avoid her. When I think back, I feel ashamed and embarrassed that Geesje then would wait until we all had our turn and she'd be the last to take her turn. When it was unbearably hot in the classroom, the teacher would again use the pail of water, add a measure of carbolineum, and sprinkle the wood floors, to cool the classroom. We did not have lesson books. The black board was used for most of our lessons. The math exercises were written on the board and then we copied them. At least, I did. This saved the teacher correcting our assignments. For writing essays, the instructor would divide the blackboard, vertically, in two halves. Then he would ask two of us, usually Huite Kok and me, to write on the black board. I loved it. I could let my imagination run wild. The class then copied our work from the black board.

---

[21] Wil(ly) de Vries, grew up with Rennie van Ommen-de Vries, and married Fedde Schurer.

[22] Fedde Schurer became a folk hero among the Frisians. Teacher, journalist and poet. His Pacifist political activites collided with his Reformed brothers. He was excommunicated by the church in De Lemmer in 1930 and he also lost his teaching position in the church's school. Fedde and his wife Willy Schurer-de Vries remained life long friends with Renny van Ommen-de Vries.

We always used the Lange Streek, the road along the west side of the waterway that ran though down town, instead of the Korte Streek, to walk to and from school. Because the public school was on the Korte Streek and they would not let us pass unhindered. Once a year there was a traditional fight. The kids from the public school would come across the water to fight us. My brother Jan was then always on the front line. They would try to hit each other with their belts, I jumped in as well, with my jump rope and a couple of knots in it, I let them have it, as a good Christian girl... However, at Kermis[23] time, we were not allowed to walk the Lange Streek because this kind of entertainment was only for the unbelievers. My cousin Rennie van der Meer once tattled on me that she'd seen me watching the merry-go-round in the Kermis. Pa always tried to provide a diversion for us when the temptation of the Kermis was upon us. But, oh, how fascinated I was with the spectacle, the music and the delicious smell of the doughnuts!

Our elementary school and teachers did not have the best tools to educate us. I had no way to measure how dumb I might be. We had no grade report cards; we were automatically advanced to the next grade.

Years later, when I received a 9[24] on my final exam from the home-ed course at the high school for prospective farmers, I was convinced that this had to be a mistake. I went to the principal, but she assured me that it was no mistake, that my tests had always been excellent. Later I concluded that my cousin Rinsje had been more studious but that I was just a little smarter.

I had to stand with my nose in the corner of a classroom for something naughty I had done. Then Mr. Funcke ordered that I was not allowed to watch that evening's slide show of stories in drawings projected with text, our entertainment before the advent of photography and movies.   Moe butted heads with Funcke and I got to see the show.

---

[23] Kermis: Kermesse, Kermes a travelling annual country fair, with merry go rounds, shooting galleries, etc.

[24] Rating system in the schools went from 1 to 10.

13. What did we wear?

Girls wore a white cotton under shirt with short sleeves, an embroidered collar. In the summertime, we wore a white camisole over the under shirt and a white cotton culotte under pant with a flap in front and in back. The flaps were fastened with strings.

Over this a "halsje", two square pieces of cloth where the one in front was secured around the neck with a lace string. The neck was again decorated with embroidery. On the bottom of this "halsje", in the back, there were strings that were tied in the front above the navel. I hated wearing them. That string around the neck would be hard and rub my neck. Particularly when I had to put on a clean starched apron on Sunday morning and the apron neck tie rubbed on the strings of the "halsje".

Over the underpants, we wore one or two petticoats, in the summer white cotton and in the winter, home knit wool with a two color, red and black, pattern. The winter camisole was also knit, in a lilac color. It did not get washed till the end of the winter. At night, we wore "night pants" and the camisole. Boys wore, one piece, cotton long underwear at night, with flaps in the back.

How I disliked the clean black woolen pants I had to wear on Sunday morning in the wintertime. These pants were always too tight and too stiff after they were just washed. The wool rubbed my skin, if only I would have just been able to wear the white cotton pants under them. Most of the girls in my school had only two woolen dresses; one for Sunday which when they could afford it, was replaced with a new one on Pentecost. Then the Sunday dress became their school wear. Many of the children came from very poor households. It was not uncommon for a younger child to get the hand me downs from their older sibling and the poor child then frequently became the target for ridicule by the more fortunate children. We "middle class" girls had several cotton dresses for the summer. To school we wore big white cotton aprons with shoulder flaps and as much embroidery as possible. At home we wore dark colored aprons. This meant lots of ironing. In our school benches were inkwells with a slide cover and if you had a mischievous boy sitting behind you, it would happen that he would open the slide cover and dip the girl's long braids or her hair ribbons in his ink well.

1910, in my school dress with Opoe and Moe

Maids were often given the hand me downs from their employer. Moe also passed her dresses down to the help, even her hat, when she had bought a new one. We once had a maid, a barge skipper's daughter, who did not accept this form of benevolence. Our maid, Popje, who was with us during my entire grade school period, before she moved in with us, would come in the morning with her work clothes across her arm. She changed in to her work clothes in the kitchen and before she returned home, she washed herself in the kitchen and change into her street clothes. We would let her bring sandwiches back home with her, there were always a couple hungry brothers and sisters she was able to please this way.

14. Ignorance

Narrow-minded ideas were a regular part of our everyday life in our upbringing. Until I reached adulthood, I had always taken for granted that we colonized the East Indies to bring the Word of God to the barbarians. We, most likely, had already heard about the Dutch Indies Company in elementary school. If I had been able to see, at a younger age, the large homes of the wealthy traders on the Amsterdam canals and the rows of warehouses filled with the products from our colonies, I might have figured out that there was more than missionary work being done. How did the song go again? The one Moe often sang:

> *Ik ben een arme negerknaap,*
> *en gans van zorg ontbloot,*
> *Ik buig voor hout en steen mij neer*
> *ik woon in 't donker heidenland,*
> *mijn ouders zijn reeds dood*
> *Ik ken geen andre God*
> *En daar ik zoveel slagen krijg*
> *betreur ik steeds mijn lot..."*

> *Translation:*
> *I am a poor negro boy*
> *and I don't have a single worry*
> *I live in the dark land of the heathens*
> *my parents have been dead for a long time*
> *I worship wood and stone images*
> *I know no other God*
> *and because I receive so many whippings*
> *I always feel sorry for myself*

What bad taste and ignorance on our part and to think that my mother came with this sort of songs out of the parsonage. You'd think that they would know better, my grandfather subscribed to several newspapers and magazines.

Every Sunday a prayer was offered up in our church for reverend van Dijk, missionary in Keboemen in Central Java. The churches had sent him there from our district. Later on, when I became member of the Christian Young Women organization, this subject was brought up with Fedde Schurer and his fiancée Wil de Vries.

At the time, I considered them a bit far on the Left; but I also started to question our national interests.

What business did we have ruling these people? Our presence there led to some grave injustices and how different was that from what we suffered during the Nazi occupation? Down in my heart I have reservations as to the need for missionary work. Why not leave them to practice their culture? But then it has also been written....

Polderdijk 1906 with Opoe, Moe, Pa, Ina on left

15. De Lemmer

We have never had running water during my growing up years in De Lemmer. A rain barrel on the side and one behind the shop provided our drinking water. The workmen drank from the barrel behind the shop, from a pail. The barge skippers that stopped alongside filled their water casks as well from our rain barrel. We used water from the drainage ditch for our laundry, to rinse fur and wool, scrubbing the front steps, etc.

The women from the working neighborhood behind us, the "Achterom" (out back) rinsed their laundry from a set of stone steps that came up from the Rien. In the morning, they emptied the bedpans in the same spot. When the water level in the rain barrel was getting low and became cloudy a "muudhoun"[25] was put in the barrel. We used a filter for our drinking water. Left over coffee and tea were not thrown out because the boiled water made it perfectly good to drink cold.

In a long dry spell, when many rain barrels ran low, water was brought in on the steam tram from Sneek. The water was sold at the tram terminal for one or two cents per pail. That was when a yoke came in handy to carry two pails. We covered them with the round wooden lids, which were also used on the crocks in which we canned string beans to keep the water from slopping out of the pails. The milkman used a similar yoke on his daily house-to-house delivery run. This was in Amsterdam in 1933 before refrigerators and even in the first years of my marriage the milkman delivered twice a day, six days a week.

Not everyone had the luxury to own a house with a cellar. Opoe had one, but it was too small to serve the whole clan. We had a storage chest upstairs in the hallway with sand on the bottom in which the winter supply of potatoes, carrots, and onions were stored. The carrots could be made into toy cars, the wheels were cross cut and attached with pins. Our choice of vegetables in the winter was very limited, besides carrots, onions and other root vegetables like turnips. On Sundays Moe would serve canned green beans or sliced string beans.

---

[25] a live fish was used to slobber up the sludge and then removed.

At canning time, a menstruating[26] woman was excused from helping because her presence could spoil the preserves. Moe would occasionally make sauerkraut. She then rented the cabbage slicer from the poorhouse.

The poorhouse was located in the "Achterom" (out back), the poor working-class neighborhood. I might have passed by it once or twice. I remember seeing several old men sitting on the steps, they were given the task of removing the weeds from between the pavement stones. The poor house was opened in 1817. It was run by the Dutch Reformed Church. Dirkje Hendriks Ages (1754-1825), my great-great-great grandmother, was one of the four first women regents. According to an entry in one of the old accounting records of the poorhouse my great-great-grandmother, then widow Trijntje Ages (1785-1842), who owned a small grocery store, had donated a wheelbarrow of dried peas. My great grandfather, Opoe's father, Tjeerd Ages, also a sailing barge skipper, was not talked about and no one was named after him. Word has it that he had become a drifter, he lays buried without a tombstone. Somehow my great grandmother managed reasonably well after her husband had left her with their three daughters, Rinsje, Dirkje and Trijntje.

This brings me to the story my Aunt Gepke, our family historian, once told us about her great grandfather, Rinze Claasesz Platte[27], born in 1767. I owe my baptismal name, Rinsje, to him. He was a young sailor on a Galleon, which was captured by the English in the Fourth Anglo Dutch War between 1780 and 1784. The British kept him and his crew in English jails for two years. This war resulted from the anger the Dutch had provoked in the British by becoming the second European nation, right after the French; to recognize the American Continental Congress in 1782 and through the material help their trading fleet had provided the new nation in their war of independence.

The young sailor went back to sea and soon after he took command of a Kofschip.

---

[26] This was a common misconception, or old wife's tale, that persisted in the 19th and early 20th century in Europe and parts of America, that the proximity of a menstruating woman could spoil the preserves or garden produce.

[27] Opoe's maternal grandfather

Kofschip

The Lemster folks went all out when it came to organizing festivities. The queen's birthday on August 31st was one of the biggest celebrations of the year. The school children, carrying flags, marched behind the brass band through the streets; decorated arches were erected over the parade route. In the evening, everyone came out to watch the boat parade. We always took part in the boat parade with our sailing yacht. This took hours of preparation; we all had to pitch in, including our workers. Moe had us make paper flowers; we cut long ribbons from green crepe paper.

The workers made hangers out of stiff steel wire to place the candlelights in. They were hung in the rigging and from the boom. The candles were set in glass jars and when the wind cooperated the hundreds of dancing candle flames lent a fairy tale effect to the spectacle. Our efforts would usually earn us one of the top awards given to the participating floats. A tugboat came to tow us and before we reached the end of the Vissersburen. The boys and young men along the route would start to sing: "And then there was Jan de Vries, hey ho, hey ho..." Besides receiving prizes Pa would also donate prizes, for example, in the sail boat races. The Lemster Sailing Club organized races for professional sailors in a number of classes such as, large Tjalks, fishing boats (Aaks and Botters) and a few more working boat classes and yachts.

Pa gave out the fourth prize in one of the races in 1915, a new ensign and a barometer. It went to Andries Scheffer on the fishing Aak 44 "Zuiderzee". Andries was not only a good sailor but, known as a fast ice skater and he could sing. He had the leading role in the three-penny opera "Geertemoer". The Lemster fishermen were known around the Zuiderzee for their sailing skills. When the sailing fleets left early Monday for their fishing grounds it usually turned into an informal but white-knuckle race for the first boat to reach the best spot.

In a following wind these 36-foot long shoal draft boats with lee boards raised would fly everything on their unstayed masts, two head sails, the large main sail and even a spanker set off the stern. In a building breeze, a sigh of relief could be heard when another boat was the first to shorten sail.

The Lemster Aak LE-64 built in 1901 by Jans Bos in Echternebrug
<u>www.spanvis.nl</u>

The Lemsters competed in the regattas held in the Zuiderzee, just outside Amsterdam, which were organized by the Amsterdam Yacht Club. They won many of the trophies. These races were held on the weekend and this meant that only the Godless fishermen could participate. Their victories were not mentioned under our roof.

16. Names and Titles

There was strict adherence to the pecking order in our town and in the way one was addressed.

Last names became compulsory during Napoleon's rule, but the custom of calling someone by a nickname or identifying them by their trade or as a son or daughter of so and so, still persisted. Pa was seldom referred to as Jan de Vries, but was known by the color of his hair, "Reade Joppe", Red John.
There was an unwritten etiquette as to how we addressed one another in our region. Men never called each other by their first name. Except the boss, like Pa, addressed his workers by their first names and the workers amongst each other would use first names.

The maid and farm hands addressed a farmer as "Farmer", the farmer's wife as "Madam". Our maid and the workmen addressed my father as "Boss" and Moe as "Madam". "Miss" was used for a female teacher and the wife of the principal. Just a few women deserved the title of "Mrs.", they were the wives of the Pastors, the doctor, the notary, the mayor and Mr. Sleeswijk, the owner of the sawmill across the water from us.

No one in my school had a father like my Pa, with so many workmen. Our father always wore a suit. The father of Boukje, my classmate, was blacksmith and he wore the leather blacksmith apron; he was always covered with soot. Our neighbor Marten de Vries, the sail maker, wore a white sailmaker coverall. My Pa talked with ship captains, he wrote post cards, went on business trips and stayed in hotels.

What made me so stuck up? Was it because Opa[28] was a preacher, the same for two uncles and one uncle a mayor? But Pa was not just anyone. I thought that he knew everything. I caught myself once in a discussion at a Meisjesvereniging (YWCA) saying: "My father says…" I might have given the wrong impression, as if we had the biggest business going in our town. I meant it for our part of town and of the families that we went to school with. The sawmill, right across the Rien from us, was much larger. We looked out at high stacks of sawn lumber and large sheds. The wings of the original sawmill had been clipped when the mill converted to steam from wind power.

---

[28] Grandfather

50

The owner, Mr. Wegener Sleeswijk, was a sophisticated gentleman. He walked with a cane and lived in a stately mansion on the Nieuweburen. His mother lived in an apartment in what formerly was known as the Grietmanshuis[29] on the Schulpen. Mr. Sleeswijk died in 1918 in the Spanish Flu[30] pandemic. Two of his cousins took over the management of the "Houtmolen" because the children of Mr. Sleeswijk were still too young.

The new managers with their university degrees wanted to reorganize the entire plant. They were also very democratic in contrast to the conservative ways of the deceased. When Queen Wilhelmina inaugurated the new steam pump station in Tacozijl in 1920, one of the new directors of the sawmill was a member of the welcoming committee. There is a photo of the festivities where Pa is part of the group of the town's delegation, dressed in long black over coats and top hats with cockades[31] pinned on their coats.

The managers of the sawmill, with their costly innovations, managed to put the once flourishing company into receivership.

The next largest employer in our town, after the sawmill, was the shipyard of the de Boer Brothers. I should say shipyards, there were two yards, one built traditionally in wood and the second was building steel boats. PaPa had gone to the public school and he had grown up with the de Boer brothers. The de Boers were members of the Socialist Democratic Labor Party (S.D.A.P.). Socialist meant Godless. We did not mix with these kinds of people, except for business[32]. Fedde Schurer's father, Bouke Schurer, worked in the shipyard. When one of the de Boers happened to be in Pa's office, he told my father: "If there is a Heaven then Bouke Schurer will go there". Isn't that a wonderful testimony? The angels must have smiled at each other when they heard de Boer say this.

---

[29] Grietmanshuis: House of the Grietman. A Grietman was a kind of regent or county councilman.

[30] Spanish Flu: the deadliest pandemic ever. It killed 3% of the world's population at the lower of the 50 to 100 million deaths estimate.

[31] Cockade: A rosette badge, with the Dutch Tricolor and orange ribbons, to honor the Royal family

[32] The Dutch have scruples but there is a price tag on it.

The de Boer shipyard workers 1911. Bouke Schurer on second row from front far left, with dark beard. Standing on right with pea coats two of the de Broer brothers.   Source: Friesscheepvaartmuseum

17. My parents

We had wonderful parents. I was not very convinced of this when I was a child, as you might expect. I received my share of punishments. Pa used his bare hand, Moe her slippers. When that happened, Moe would be very angry and she would call me "fanke". This sounded just like the opposite of "famke"[33].

Jan, my oldest brother, was always teasing me. He was sixteen months younger and I could keep him under the thumb for a number of years but when he reached ten, he had become stronger than what I could handle. Yet, we continued to walk to school together; Folkert de Vries, our neighbor from the sailmaker, joined us every morning. Folkert was a very kind boy; he died in 1927 when he was only twenty-four years old.

---

[33] Famke: Frisian for girl.

Jan and I had become used to playing together until the two cousins, Rennie (or Rinsje) and Hanna, came to live with Opoe and Aunt Trijn. I might have become even more stuck up without Opoe playing "our" Rinsje out against me. "Their" Rinsje did everything so much better than me.

I was fortunate to have a mother who did not make me finish a given number of stitches before I was allowed to play outside. Moe always stood up for us, even before Pa. One day Oma van Anken was visiting with Moe's still unmarried sister, Aunt Rien; Moe relayed to Pa that evening something to the effect that the visitors thought that we were not all that bad after all. There was hope….

Pa had bought a second-hand bicycle for me, but I was not allowed to try it out until I was able to play "The Lord is my Shepherd" on the harmonium. But Moe was getting impatient, one day when Pa was away, she suggested that she would teach me to ride the bicycle. She ran up and down the Polderdijk behind me until she was completely out of breath. From then on, I used the coils of wire rope stacked in front of the chandlery to hoist myself on the saddle. A skipper's wife stopped and offered to help me, but her kindness turned out to have an ulterior motive: "May our Aafje have a try now?" That was the end of my bicycle practice.

To get back to my oldest brother, Jan, he was given some special privileges as the oldest son. He had a toy steam engine; I did not get such fancy toys, but I do not believe that jealousy belonged among my many vices. Jan might have received some of these toys from our Uncle Jentje who did not have any sons.

When I was still a tot, Uncle Jentje paraded with me on his arm through the store when a customer asked: "de Vries, is that your first child?" and he responded: "I am not getting married if I knew that I would get daughters". As it turned out he had two daughters and no sons, whereas his older brother, my Pa, had three sons and four daughters. Pa was very fond of my younger sister, Ina, He called her, in Frisian "zijn typke" (his type). He named his day sailer "Ina". She was shy and a picky eater. For example, I had to take her to the toilet in the back of the schoolyard when she had to go.

53

Around 1910, in front of chandlery, L.R.: Opoe, me Rennie, Moe, Pa with Ina on his shoulder. Blacksmith shop on right, girls of the neighbor Marten de Vries, the sailmaker.

Pa with Ina, round 1910, in the "Ina" in front of Polderdijk

1905 In Urker costume, for the occasion, L.R. my brother Jan, Moe, me (Rennie) and Pa

18. Urk

Urk was then still an island in the middle of the Zuiderzee. After the Aflsuitdijk was completed in 1932, the sea became a large fresh water lake and has since been reclaimed into polders. Urk is now locked to the mainland as part of the dike system that formed the North-East Polder.

I have many memories of Urk, from visits and stories that Moe told us from the time she lived on the island.

On a clear day, we could see the island from our second floor living room windows. Because the Urker fishermen were an important part of the business for us, the island and its people often came up in our discussions. As a young girl, I spent many vacations in the parsonage of my grandparents on Urk. My first recollections are of hiding under Moe's skirts when we sailed across in stormy weather. That was a good place to hide, nice and warm. Married women wore long skirts. Moe was seasick and lateron I heard that was in the time that she was expecting my sister Ina.

Opa van Anken was the Reformed Pastor in the Bethel Church, on Urk. He married Pa and Moe in this church in 1900.

I remember playing with a girl my age in a courtyard, when I stayed on the island. We had shelled peanuts, which were called "sausjes"[34], in a blue enameled drinking cup with water.

In contrast to the fishermen from other harbors who fished primarily on the Zuiderzee, the Urker fleet fished with a larger and sturdier Botter on the North Sea out of the North Sea harbors, den Helder and IJmuiden. They would be away from Monday morning to Saturday. When the herring and anchovy spawning runs ran in the Zuiderzee then the Urkers caught their share of it on the Zuiderzee. They worked and slept all week in the same clothes. On their arrival on Urk, the women lit the kerosene burners under the large galvanized tubs and peeled their men out of their many layers of flannel to scrub them clean.

There was no gas and no electricity. On the highest point of the island a large storage tank was filled with heating fuel before the start of winter because the island became often cut off when the Zuiderzee froze over. When that happened, the men would pull a large sled over the ice to bring the mail and emergency supplies to the mainland.

The sled was built like a rowboat and could be used as such when it broke through the ice. This could become a very hazardous undertaking.

---

[34] Sausjes: derived from Curaçao.

At times, it was the only way to evacuate patients for which there were only limited facilities on the island.

Moe told us of the time that Opa received 28 daily newspapers all at once when the men of the "ijsvlet" had finally managed to make it back across from the main land. The homes were all built on the higher ground of the island, squeezed together, there was no room left for a garden. The lower parts of the island were used for agriculture such as food, crops, and sheep, but they would often flood in the fall and winter storms.

In De Lemmer and elsewhere the laundry was dried and bleached on a grass lawn. On Urk wires were strung across the narrow streets and it made for a colorful sight to see on Mondays, particularly with a good breeze.

Hygiene was always a problem. There was no running water, no sewage system. Grey water ran down and accumulated on the lowest level of the town. Cholera and Typhus have raged through the island repeatedly.

Opa had to go house to house to visit the sick. When he returned to the parsonage there would be a fireproof dish with burning coals with a bowl of carbolineum on it. His coat was hung over the steaming concoction that served as a disinfectant. No one fell ill in the minister's household.

The botters were all lined up, bows out, scrubbed and their oak hulls freshly oiled, signal flags dressed from boat to boat and orange, the color of the house of Orange, and streamers from the mast heads. The town was also scrubbed and freshly painted. Welcome arches had been erected everywhere, built out of new anchovy kegs, decorated with ships anchors, draped with new silk fishing nets.

The men in their black woolen baggy pants, the silver belt buckles polished; the women parading in their colorful multiple skirts, aprons and starched white lace caps. We watched the H.M. "Hydrograaf", a navy vessel, drop anchor off the island. The queen and her party went down the gangplank into a rowing launch that came along side. On command, the sailors brought the oars up and down in perfect synchronization. I had never seen such a spectacle.

The queen and her entourage made the rounds of the town and performed the ribbon cutting.

Queen Wilhelmina and the "IJsvlet" Photo Elsevier collection

The volunteers of the "ijsvlet" enacted their trip across the ice. The sled/row boat was pulled on the harbor square.

Big blocks of ice from the ice plant, where the ice was produced to keep the fish fresh, where laid out under the "ijsvlet" to simulate the winter scene. The crew sang the songs they were accustomed to when pulling the sled.

But what I will never forget, and tears of emotion still well up when I think of it, was the way the Urkers sent the Queen off. At the end of the day, after farewell speeches from the mayor and other notables, the brass band broke out with Psalm 134: "Dat Heeren's zegen op U daal, Zijn gunst uit Sion U bestraal" (May the Lord's blessing descend upon you, may His favor from Zion shine upon you") and all of Urk sang this blessing to their queen. The Urkers are known for their singing. There are a number of all men choirs on the island that have earned international reputation.

When I was a teenager, I had some friends staying with us in De Lemmer. Pa was always clever in coming up with surprises.

He had advanced money to install a motor in the sailing vessel of the skipper of the weekly ferry service to Urk. Pa arranged for our whole group to make the first motorized trip to Urk.

Under sail one never knew how long the round trip would take. We were all back in De Lemmer before dark.

The expression: "A preacher is passing by", used when there is an awkward lull in the conversation, originated in Urk. When a fisherman had drowned, a telegram would be sent to the harbormaster who would notify the family's Pastor.

When the women saw the Pastor approaching, through the narrow streets, their conversations would stop: "Which house is he heading for?" My Opa had to be the bearer of this sad news on many occasions during his service on Urk.

The crew of a botter was made up by the owner as the skipper, one or two mature crewmembers and the son or nephew of the skipper. On the last day of grade school, when they were just twelve years old, the father or uncle would show up and officially take the boy under his wing. The Dutch-American, Jan de Hartog, author of many sea stories invented a name for these young sailors, "Bramzijgertjes" and in his English version called them Sea Mice.

1717	HENDRIK WILLEMSZ	30 J.
1751	ALBERT WEERSTAND	18 J.
1779	PIETER BRANDS	43 J.
1825	ALBERT BAKKER	19 J.
1830	KLAAS de VRIES	8 J.
1835	HARMEN TIMMERMAN	24 J.
1836	OKKE WAKKER	10 J.
1850	JAN WILLEMS	18 J.
1863	WILLEM WEERSTAND	58 J.
	JAN WEERSTAND	22 J.
1865	HENDRIK MOLENAAR	36 J.
	HEIN MOLENAAR	25 J.
	JACOB MOLENAAR	22 J.
1866	RIEKELT BRANDS	45 J.
	JAN BRANDS	14 J.
	LUBBERT ROMKES	37 J.

One of the plaques on the fishermen memorial on Urk. Note ages as young as eight years

19. Zeeland

Pa expected me to help him with his office administration, but at age eleven I still needed more schooling. When I was done with grade school, Pa offered to have me study to be a teacher. I was dead set against another four years of school but I could not expect much of a future without more than grade school.

De Lemmer had nothing to offer beyond the elementary level. I had already made myself useful in the store and started to earn my allowance by sewing the many different flags and pennants which were used by our customers. All were made from woven wool; ensigns, signal code flags, burgees and pennants for special occasions to announce, births, deaths, etc. Mourning pennants came in a Protestant and a Roman Catholic version, in black and white with white sash fringes.

Moe also had me help her sew the workmen's brown corduroy pants on the foot pedal machine. Just before the annual Kermis they all were given new pants. Because you did not want your workers seen sitting on the steps of the shop in their old pants as the town folks would pass by our buildings on the Polderdijk.

When in the first year Kermis time approached, after we had moved in on the Polderdijk, Opoe let Moe know: "We always sew them ourselves!" And Moe didn't think twice: "I'll show her!" She took one of the old pants apart and used the parts as patterns for the new material.

Before I had finished my sixth grade my parents decided to send me with my uncle, Jan Pottjewijd, and Aunt Tine, Moe's youngest sister, to Kapelle-Biezelinge in Zeeland.

Zeeland is the province in the S.W. corner of the Netherlands, on the Belgian border. I was eleven. My uncle and aunt had no children of their own.

Uncle Jan was the principal at the Reformed elementary and high school. I would finish my education here and be taught French by my uncle and receive organ lessons from Aunt Tine. [35]

My parents' decision must have also had something to do with the fact that I did not get along well with Mr. Funcke, the principal in De Lemmer. I came home during vacations because my aunt and uncle spent their vacations with his family in Winschoten, which is not far from De Lemmer. Uncle Jan's father, Boele Jans, was one of the first professional photographers; he earned the distinction of Court photographer in 1901. The business he started is still being run by his descendants and is the oldest family run photography shop in the Netherlands.

One time I returned to Kapelle all by myself. I was quite proud of my accomplishment. I had to change trains in the Utrecht station and pass through a tunnel to get to the right platform. I was the only child at home in Kapelle and liked the attention they gave me. I was treated quite differently by my aunt and uncle than I was at home from how my parents brought me up. My new classmates also treated me with a certain amount of respect because I was the head master's girl.

The area around Kapelle Biezelinge is known for its fruit orchards crops, cherries, plums, apples and pears. In the Spring, it turns into a sea of white blossoms. In the early summer, around June, the schools were closed for "kezzenwaggen"; local dialect for guarding the orchards from starling attacks. This was done by hanging a tin can, filled with pebbles or broken pottery pieces, in the cherry tree. The can was then connected with ropes to another ten cans in neighboring trees. A child sat all day in the orchard and as soon as it saw a flock of birds trying to land in the trees it would pull the rope setting off a loud racket that scared the birds away. With my special privileges as the principal's niece they'd let me into the cherry orchard to eat the ripe cherries. That was a feast.

---

[35] Aunt Tine= pronounced: Teene

The Reformed church in Kapelle Biezeinge around 1912 Goes Gemeente Archief.

1911 Kapelle Uncle Pottjewijd far right, to his right Adriana Balkenende, behind her brother Dirk B. and to her right Jan B. Adriana Dees on her knees behind the sign

Soon after this vacation there was another one, "Beierstrokken" (local dialect for Berry Picking), when the berries, red and black currents were ready to pick.

In my poetry album that I kept from my tenth year through my twelfth birthday, I find entries of some of the friends I made in Kapelle, Adriana Balkenende[36], Maria Nout, Andries Nout, T. Ossenwaarde, and Adriana Dees.

Occasionally my aunt sent me to get butter and eggs from a farm out of town; Wisse was the farmer's name. Farms often had turkeys and peacocks running around in the front yard; I believe that this was a kind of status symbol. The turkeys would hiss at me, I was deadly afraid of these birds.

At that age, I was also afraid of the people that travelled with the Kermis, in their horse drawn wagon homes. I classified them all as gypsies. According to my neighbor friend's grandmother, Beppe Dam, there were "bennedieven" (child molesters) amongst them. Beppe Dam walked with us along the Polderdijk in the summer evenings and when it started to get dark we had to go home because of the "bennedieven". Beppe Dam slept with three of the grandchildren in the bedstead, one more in the foot of the bed and an infant in the crib above. She was crippled on both sides and when she went on her walk she'd be knitting for the large family, she carried a quiver in her apron belt for her knitting pins. We brought them regularly a basket full of thick wood shaving from the shop for firewood with strict orders from Moe that we were never to accept any money for this.

---

[36] Adriana Balkenende became the great aunt of Jan Pieter Balkenende, Prime Minister of the Netherlands from 2002 till 2010

20. The First World War

We were confronted with the First World War during the summer vacation of 1914.

It was still six years before the radio was introduced and we were not well informed as to how this might affect us. I was just shy of thirteen years. We had been swimming, or in my case bathing because I have never learned to swim, at the beach on the Zuiderzee. There was a roped off area on the East Dam and a facility to change clothes. Cork floats were available for those who wanted to teach themselves to swim. We have spent many happy hours in this spot. Moe would come along at times. She had made a sort of jumpers for us from flannel. And when they were wet, they did little to hide the shapes of our buns and bumps.

Ladies and gentlemen had separate opening hours. This did not keep the fishermen boys from changing outside of the bathhouse and jumping into the water next to the organized facility and mixing in with the shrieking girls. But once, that turned out to the benefit of Griet Tieleman when she lost her dentures in the swimming area. One of the boys recovered her false teeth.

Anyway, I was saying about the start of the war, we were coming back with wet hair; when we came closer to the ferryboat to cross the Rien we saw groups of women huddled. They were the wives of the sawmill workers who lived in small one -room house on the sawmill property along the Rien. They stood crying because their men had been called up for military mobilization. Holland remained neutral in this war. In the beginning, many in Holland were pro German or, possibly better put, anti English. The Boer War in South Africa was still fresh on most minds.

When I was back in Zeeland, a couple months later, we could hear the thundering guns of the drawn-out battle that took place in Flanders between the Germans and the Allied troops. An English pilot accidentally dropped a bomb nearby on Goes, which killed a pharmacist. When the war came closer to the southern Dutch border it was decided that I should move back North again, but I was still short of completing my education. It was towards the end of 1914 and I was just thirteen years old. Pa had placed an ad in the Frisian Daily looking for a combination live-in and part time office work.

This brought me to the Zeijl family on the Koemarkt in Sneek. Mrs. Zeijl was a farmer's daughter; she had brought some money with her into the marriage.

With his wife's money, he managed to set himself up in the banking business. His official job was with the Boaz Bank, a bank that was organized by a Christian Association.

When the farmers came in to make deposits and they did not specify that the money was to go into the Boaz Bank, he would deposit it into the W. Zeijl Bank. When the bank's board caught wind of this, they relieved him of the bank's management. But by then he had managed to build his bank to where he did not need help any more. This happened after I had left them.

I sat on a tall stool in the Zeijl office every morning and kept the books of a chrome-plating factory. The afternoon was for my homework that I had to turn in at the nightschool, a home education course for future farmers' wives. I had lessons in First Aid and learned costume sewing. In addition, I completed an accounting course. Saturday afternoon I took the tram back to De Lemmer and returned to Sneek on Monday afternoon.

The moment I came home there was work to do. Moe was expecting Rientje, my youngest sister. Anna the maid, a barge skipper's daughter, had been seriously ill and was not allowed to do any strenuous work yet. I started washing the exteriors of the twelve windows in our buildings. This included the windows on Opoe's living quarters; I considered that the job for my unmarried Aunt Trijn who lived with her and she was then just thirty years. Next, I had to scrub two of the sidewalks. Monday was laundry day. This was done in a wooden tub with a lid through which a hand crank was stuck and I had to pump this crank 135 times up and down. Once in a while I cheated but this did not go unnoticed. Anna found a job in an institution where she would be addressed as "Miss". I felt it my duty to quit my school and job in Sneek and come home to help Moe out. My parents were a little stunned by my action. We did get domestic help again a while later. Pa put me to work in the office with Sybrant (Siebren) Lighthart, who worked in the dark room in back of the chandlery, always singing Hymns and Psalms. He kept the books and copied the correspondence. Carbon paper had not yet been invented. Letters were written with copy ink and then pressed between thin sheets of paper in a book with numbered pages. I was able to show Lighthart what I had learned in my accounting lessons, like double bookkeeping. I liked Lighthart and we got along well.

He was well read; he was a deeply committed Christian. His job was a blessing for his family. His father had owned a Barque ship, which had broken up in a storm in the Atlantic. There were no survivors. The widow was left with two young children. She started a small grocery store; she was too shy and she attracted the wrong customers who would not pay their accounts when payday came. She lived between baker Oldendorp and baker van der Geest on the Old Harbor. When I was a child, I visited their home and I was shown old prints of big ocean-going sailing ships that sailed to lands far away and that is when I heard the story of the last voyage of captain Lighthart and his crew.

Besides the care of their mother, Siebren and his sister Dieuwke, they also looked after two dementing aunts. Dieuwke dabbled in making hats and at that time Siebren went house to house collecting premiums for the social health care fund. After Siebren passed away Dieuwke could no longer afford to operate the store and ended up selling from a "bölekoer" (basket) in the streets. Later she moved up to a pushcart. Luckily, she was able to live a few better years in Hilversum with my Uncle Jentje as an assistant to an elderly gentleman who lived in the rest home my uncle operated.

The neutrality of the Dutch during the First World War brought higher earnings to many of the Dutch businessmen, Pa included. At the outbreak of the war in 1914, we had eight men in the shop. By the war's end this number had increased to twelve workers and lasted through 1920 but came back down to eight a few years later. Our Pilot Cutter yacht "Top" had a lead keel. The war had driven up the price for lead. Pa decided to sell the lead keel and replace it with a cast iron keel. But this clever exercise on Pa's account ended up instilling a fear of sailing that stayed with me for the rest of my life. On the way back from Urk, shortly after the keel switch, a storm came in unexpectedly from the North East.

It was just Pa, Huite Zijlstra, and I. Huite quickly reefed the main sail, but we soon discovered that the boat had lost much of its stability with the lighter keel. Pa ordered me below and I saw the green water rush along the lee side port holes. The shallow Zuiderzee is infamous for the short distance between the swells. "Top" was bucking the waves like a rodeo bronco. I was cold, scared, and sea sick, coiled up on the lee cabin berth. Pa came down out of the cockpit and I sensed Pa's concerns of the situation.

66

But, seeing Huite, through the companion way, standing at the helm gave me new courage. He knew what he was doing. Our yacht has never had an engine; there was no radio yet.

We made hardly any headway with the wind right on the nose.

Darkness set in and sailing into the narrow De Lemmer harbor entrance surrounded with shallows was not an option. Huite had no other choice than to make long tacks, between the lights of Urk and Schokland, hoping for the wind and seas to ease up.

At daybreak, the storm had indeed weakened and Huite managed to sail into the protection of the breakwater of the De Lemmer harbor entrance. As soon as we got to the locks, I climbed out and sprinted to the Polderdijk. Moe had been worrying all night.

"Top" at Kampen in 1917. From stern Pa and Moe in the cockpit with Huite Zijlstra. On boom brother Jan with Riek(?) Seated on house Fenny Jonker, Gezina Sijbesma, me (Rennie) with hat, Albert v/d Berg(?) with cap. Crewman on bow.

The fishing boats that fished on the North Sea had "HOLLAND" painted on their hulls to ensure that combatants in this war left the neutral fishermen and sailors in peace. In 1916, the "Lemmer" IJM-282, a two masted sailing lugger fishing boat was launched at the de Boer yard. This was a good excuse for another festivity. Our shop supplied the spars, blocks, and rigging; the sails came from M.F. de Vries the sailmaker next door.

The sailmakers are the ones dressed in white in the below picture.

IJM-282 the fastest sailing fishing boat in the IJmuider fleet.

The engineless boat was towed to sea by the Koningsveld tug. One of the IJmuider young crewmembers had developed a fondness for the tug skipper's daughter, Margje. He decided to pay her a visit; he shimmied down the tow hawser, but when Koningsveld realized what the boy was up to, the skipper reduced speed, the towrope slackened and the resourceful Romeo presented himself soaking wet at the feet of Margje. Any combatants, like deserters or shipwreck survivors, who intentionally or accidentally crossed the Dutch borders and were caught, ended up in a detention center. On Urk was a detention center for officers of the allied forces, mostly Belgian, some French and British. All ships that left Urk were thoroughly searched for possible adventurous internees. Our boat was turned upside down on several departures from Urk in the wartime.

Internment camp on Urk. Photo from light house, Dutch Reformed church in background   Photo collection museum Het Oude Raadhuis, Urk

Opoe worried that Uncle Jentje, in Holtenau, might be called up to serve in the German army, but his Dutch citizenship exempted him. He obliged his German hosts by smuggling German seamen stranded on the Dutch shores back to Germany. The Kaiser's government awarded him the Iron Cross for his services. He became a German citizen shortly after the war to facilitate owning property in Germany. The other Mastmakers' Daughter, my namesake *Rennie* de Vries, elected to be naturalized as a German when she reached age twenty-one. When I was living in Groningen, the most N.E. province of the Netherlands, in the last years of the war, there was an internment camp behind the Sterrenbos, near where I was staying, for 1,500 sailors of the First Royal Naval Brigade. They arrived in the beginning of the war in October 1914.The Germans had cut off their water escape route at Antwerp. Instead of being made prisoners of war by the Germans the commander chose to take refuge across the nearby Dutch border.

I recall the colorful morning parades when the Tommies marched behind their brass band through the town. This was a very festive sight; the young women liked this in particular.

1917 taken in garden Polderdijk. l.r.: Maria (Mieke) 1911, Jan 1903, Moe 1875, Rientje 1915, Rennie 1901, Pa 1876, Gezina Jantina (Ina) 1905, Siebold 1908, Jentje 1912

There was little more for me to learn in De Lemmer and after Moe had found another domestic help, I moved in 1917 to Groningen, the capital of the province by the same name. It is the largest city in the North of the Netherlands and the Royal University of Groningen, founded in 1604, is the second oldest university after the Leiden University.

My Greataunt Garreldina Spiering took me in as a boarder. She was the youngest daughter of Moe's grandfather, he remarried as a widower and Garreldina was born from his second marriage when he was fifty-nine. This way she was only nine years older than Moe and I considered her more as an Aunt than as a Greataunt. Their daughter, Gezina, in reality my aunt, was a year older than I was. We became close friends. The Spierings lived in the Boteringstraat. From their house, I could hear the fire lookout who was stationed on top of the Martini Tower. Starting at 10 p.m. the lookout would blow an air horn every fifteen minutes to assure the city that all was well.

What would happen, I wondered, if he fell asleep; would someone have to climb the 323 steps to wake him up?

I liked living with them, but one day Aunt Garreldina told me to look for another home. No one knew her reasons. She ended up taking a farmer's son into her home who could probably afford to pay her more, but it might also have had something to do with the fact that she observed her son Adriaan taking a liking to me. As a girl from a large family with modest means, I might not have fit her expectations for her son. Adriaan initiated me in the art of kissing but when he sought contact with me again after I had found another boarding home, he smelled of smoked herring.

It was November 11, 1918. It was also the feast of Saint Martin, which even though it is a Catholic feast day it remains a tradition in the North of Holland. Children were going house to house with jack o'lanterns singing their songs for a treat. The American Halloween evolved from the old European St. Martin tradition. On the 11th hour this 11th day of the 11th month the First World War ended. The entire country, on this Monday, went to church to give thanks for an end to this brutal and costly war and to remember the many victims.

In the meantime, I had found an office job at the provincial delegation of the Dutch government. I was an assistant correspondent. I liked the work. The young chef and I got along well without allowing the relations ship to become too personal. I missed the friendship with Gezina Spiering that broke off when I moved out. She had in the meantime become very involved with a new boyfriend. I spent my time in the library reading, especially poetry and I followed courses at the city college. When the manager of the office sent for me too often for dumb tasks, I turned in my resignation and gave my notice to my boarding house. When I showed up in De Lemmer on December 1[st,] 1918, my folks where once more a little awkward about my sudden reappearance.

It was not that I was not welcome but that story about the manager in Groningen had to be a figment of my wild imagination, tending on sensationalism. Now that was a peculiar reaction from my parents when I think back to the time when I was ten years old. I came running home one evening form my neighbor, Boukje van Putten's home, in tears because a van Slagteren boy had kicked me with his fist under my skirt. Pa called on his parents the next day.

A year later, I got involved with a group of girls who were paring up with boys. They told me that I also had to have a "feint". They hooked me up with a boy and I remember the first kiss.

71

When Pa got wind of this, he called me into his office and read me the riot act and even dropped the word "whore".

He made me write a letter to the boy. In retrospect, I think that Pa's reaction was more fear than anger when he was confronted with the fact that his little girl was growing up.

Pa took me to Ugchelen in Gelderland to his sister Dukke and Uncle Manus. My two cousins, Rinsje and Hanna van der Meer, with whom I used to play hide and seek on the Polderdijk, had moved there with my childless aunt and uncle. Their parents sailed a two masted 330-ton clipper on the inland and coastal waters. The clipper replaced the Pavilion Tjalk "de Onderneming" in 1902. Reinder's son, Rudolf, sailed on the clipper until 1935.

A 2006 picture of the clipper "Iselmar", formerly "De Onderneming" in the Brandaris race, now in the charter fleet in Harlingen www.iselmar.info

Pa informed the whole family in Ugchelen of my loose morals and I was to be watched. But my stay turned into a nightmare, Uncle Manus would take me on his daily delivery runs for his grocery store and had me sit next to him on the horse and buggy. And that was just so awful. The memories have haunted me until the pervert died prematurely in 1938.

In the last month in Groningen, I met Henk. Little did I know then that this was the beginning of a long road to nowhere. Just before that, I had a short crush on Jelle a midshipman from Heerenveen. Romance from the very first encounter, but my parents did not have any "faith" in it because he was not a Christian. Pa travelled to Heerenveen to meet his parents, but he did not get anywhere. Jelle's parents did not have any objections for their son to date a Christian girl.

So, I broke it off.

21. Amsterdam

Henk and I fell madly in love. I was barely seventeen and he was ten months older. My parents did not approve of the relationship.

I would secretly intercept the mailman for Henk's letter.

Pa suggested: "Send a post card". But when I was going to be confirmed it was Moe who asked me if I would like to invite Henk to be a part of this occasion. This became the first meeting between Henk and my parents. We became officially engaged when Henk started his medical studies at the Royal University of Groningen.

I worked for Pa in his office again. I was looking for something else to do. With the idea of getting a nursing training so that I could be of help to Henk, I left for Amsterdam.

Moe arranged, with the help of her cousin, Karel van den Berg, who knew the director of the Valerius Clinic, to get me into a training position at the hospital. The nurse trainees had to mop the stone floors, wash the inside of storage cabinets, and do windows. We had to do the floors with worn out mops because the recent world war had caused a shortage of many common household items. We could not get the job done in the time expected with these worn-out rags. It did not set well with the other trainees that

I was allowed to start the nursing classes ahead of them while they still had to take the preparatory courses. I also irked them with some of my habits. What was my reason for having an English bible on my nightstand? I spent many an hour visiting the van den Berg family on the Jacob Maris Square. It was a big family. The oldest son Bé took me to visit the many museums in Amsterdam. We discussed Schopenhauer, August Strindberg, Heijermans, Raden Mas Noto Soeroto, Rabindranath Tagore, etc.

We had become good friends, but I was engaged.

When Bé was at the point to be sent off to the Dutch East Indies my engagement with Henk had been broken off for the second time.

Bé proposed to me very officially in writing. Though he was not a church going man his last sentence in the letter was: "And trust with me on the help of the Almighty God". But, it had to be: "No", because I loved Henk too much.

Years later I heard what had happened to Bé. He got married in the Dutch Indies in 1927. His entire family was imprisoned in concentration camps during the Japanese occupation in the Second World War. They made it back to Holland after the war but Indonesian terrorists in Sigli, on the island of Sumatra, had murdered Bé in 1942.

Bé standing second from left in 1918, with his 13 siblings.

Because I felt that I could not last through the rest of the training course at the Valerius Clinic I started looking for other options. I found a position as a companion/chamber maid to Mrs. Berber Lucretia Hajonides van der Meulen-Taconis. Mr. van der Meulen was a wealthy grain dealer; they lived in a monumental home on the Over de Kleders in Leeuwarden, the provincial capital of Friesland. She came to pick me up from the train station in an open surrey and told the coachman to first give me a tour of the city.

I was impressed, but it might have had something to do with preparing me for the surprise that her kitchen maid had run off. Two sisters had assisted her, one in the kitchen and the other for housework. She intended to replace the one sister who did the house work with someone who could also be of company to her. But this plan had apparently backfired and the second sister quit in sympathy with her younger sister. She found a young lady, who had previously worked for the provincial deputy of the Queen, to work in the kitchen for five days of the week. For Saturdays and Sundays, she had the meals catered. The laundry was done every Saturday by a cleaning lady; she did my laundry every other week. In order to be closer to Henk I decided to move back to Groningen.

I found a position as a governess in a lawyer's family household. It was difficult in that period for a woman to find a more challenging job other than teaching or nursing.

22. Drenthe

Drenthe is the province just to the east of Friesland and south of the province of Groningen. Henk's parents lived in Nieuwe Weerdinge, between Emmen and Stadskanaal. I came to visit them regularly and Henk also travelled to De Lemmer occasionally.

This part of Drenthe was a comparatively isolated rural area. In our small town of De Lemmer we ran behind the more urban areas but we were far ahead of the people in Nieuwe Weerdinge. They had never heard of tomatoes, they ate lettuce with sugar on it, the same with brown beans. A Sunday dinner consisted of boiled potatoes with meat and gravy and for dessert you were served rice with butter and sugar and stewed pears. No vegetables.

Pa Noorlag and Henk's older brother had a construction business, just like Henk's grandfather who still lived in Musselkanaal. They came from Groningen and had followed the peat diggers down south into Drenthe. Dairy and produce farmers would move in once the peat had been removed. This meant plenty of work for people in the building trades. Pa Noorlag had done well. On Sundays, the announcements were made from the pulpit in Nieuwe Weerdinge as to where the church elders and the Pastor would make their home visits that coming week.

The church members could then start planning their meal that the visitors counted on. Pa Noorlog was a church elder; he had been retired for some time and this church work suited his schedule well.

One day, coming back from one of these house visits and the obligatory meal, he relayed that to his astonishment a common labor family had treated them to: "brune bonen, dik onder het vet en nog soepenbrie tou" (Groninger dialect describing a meal that befitted a higher social class.)

I cannot remember anything nice to write down about this man. What still bothers me to this day is overhearing the following dialogue between Pa Noorlag and his wife. Moeke[37] Noorlag asked: "Willem willst mie wat in't knipske doun?" To which replied Pa Noorlag replied: "D'hest gusteravond nog viefentwintig stuuvers van proam beurt." (She asked her husband to put some money in the household kitty to which he replies that she, on the previous evening, had received five nickels for renting out their canal scow.)

Moeke, Geesien Noorlag-Schmidt, was a sweet woman but life had not treated her kindly. Her mother passed away when she was three and her youngest sister seven months.

Her dad, Date Schmidt, remarried in 1867, she grew up with two more step brothers and a step sister from her dad's second marriage. Moeke Noorlag's father died when she was fifteen and shortly after her stepmother, Jantje Bouwman, remarried a farmer Eernst de Graaf, who was twelve years younger than his new bride and only fourteen years older than her oldest sister. Her two step brothers learned to be farmers from their new step dad and then emigrated to America in 1887. Just a year later the rest of the family followed them to America as well; Moeke's stepmother together with her farmer husband, her stepsister and two more daughters born from this last marriage. Moeke and her two sisters had by then already moved out and gotten married. Jantje was the only mother Moeke had known, who had raised her from age three. She and her sisters never saw their stepmother again A cousin had visited the family in America and he told the following story:

---

[37] Moeke: Mother in Groninger dialect

The stepmom, Jantje de Graaf-Bouwman, had dressed in her Sunday dress and was searching for her Psalm book, on the first Sunday after they had arrived at the home of her two sons in America, when the sons asked her: "Wat wil ie moetje?" ("What do you want, Mother?")

"Noar kerke tou natuurlijk!" ("To go to church of course!")

This prompted the boys to burst into laughing: "Hier is gain kerke!" ("There is no church here!") to which "Moetje" replied: "Wat douwn wie hier dan?" (What are we doing here then?)

Henk's father also had an uncle who emigrated in that same period, in 1891, to Chicago. When I visited my son in 1979, at his home in La Conner, Washington, I came across the name Neal Noorlag, a bulb grower in the Skagit Valley, who turned out to be Henk's cousin.

Henk's parents never felt the need to meet my parents during our twelve-year engagement. They were so damned smug. Was it a wasted time of my life? Yes, it was; the time I waisted waiting and the disappointments, especially when Henk was falling behind the other students. Maybe he could not help it. I heard later that his father, as a young man, had a drinking problem. This was common in the area at the turn of the twentieth century; when the peat had all been removed, there was little other work available, unemployment ran high and without a public safety net many of these families ended up in misery. The men resorted to drowning their frustrations in alcohol.

The area became a hotbed for radical socialism. Similar conditions that led to the 1917 October revolution in Russia. Lenin's rhetoric had a growing following here as well. One of his best-known Dutch disciples was a Lutheran preacher, Domela Nieuwenhuis, who preached the gospel according to Karl Marx. Nieuwenhuis accentuated his rhetoric with liberal use of bible texts. The Frisian peat workers elevated Nieuwenhuis to hero status with their Frisian nick name for him: "Us Verlosser" ("Our Redeemer"). A sample of his orating skills is a slogan he made popular: "Thinking workers don't drink and drinking workers don't think".

The working conditions, hours, and pay also improved for the men in the mastmakers shop through the efforts of the elected representatives of the workers. In some instances when the workers did not feel that their demands were met, violence flared against their employers. We had one worker who was a member of the SDAP (Social Democratic Labor Party). When Pa told him: "If they show up here to raise hell, I want you to stand behind the door with an axe to keep them out". He replied: "Yes boss, that's what we'll do here".

It was the start of the industrial revolution. Steam power was being replaced with electricity in the trains and with diesel engines in the ships and factories. The Philips light bulb factory in the south of Holland was drawing laborers from the unemployed peat workers in the North. Little by little the signs of laborers having a little more spending money became noticeable. Pa Noorlag asked himself: "What in the world does a laborer think he needs to buy a harmonium for?" Henk's parents moved back to city of Groningen. This way they did not need to pay for a boarding house for Henk.

In those days, the students practiced an old custom, which now appears bizarre, on graduation day or when a student had earned his doctorate, they would rent an open surrey to go for a ride through the city to celebrate the event, a large coach drawn by two horses. The horses wore large feather headgears in the colors of the fraternity. The students would throw pennies so that a long line of young boys would follow in their wake to gather up the coins.

It all could have been so good, because we were very much in love.

I have never had any regrets during my marriage to Dick that I broke the engagement to Henk after twelve years. But when I attempted to make contact again, a couple years after Dick's death in 1956, it still hurt when I found out that he had also recently been widowed and then already had plans to marry again.

1927 Bondsdag in Groningen. Board members of the YWCA, guest speakers and their partners, Rennie de Vries second from right, Henk Noorlag standing behind her.

23. Challenging Man's World

Christian and Socialist women groups pushed for blue laws and women's suffrage. The women in Holland finally gained voting rights in 1919. That same year, when I was eighteen, I joined the newly formed Reformed Girls Association (Gereformeered Meisjesbond), comparable to the YWCA, for young women in the ages sixteen to twenty-five. It opened a new world for many young women and me. We chose our own board of directors and we drew up our programs and platforms without any help from the men. This was a radical new concept for the men and intimidating to the more dependent women.

Henriëtte Kuyper was the Honorary President of the Meisjesbond. She was the daughter of Abraham Kuyper. Abraham Kuyper was the preacher who had differed on the doctrines of the Dutch Reformed Church and formed the Reformed Church in 1886. Henriëtte Kuyper was in a way to Holland what women like Susan B. Anthony and Alice Stone Blackwell were for the American women's suffrage movement. Kuyper had made several trips to the U.S.A. She brought many of her progressive ideas with her from America. The Dutch government sent her in 1919 as their delegate to the conference on women's rights that was held under the auspices of the League of Nations, the forerunner of the United Nations.

A young man wrote in 1913 in het "Jongelingblad" (Youth Forum) his thoughts on this new phenomenon: *"I have no objections when the young ladies are better informed. But there is no need for a young ladies organization. No, because this is really the task of a Youth (boys and girls) association. Because then we will be more effective with the knowledge gained from our sisters, and we do not keep this to ourselves, and have the ladies start something for themselves. The attraction of the youth is our strength. The power of our word should never be taken away from us. Should we, as future heads of our families, allow a woman to silence us? No, my friends, I think that the girls generally will find a better purpose than to join a young ladies auxiliary. A woman, a real woman at least, will find a different calling than to study literature, etc., etc. She shall learn how to run a household and the girls should be sewing and knitting.*[38]*"*

---

[38] From: 30-year Jubilee issue 1918-1948 of the association of Girl Clubs founded on the precepts of the Christian Reformed Church.

I was elected to the regional board of the Meisjesbond and in this function attended several of the annual national conventions.

Around 1925 at the national head office of the Meisjesbond in Utrecht. Rennie de Vries on far right. Standing in rear at doorpost is Riek Brandenburg whose name comes up in the last chapters.

24. The German Mastmaker

The losers of the First World War were heavily burdened by the war restitutions imposed on them by the victors. The Mark's value had dropped to little more than the paper it was printed on, through hyperinflation. Uncle Jentje hired August Arendt, who had served in the nearby naval base as a master carpenter, maintaining the spruce airplane frames. He had flown aboard bi-planes in the recent war as an observer/photographer. With his wood working skills, he quickly adapted to making spars and wood rigging blocks. August was born in 1897 in East Prussia, in Schillgehnen, which was returned to Poland after the Second World War and restored to its original name Szleny. August was a handsome man. A stunt flight with one of the navy bi-planes under the Prince Heinrich Bridge in 1920 resulted in him doing time in the Navy brig at the Holtenau Navy base.

The bridge through which August Arendt made his stunt flight.

The depression started to affect the business in Holtenau as well. Uncle Jentje and Aunt Grada started a café in a building next to the chandlery. Aunt Grada was the driving force, she cooked and served and Uncle Jentje walked around in his suit and tie chatting with the clients, passing through barge skippers and some local folks.

November 7, 1917 August Arendt in France during First World War

I remember Aunt Grada as a kind and funloving woman. She liked to attend the dances at the Kaiserliche (Imperial) Yacht club. Uncle Jentje would sit there watching her waltz and polka with the German navy officers and club members. Holland fared much better economically and America experienced the Roaring Twenties.

Jobseekers from Germany came across the border to Holland. Many of the Dutch households had German girls as servants in those years.

Uncle Jentje had developed a hernia from work in the shop, he wore a truss the rest of his life. This excused him from doing any physical work.

The Navy air base at Holtenau. Picture taken by August Arendt. 1920

They kept a cow, "Elze", in a pasture behind the buildings.

In the end, there was so little work in the mastmaker shop that August exchanged his leather wood working apron for a cotton waiter's apron. The tax rolls in Kiel-Holtenau for 1919 already listed Uncle Jentje's profession as a "Gastwirt" (innkeeper).

But by 1924 Uncle Jentje had lost all hope for a turn around and he closed shop.

He traded his inventory and tools for antique furniture since even a wheel barrow load of devalued German Marks would not buy much any longer in Germany. He decided to return to Holland.

In the meantime, *Rennie*, my namesake, and August had fallen in love. *Rennie* was then twenty and August was seven years older. Uncle Jentje came back with Adri, his younger daughter, to arrange for their return to Holland. *Rennie* had given him specific orders that she was staying in Holtenau until her dad had found a job for August and a place to live, complete with a piano for her to play on. A millwork company in IJsselstein, just south of Utrecht had a job for August and Uncle Jentje rented a nice apartment in Utrecht on the Wijkkade.

Utrecht, the capital of the province with the same name, sits right in the center of the Netherlands. Instead of buying a piano, *Rennie*'s father rented one for his daughter. She was an accomplished musician and played both classical piano and popular music. She spoke Frisian well, even though she left Friesland when she was just four years old and her mother only spoke Dutch. During the few years that Taeke Bijlsma worked in Holtenau she would have spoken Frisian with him and her father and with the Frisian barge skippers who were an important part of their regular customers.

The German mastmaker and his family moved in again for a while on the Polderdijk. I was working for Pa at that time. Adri and I got along great but we two Rennies, did not have much in common. Uncle Jentje traded his German passport in again for Dutch citizenship in 1926. *Rennie*, my cousin, kept her German nationality.

My uncle found a new career as a director of a retirement home in Elburg on the Eastern seashore of the Zuiderzee.

The "Feitenhof" was a foundation set up by Maria Catharina Feith (1664-1740 night in), financed mainly from the proceeds of the tenants on thirteen farms she owned. It was a very dignified home, befitting her legacy and a perfect place for our uncle who had so little in common with Pa and was awkwardly cast in a mastmakers business. We called him the "baron". There is a story that at one time he had just settled in for the night in a hotel in Valkenburg, in the very southeast corner of the Netherlands;

there was a knock on his door and he was told that he needed to turn his room over to a very important guest who had just arrived, some ambassador, who had not made a reservation. But the "baron" did not even consider moving and retorted: "Does a Frisian country squire have to move for an ambassador?" The ambassador did not get this room.

The "Feitenhof" was governed by the regents, Pastors from a combination of the different protestant churches in Elburg. The widow had stipulated a couple specific rules in her testament. For example, it was forbidden to speak while the Bible was being read. On the feast of Saint Martin, November 11, all the guests were to be poured a glass of red wine from crystal goblets that she had left for this purpose. The house had two chauffeured limousines; one for Uncle Jentje and one for the regents.

1927 wedding *Rennie* de Vries and August Arendt (with his WW-1 decorations).in the Dutch Reformed Church in Utrecht in 1927

25. The Big Move In 1928

Pa had counted on his oldest son Jan Siebold to take over from him. Jan went from the grade school in De Lemmer to a vocational school in Leeuwarden to become a marine engine mechanic. Pa had plans to expand the blacksmith shop with a marine engine repair facility.

The sailing barges were starting to add auxiliary inboard and outboard diesel and gasoline motors. It would offset the reduced demand for masts and spars and rigging that was starting to affect Pa's business. New building of traditional commercial sailing barges was slowing down in favor of motorized ships.

My oldest brother went on from Leeuwarden to Amsterdam to do an apprentice-ship with the StorkKromhout Marine Motor division on Oosterburg in the Amsterdam harbor. He boarded with the van den Berg family on the Jacob Maris square, with Uncle Karel, the same uncle who had helped me years earlier with the nurse training session at the Valerius Clinic and where I was befriended with Bé van den Berg. Jan had no desire to be a mastmaker. In 1926 he started an automobile business in Beverwijk, 20 miles west of Amsterdam.

The shop in Amsterdam. Mastmaker Scholing, photo taken around 1948

Pa had already started a mastmaker shop in Amsterdam in the Houthaven in 1921 and a chandlery store as well, nearby on the Houtmankade 37.

Jelle Rijpkema transferred from the branch in Heeg to Amsterdam. Jelle had taken over in Heeg when we moved back to De Lemmer from Heeg in 1902.

Plans to reclaim large sections of the Zuiderzee for agriculture had already been in the works before the end of the 19th century and were finalized in 1918. Construction on the Afsluitdijk, the dike that enclosed the Zuiderzee commenced in 1927 and was completed in 1932. New building of fishing boats operating on the Zuiderzee was cut back drastically from as early as 1900. At the turn of the century the fishing fleet, fishing from the various harbors on the Zuiderzee, counted roughly 1,400 boats of the dimensions that required the type of masts we made on the Polderdijk. Masts for new fishing boats were our bread and butter. The handwriting was on the wall.

The worldwide depression started to affect us as well. There was not enough work for our crew. I remember typing a long letter to the "Fryske Greidboeren" in the surrounding countryside. There was a tone of desperation in Pa's sales pitch. He was appealing to the farmers to buy their "bea ponters, fym-peallen", etc., from him to help him keep his mastmakers employed.

The letter, dated February 1924, is still in the old store files. I see from the letterhead that we then owned the 19th telephone in De Lemmer. Pa closed the shop and store in Heeg in 1925. Opoe passed away on November 22, 1925. Bosma, one of our workers, built her oak coffin; Fl. 100 was properly charged for the coffin to the family private account by the business that carried Opoe's name.

Pa decided that this was the right moment to sell the main store and shop on the Polderdijk. This way he could fairly divide the shares his brother and four sisters inherited.

The sale was made to a long-standing business acquaintance, the mastmaker van der Neut in Alphen. The first investments had already been made in Amsterdam. Pa figured that he needed to switch his dependency on the Zuiderzee fishermen to the commercial cargo sailing fleet. Amsterdam was to become the new home for the main office and stores.

He leased space in an old building on the Singel Canal, close to the Amsterdam seaport and the area where all the terminals were for the scheduled sailings to all parts of the country. The lease commenced on January 1st, 1928.

My youngest sister, Rientje, was thirteen years. Jan had already started his automobile business in Beverwijk. My oldest sister Ina worked and lived in Amsterdam on Vondelstraat. That left the seven of us to make the big move in the middle of the winter. All our belongings had been stowed aboard the Lemmer-Amsterdam ferry boat service.

By the time the s/s "Groningen IV" was to depart the harbor was frozen shut. All our crates and footlockers were hoisted out again and brought to the tramway station. This was the only connection to the nearest railway station in Stavoren. Notwithstanding the extreme cold, our entire crew with wives and children and many friends came to wave us farewell.

It was an emotional moment. Three of the men had worked over twenty-five years for Pa and Opoe. Gurbe van Brug started in Heeg the year before I was born there. Huite Zijlstra the rigger and skipper on our boat; the one who had given me the reassurance I needed in that storm when I was a teenager aboard "Top", Frens de Vries as the third longtimer. Fortunately, most of the men had kept their employment on the Polderdijk under the new owners.

Railway porters transferred our cases to the baggage car and we boarded the first-class section. The harbor of Stavoren was still open and the rail ferry s/s "Stavoren" took us across the Zuiderzee narrows to Enkhuizen from where we travelled the short distance to Amsterdam.

Our new home was in complete contrast to the Polderdijk. No longer would we have an unobstructed view across the Zuiderzee, no farmlands and grazing sheep, no longer would everyone in the neighborhood call me by name. Here my family's social status was just one of thousands instead of less than a hundred in De Lemmer. But at age twenty-six, I was looking forward to the new experience. The building on Singel 2^a was built between 1601 and 1603.

Singel 2 ª. My brother Siebold 5th generation Mastmaker on steps of the chandlery on the left side. Photo around 1956

Gable Stone

Photo: Vereniging Vrienden van Amsterdamse Gevelstenen

It was built right on the edge of the bay that was directly accessible to the Zuiderzee until a manmade island was built for Central Railroad Station which stands between it and the bay now. The building is known as the Spanish Gable, and it has an interesting lineup of previous owners and occupants. Hendrick Janszoon Cruywagen and his heirs owned it from 1641 until 1669. The name translates to wheelbarrow and is the reason for the decorative gable stone portraying a wheelbarrow. Hendrick was a sailmaker and operated his loft a ½ mile to the east, on the same water's shore, on the Prins Hendrikkade 34. The brick exterior was built on a frame of massive pine timbers. The floor and ceiling joist are rough-hewn and measure roughly 12 x 20 inches. The wall frame timbers are larger yet. Originally, all four floors above the ground level were warehouse floors. On the street level were then two residences and they were later used as retail stores, traveler's inn, ferryman's home, etc.

The office was on the second floor right above the chandlery; next to it lived the couple that operated the cafe below them. We lived on the entire third floor and a couple small bedrooms were built on the fourth warehouse floor for my younger brothers and sisters. The stairs in the building are steep and narrow. All of our belongings were hand hoisted up with the block and tackle that ran over a large wheel from the top floor. The big double warehouse doors opened flush with the floors and standing close to the edge looking down to the street was a scary experience.

The small chandlery had little room for storage; the backup supplies were stored on those upper floors and frequently they had to go up and down by way of the outside hoist.

The chandlery in 1956 Carol de Vries 6th Generation at counter. Rob Koop, 1995 ©

Later, the upper warehouse floors became the places where my children, nephews and nieces played similar games just like I did in the shop on the Polderdijk with my cousins. Great places to play hide and seek and let your imagination run wild.

Our views from the living area were the Haarlemmerdijk, Central Station, and the green oxidized copper roof of the Koepelkerk (Domed Church). I had to get used to all the new noises, the constant coming and going of trains on the nearby track over the steel bridge in and out of Central Station. The Haarlemmerdijk is a busy shopping street and the cafés were filled until late in the evening. From farther away we could hear the ships' steam whistles of the busy Amsterdam harbor.

I worked in the office again. Every other weekend I took the train to Groningen or Nieuwe Weerdinge to visit Henk. I wanted to start something for myself and I wanted to live on my own. That next year after we had moved to Amsterdam and with the financial help from Pa, I bought a small store on the de Clerqstraat 119. I sold delicatessen, mostly lunchmeats. Construction had just started on the new main Post Office on the Kostverlorenkade.

The construction crews became regular lunch customers for my ham sandwiches. The ham I boiled myself, two hams in a large kettle. A local barrel organ player always stopped to take the side cuts from the ham, which I saved for him, on his weekly run through the neighborhood. I lived above the store. For company and security, I took on a dog.

But my expectations, that this would solve the dilemma I was in with my never-ending engagement to Henk, became another disappointment. I was twenty-nine and if I had waited one more year I would not have needed to ask my parents any longer for their permission to be married. Finally, I had enough of all the waiting. I took the bull by the horns and broke off the twelve-year engagement.

The plan was to have my youngest brother Jentje take over the store. He had worked with me for a while, but that did not work out. I sold the shop to a Frisian couple from Haulerwijk but they were unable to make a go of it. Later, a sewing machine shop ended up taking over the space.

Then, just when I was familiarizing the new owners with the store, I met Dick. He had also been engaged previously and was no spring chicken either. Dick was three years my senior. He was an usher in the Keizersgrachtkerk church and I had noticed him when he did the collections. We were introduced to each other through Ginus Bosman who shared an apartment with Dick. Ginus was related to the van den Bergs on the Jacob Maris Plein, where I was often at home. Dick was born and raised in Amsterdam. He worked as a cashier for the Amsterdamsche Bank's branch near Dam Square. He had travelled to different parts of Europe as a member of a travel club. Dick also liked to sing and had a good voice; we both members of the KCOV, Royal Christian Oratorio Society. We were engaged on May 10th, 1932 and were married on the same date a year later. My brother-in-law, Jan Hartkamp, the Reformed minister in Alphen, officiated in the Keizersgracht-kerk.

My parents moved from the Singel 2ª to a home in NaardenBussum. Bussum was a bedroom town for many middle and upper class families whose breadwinners worked in Amsterdam.

As we could have predicted, Pa missed the water and the hustle and bustle of the maritime activity. They moved back to Amsterdam and rented two floors in one of those stately old Amsterdam merchants' homes on the canals, on Keizersgracht 54. It was just in time before our wedding to make sure that I could help with their move. The home had a long black and white marble floored hallway and polished brass stair rails. There was a roof terrace in the back from where you looked out upon the gardens and on the rear of the homes on the next canal, the Prinsengracht.

It was an easy walk to the Singel 2ª, where Pa would catch up with some of his old friends and the skipper customers for a cup of coffee or a beer next door in the pub. The store had become a place where many an old Lemsters would meet and trade lies in their own Frisian language. Jobs were becoming scarce with the diminishing fish catch and many came from De Lemmer to the big city to find work. Pa had transferred his responsibilities of running the business to my brother Siebold on February 1st, 1937.

We made our first home in the Pieter Basstraat, near the Concertgebouw, for the first two years of our marriage. Karolien (Lien) our first child was born here in 1934. At the end of 1936, we moved to a brand new apartment in the Alblasstraat 41 on the very southern edge of Amsterdam.

My oldest sister Ina was the first of us to have children. Siebold and his wife Saakje were next and by 1937 when our twins were born it started to become a lively gathering place on the Keizersgracht where we had birthdays or other occasions for the whole clan to come together. Pa would take our boys for walks to the harbor and teach them the names of all the different types of the traditional sailing barges.

26. The other Mastmakers' Daughter

The Great Depression started officially in 1929.
Unemployment had reached 20%. In Germany it was much worse;
by 1932 44% of the work force was without work. This is where
Hitler came in with his scheme to return Germany to greatness
after being humiliated in the First World War. Hitler was elected to
chancellor of the Reichstag in 1933. His popularity and his National
Socialist Democratic Labor Party (NSDAP) drew great crowds and
new members. *Rennie*, my cousin, joined Hitler's party. Her
German husband, August, never became a Nazi member.

Their first son, Georg, was born in 1930; years later he
recounted how, when he was four years old, his dad took him for a
bicycle ride to Doorn and pointed out to him the villa where the
exiled German emperor Wilhelm II was living. His dad had tears in
his eyes when he told his son that this was the leader he had
fought for in the First World War.

Rennie's dad, my Uncle Jentje, had a falling out with the regents of the
chique retirement home he ran in the "Feitenhof". He found a similar
position in Hilversum, about 20 miles east of Amsterdam. The Dutch
Reformed Church in Hilversum built a brand new retirement center on
the Vaartweg and opened its doors on May 31st 1930 with Jentje de Vries
as its first director. It became known as the "Boomberg" and still operates
to this day under this name.

**May 31st, 1930. Uncle Jentje in center planting a tree. Aunt Grada far left and
my cousin Adri de Vries on far right.** Photo Historisch Hilversum.

My uncle kept charge of the new facility until 1935 but in the meantime, in 1932, he set up his own private retirement home in Hilversum with his share of Opoe's estate.

August Arendt was put in charge of the "Hoffwerk", assisted by his wife *Rennie*. The Arendts, with son Georg, moved from Utrecht to Hilversum. "Hoffwerk" was a stately old mansion on the Boomberglaan 13 in a large park like setting with big old Beech trees and an undergrowth of Azaleas and Rhododendrons. The third floor was a tower penthouse where the Arendts made their home. Many of the occupants were retired repatriates from the Dutch East Indies where they had been in colonial service. This was a chic set-up be-fitting our uncle the "Baron". He used many of his antique treasures that he had brought from Germany to dress up the facility. Several of the guests had brought their chambermaids or butlers with them.

Dieuwke Lighthart, as I wrote earlier, came here from De Lemmer to serve as a social assistant to one of the Gentlemen guests.

1932 Opening of rest home "Hoffwerk". Center rear Jentje and Grada de Vries, far right *Rennie* (Rinsje) and August Arendt.

Huize „Hoffwerk"   *Hilversum*

    Rennie possessed extra sensory abilities. She communicated with the dead, with departed family members from both her father and mother's side. She spent many hours in room #1, with the Nout couple, who had spent most of their adult life in the Dutch East Indies. She was fascinated by their experience with spiritualism from Eastern cults and Buddhism. They held psychic séances and *Rennie* would revel in her role as a medium. When Georg was ten, his mom introduced him to her world of hocus pocus and he reluctantly discovered that he had apparently inherited some of her bizarre talents. August had enough of this difficult woman and left her in 1934. In a letter, she wrote to Georg in the sixties, she writes that she was all alone with Georg at Christmas time in 1934. She bore her second son, Gerard, in May 1935. But in all likelihood August was not his father. She told the boys later that their father had been killed in an airplane crash at Tempelhof Airport in Berlin in the accident of the KLM DC-2 the "Uiver". That did not quite check out because that plane had crashed in Iraq on its return flight from the Dutch East Indies. How could a six and one year old have known any better?

    The divorce became final in the first week of 1935.

The municipal records for Utrecht show that August checked out in October 1935 destined for Charlottenburg, a Berlin suburb. The story that did the rounds in our family was that August had taken off with the maid. This could have been the German woman they hired in 1931, a year after Georg was born. Maria Elsa Dombrowski moved in with the Arendts on the Roerplein. She was born in Goldap, Poland and came from Neuendorf in Germany to the Arendts. She was two years younger than *Rennie*. Miss Dombrowski moved to Jutphaas near Utrecht when the Arendt family moved from Utrecht to run the "Hoffwerk"

Adri, *Rennie*'s fouryear younger sister, had stayed with her parents when they first lived in De Lemmer and later in Elburg and at the "Boomberg" in Hilversum. Adri met her husband while attending a meeting of the "Fryske Krite" in Bussum. This is a social club for Frisians living beyond the Frisian borders; similar to the many different clubs for immigrants in North America. At these gatherings, they can speak in their own Frisian language.

Frisians take serious offense to anyone calling their language a Dutch dialect. Adri was born in Holtenau and only spent a limited time on their return to Holland in Friesland. Their father spoke Frisian with them; their mother only spoke Dutch and their Holtenau neighbors and playmates German.

Adri's husband, Kees Bakker, came from Leeuwarden, Friesland; born in 1913 in Baarderadeel, he was five years younger than Adri. Bakker worked as a mechanical engineer for a linoleum floorcovering producer "Balatum" in Huizen. They were married in 1938 and lived in Blaricum. Kees Bakker joined the Dutch Nazi Party (NSB), much to the displeasure of his new wife. When he came home in his NSB uniform she cut it to pieces. With August out of the picture, Uncle Jentje resigned from his directorship at the "Boomberg" and took over the running of his rest home on the Boomberglaan, the "Hoffwerk". And in order to support his oldest daughter he leased another large villa in 1936, the "Limborg", on the Gravelandseweg 61, also in Hilversum. He put *Rennie* in charge of it and used it to also provide assisted living to older folks.

The "Baron" still had enough of his antique furniture to dress up this home as well in the style of his trade.

Huize „ de Limborg"   *Hilversum*

One of the guests in the "Limborg" was Sjoukje Troelstra-Bokma de Boer, better known under her penname Nienke van Hichtum[39], a well-known Dutch author of children books. She adapted Winnie the Pooh into a Dutch version. Sjoukje was the daughter of a Dutch Reformed minister, born in Friesland. She was a member of the most left leaning political party the SDAP, in sharp contrast to the political convictions of *Rennie* Arendt. But, yet the two were the best of friends. The author passed away in the "Limborg" in 1939.

There were Jews among the occupants of both rest homes. Uncle Jentje was able to help several of them through his connections with the shipping industry to find a way to get across to England before the Germans overran the low lands. The Wehrmacht demanded possession of the "Limborg" in October 1940.

As far as I know, *Rennie*, not withstanding her NAZI association, has never cooperated with the invaders at the expense of the Jews or aided in the persecution of her one-time compatriots.

---

[39] In 2001, the movie "Nynke" came out about the life of Sjoukje Bokma de Boer.

1938 at Schiphol airport for an excursion flight in the DC-2 "Kiewit" see below insert

L.R.: front Georg Arendt, his opa Jentje de Vries, Gerard and chauffeur/servant.

1940 just before the Germans claimed the KLM DC-3 "Roek". A similar outing at Schiphol. On the left Folkert de Vries the sailmaker neighbor of Jan Siebold de Vries on the Polderdijk and Folkert's wife. The second couple from left are my parents Jan S. de Vries and Karolien de Vries-van Anken.

1939: Georg, with pen, in Kaiser Wilhelm Schule, Amsterdam

Jan and Jaap at baptismal. L to R or R to L??

27. Twins!

On the last day of February 1937, it was a Sunday, we were presented with a surprise. After I had delivered a healthy baby boy, doctor Lybrants announced: "Mrs. van Ommen, you are not done yet!" An hour and a half later his brother made his surprise appearance. Moe had to quickly get her knitting needles busy again and Dick and my sisters were given another shopping list.

Dick had a backache when we were getting ready to go to church for the baptismal; I had to help him get his socks on and kidded him suggesting that I should leave him home. Our minister, Sikkel, remarked that if it were his children, he would have waited another week for the mother to come along, where upon Dick responded that if it were for him, they would have been presented the week before. Yes, sure, Dick!

Moving to the Alblasstraat turned out to have been a good choice. It was a brand-new neighborhood right on the southern edge of the city. It was and remains one of the most grandiose multipurpose city plans ever attempted. It was the brainchild of Hein Berlage and was called "Plan Zuid" (Plan South). The part we lived in is called the Rivierenbuurt (Rivers section) and every street, boulevard, and square bears the name of a river or waterway.

Our apartment block was a Protestant housing cooperative; across the street was a similar apartment block of a co-op for Roman Catholics. Most of the residents were young couples moving into their first apartment. This way the children had lots of playmates their age to choose from. Because the majority belonged to the same church and the church operated schools, they spent a large part of their growing up years together. At the end of our street was the biggest sand box a child could ever have wished for; farmland that had been covered with sand dredged from the North Sea, to be the foundation for future home construction. Beyond this were farmlands with drainage canals to fish in and to skate on in the winter. The Amstel River was fifteen minutes walk away; it offered a great choice of paths along the river and through the countryside to walk and ride our bicycles.

A few blocks away between us and the Amstel was a large open-air public swimming pool where the neighborhood kids spent most of their summer days for a ten cents entrance fee.

August 31st, 1939. Our street. L.R. Lientje (Karolien) Jan or Jaap, Dick Jaap or Jan. The last time that the flags came out for the Queen's birthday, until 1945.

Many Jews, moving away from the threat in Hitler's rhetoric in Germany and beyond, found ample housing choices in this new section of Amsterdam. A brand new stark modern sjoel (Synagogue) was consecrated in 1937; it was just a few blocks away from our street. None of us knew then that this peaceful setting would become the scene of the cruel raids, deportations and extermination of so many from this neighborhood, including the Frank family. The Rivierenbuurt was also the home from where a Jewess betrayed her own people. Ans van Dijk is the only Dutch female traitor who was executed after the war for her vicious service to the enemy.

Part Two: The Second World War

28. Two Rennies - Two different drummers

Germany declared war on the Netherlands in May 1940. The Dutch mobilized their army. The leader of the Dutch National Socialist Movement (NSB), Anton Mussert, and most of the NSB members were rounded up. My German Nazi cousin, the other *Rennie* de Vries, ended up sharing her detention cell in de "Krententuin" (Currant Garden) prison in the town of Hoorn with Mussert's wife. Later, after the Fascist troops overran the Dutch defenses, she boasted of the company she kept in her detention.

A glorious period began for my cousin *Rennie* and her Dutch Nazi sympathizers. Nazi *Rennie*'s oldest son, Georg, or "Bubi", was ten years old when the Germans invaded the Netherlands. He had started elementary school in Hilversum at the "Groen van Prinsterer Instituut", a private Protestant Christian school. Once the Germans ruled the Netherlands his mother decided that Georg should attend the German "Kaiser Wilhelm Schule" on the Nieuwe Looierstraat in Amsterdam. In 1941, after the Germans had established their own Nazi doctrine school in Hilversum, Georg could forego the twenty-mile train ride to Amsterdam.

Georg finished his sixth grade there that year and his younger brother, Gerard, started first grade. The Nazis poisoned these youngsters with their propaganda and hatred towards the Jews. The little Arendt brothers scratched anti Jewish slogans on the walls of the toilet in my parents' home on the Keizersgracht. Georg joined the Hitler Jugend at age eleven.

Their uncle, Kees Bakker, married to Adri the younger sister of *Rennie* Arendt, took a chapter out of the life of Adri's Great-Great Grandfather Sybolt Ottes de Vries, whom you read about in the first chapter of this book. Sybolt was conscripted to fight the Russians under Napoleon in 1812 and managed to be one of the few to return with Napoleon's decimated "Grand Armée". Kees Bakker joined the Dutch Waffen SS Legion and lost his life in the spring of 1942 at the small town of Pyatilipy, near Novgorod; before the battle for Leningrad in 1943.

Sterbeurkunde

(Standesamt I Berlin — — — — — — — — Nr. 4829/1942

Der Legions-Sturmmann Cornelis B a k k e r—

— — — — — — — — gottgläubig — — — — — — — —

wohnhaft in Blaricum in den Niederlanden, Huizer — weg 29 — — — — — — — — — — — — — — — — — —

ist am 4. April 1942 — — — um — — — Uhr — — — Minuten

in Berlin Pistilipy in Rußland auf dem — — verstorben Hauptverbandplatz verstorben. — — — — — —

Der Verstorbene war geboren am 15.April 1913 — — —

in Baarderadeel in den Niederlanden. — — — — —

(Standesamt — — — — — — — — — Nr. — — — — —

Vater: Auke Bakker,zuletzt wohnhaft in Leeuwar-den. — — — — — — — — — — — — — — — — — —

Mutter:Akke Martin,wohnhaft in Leeuwarden. — —

— — — — — — — — — — — — — — — — — — — —

Der Verstorbene war — nicht — verheiratet mit Adriana — Anna de Vries. — — — — — — — — — — — —

— — — — — — — — — — — — — — — — — — — —

Berlin — — — — — — — — — —, den 16. Mai — — — 1949

Der Standesbeamte
In Vertretung

The Death Certificate of Kees Bakker. It states that he was Christian and that his parents were Auke and Akke Bakker from Leeuwarden.

Bakker was buried in Hilversum with full military honors. His widow moved from Blaricum to Hilversum, Emmastraat 43, into a home that had belonged to a Jewish family. Adriana, who had no sympathy for the Nazi convictions of her husband, was totally devastated and ashamed; she took her life by opening the gas valves of her kitchen stove.

Rennie then moved into Adri's larger home. Adri's father, my Uncle Jentje de Vries, reburied Adri's remains in the family grave in 1951 after her mother's death.

Rennie favored Gerard over his older brother Georg

In an earlier chapter, you read that most likely Georg's father, August, was not the father of Gerard. Georg reminded her too much of the man she was unable to keep. She could never forgive August and took her spite out on Georg.

Rest home Hoffwerk" Hilversum, *Rennie* with Swastika insignia, Gerard and Georg (in Jugendsturm uniform.) Mother's Day 1941

August Arendt in 1920

29. In the Resistance[40]

    In the first year of the occupation life appeared to go on along the old routines. But slowly the screws were tightened on the Dutch population. Henk Dienske was the leader of the L.O. (national organization for assistance to "onderduikers"[41]) in the province of North Holland, which includes Amsterdam. All men between the ages of 18 and 45 were to report for conscription in the forced labor force. Many went into hiding. The biggest challenge was to be able to provide them with falsified ration coupons. All food was distributed on these ration coupons and without an identity card they had no access to these rations. The Resistance stole these coupons or printed bonus copies and also made up falsified I.D. cards for the ones in hiding. Jews that went underground were also provided the same documents and ration coupons by the Resistance.

    Henk Dienske was six years younger than I was; he had served as an officer in the Dutch Army that had tried to stop the German invasion. The Dienske family were members of the same Christian Reformed Church, the Waalkerk, which we belonged to. We all lived in the same neighborhood. One of Henk's daughters was in the same grade school class as our twins. The parents of Henk lived right across the street from us. I was recruited by Henk and acted as a redistribution link in the flow of these clandestine documents. Couriers, mostly young women, often students, would deposit their contraband at our address. We lived on the third floor in an apartment building. A stone stair led up to the second floor from where they would ring our doordoorbell. I would then open the second-floor door remotely and leave the door open to our third floor flat, we never had any visual contact; they knew where to deposit their deliveriedeliveries, which they usually hid inside their underwear and bras.

---

[40] In **Part Three** you will find valuable background information to this part of the book. Information that was compiled after these events in part Two took place.

[41] Onderduiker=diver, the men who went into hiding to escape German forced labor.

They left their contraband behind the commode in our toilet. Another courier would take the same shipment further to another destination. Again, there was no physical contact between the courier and me. But there were also times that a number of incoming shipments were split up at our home before they were being taken to their final destination. Henk and others would then come to oversee the redistribution.

My I.D. or laissez passer as a member of the Dutch Resistance, L.O.

30. **My husband arrested**

A black car drove slowly into the Alblasstraat where we lived on the evening of the fourth of April 1944. The car stopped near our address. A civilian stepped out and asked our daughter Lientje, who was playing in the street: "Can you tell me where I can find the van Ommens?" Now, that was not that difficult for an almost ten-year-old.

The civilian happened to be Maarten Kuiper, a Dutch traitor, who was accompanied by Friederich Christian Viebahn, Staffelsturmscharführer. Later on, we discovered that we had earned the distinction to have been visited by a notorious posse of the German SD (Sicherheits Dienst). These same two men arrested the Anne Frank family four months later. The Frank family went through the same routine as my husband via the SD headquarters in the Euterpestraat and then sent to the prison on the Weteringschans. Maarten Kuiper was also the one to empty his pistol on the legendary Resistance heroine Hannie Schaft, two weeks short of the end of the war. His bloodthirstiness became the fatal fate for the many men picked at random in the "Silbertanne" executions at the end of the war. Kuiper was sentenced to death by the Dutch war court and executed right after the war.

The black booted gentlemen rang our door bell and announced themselves as: "Police" and then explained that they were looking for housing for people that were being evacuated from the coast line, where a defensive system was being built to keep any invasions from the North Sea at bay. Dick happened to be on the fourth-floor attic listening to his clandestine radio transmissions from the BBC. After tramping through our apartment for a half hour, they disappeared across the street to pay a visit to the street level apartment of Henk Dienske's parents. But twenty minutes later Kuiper with a German soldier came back up our stairs. The soldier had his rifle drawn. They arrested Dick and took him across the street to the Dienskes. It was obvious that they were on a wild goose chase. Dick had never been involved in any of my resistance activities, and for every one's safety, it was not discussed between us. I was hoping that it all would turn out to be an error. It was obvious that they were on a wild goose chase.

They did not seem to be clear in what or whom they were searching for. Dick had never been involved in any of my illegal activities, and for every one's safety, it was not discussed between us.

But yet the thoughts of what the Germans could be up to frightened me and my praying started in earnest.

The old Dienske, Johan, Henk's father was not home yet. Another man, a certain van der Most[42] out of the Deurlostraat, was being interrogated, in the Dienske home, by Emil Rühl, second in command at the SD Amsterdam headquarters. Dick was brought, with van der Most, to the SD headquarters. Dick was asked what he knew of a certain "de Ridder". This was the alias of Henk Dienske. Dick did not have a clue. The only "de Ridder" he knew was our milkman who came daily through our neighborhood to deliver fresh milk. Johan Dienske was brought later that evening to join Dick and van der Most. When the old Dienske arrived home, Kuiper was waiting for him. His wife, Jo, had a plate of cereal ready for him and Kuiper let him eat it and mocked him: "Don't you need to say grace first?" The threesome, Dick, van der Most and Johan, were brought over to Weteringschans prison, near the Rijksmuseum. Each was in a separate but adjoining cell with van der Most in the middle cell. Johan was transferred to a different part of the prison the next morning. Dick's cell number was B 2.16. Johan's wife, Jo, was also arrested and brought to the women's section of Weteringschans prison. Dick shared his cell with an "onderduiker" and Sponmoelee[43] who had been imprisoned for more than two years. The first thing his new cellmates asked was: "Do you have any cigarettes or tobacco?" No, Dick had neither. Dick slept reasonably well on his straw mattress that first night in prison, considering his predicament. Their daily routine was to be woken at 7 a.m. and then to wash their faces from the water pitcher. Each had four thin slices of bread and tasteless coffee for breakfast. The best that could be said for the coffee was that it was warm. Lunch consisted of potatoes and cabbage that floated in warm water. Every other day they were served soup that did not taste bad, but was far too little. Dinner was identical to breakfast. On Saturday, the prisoners received 25 grams margarine, a small chunk of cheese, and a tiny measure of sugar, which was meant to last for a week.

When Dick paced himself, it could last him through Tuesday.

---

[42]Philippus van der Most. Dick van Ommen wrote in his diary that v/d Most was very scared. His name has never come up again.

[43]Most likely the name is Sponselee and a memory or writing error in Dick's Diary

Every two weeks, on Wednesday, the Red Cross distributed a package to every prisoner. That was a feast! The package contained six slices of bread with sausage, two slices rye bread with cheese, one boiled egg, sugar, two pounds apples, two pounds spice cake, a cube of lard and vitamin C tablets.

De "onderduiker" was sent to the prison camp in Amersfoort. Sponmoelee was a typical ordinary Amsterdammer and a very nice person. He was married and had a young daughter. He could tell some great tales about all his experiences, especially about the cellmates he had seen come and go in these two years. He had been sentenced to two and a half years for his participation in the General Strike in February 1942[44]. Sponmoelee had shoveled coals in a steam plant at Schiphol airport.

On April 7th, Good Friday, they received a new fellow cellmate named Voogd. He was a member of the Dutch National Socialist Party, the NSB. Voogd was an officer in the W.A., a paramilitary auxiliary of the NSB. He was a strange and seedy character and his shady dealings apparently got him into this prison. He was a fourty-eight-year-old widower. He had six children; his oldest daughter was twenty-five. Voogd told us that he slept with a nineteen-year-old. She was the mother of a child she conceived with a German officer who had in the meantime been killed on the Eastern Front.

Voogd demanded constant attention. At times, he was totally disoriented and could not sleep. He'd either talk non-stop or just sat there and stared at the walls. He had been raised in the Orthodox Reformed Church and had been going to church with his children regularly until he joined the NSB. When he saw Dick and Sponmoelee, who was Roman Catholic, praying together, he joined them.

On that same day, Good Friday, I rode my bicycle to the Euterpestraat, with a set of clean clothes for Dick. I did not know yet that Dick and the Dienskes were being held at Weteringschans prison. I lucked out, Viebahn the SD officer who had arrested my husband was willing to see me at Weteringschans prison and told me that I should bring the change of clothes with me.

---

[44]This "February Strike" was called for by the Communist labor party and managed to halt practically all public transportation and seriously disrupted the NAZI war machine. The German reprisals were brutal.

I needed to get the keys from Dick, including the one to our safe. No, we did not have any jewels in there, but I'd rather not had the SD keep these keys. Dick also had meat ration coupons with him when he was arrested.

Viebahn took me into a small office and tried in vain to interrogate me and I learned from it that they were still trying to identify whom "de Ridder" was. Viebahn then went to get the keys and the food rations coupons. After that he directed me to where to leave the package for Dick. I told him that there was a Bible in the package. "No, Mrs. van Ommen that is strictly verboten". When I gave the package to a prisoner at the gate and I mentioned the Bible, he said: "Oh, just keep it in there, sometimes, they close an eye". And sure enough, it did work. Much later, Dick related to me that they read from this little Bible every day.

At that same time, while I was there, Viebahn had Dick summoned from his cell: "Your wife is here to get your keys and ration coupons". Then he asked him once more: "And who exactly is de Ridder?" And once again he was unable to satisfy him with that question. Viebahn told him that falsified ration cards were being distributed at our apartment. Dick retorted: "That is a total surprise to me!" He did not get a chance to ask if he could be allowed to see me.

One day Voogd went totally off his rocker. It was so bad that Dick and Sponmoelee called for the doctor to tend to the poor man. After the doctor left, he asked if Dick could read him a part of his Bible. He read him Psalm 42: "As a deer longs for flowing waters" and in particular the verse:

How sad are you, my soul,
and restless in me.
Base your hope on the Lord,
in days to come I will praise Him again,
my God who observes me and rescues me.

Dick recalled this as a touching and memorable experience. From that moment on Dick read him a chapter from the little Bible every morning and evening.

Emil Rühl took his turn on April 21st to interrogate Dick. Rühl was the one who had been at the parents of Henk Dienske's house the day of Dick's arrest on April 4th. The German asked him once more who "de Ridder" was and there was a new name: van Bergen. And once again Dick had to disappoint his interrogator.

Then Rühl asked him: "Do you know Dienske?" When Dick acknowledged in the affirmative, he was told: "We have him already!" "Well, well" answered Dick.

Next Rühl asked: "Does he ever come to your home?" "No, never" replied Dick. Within seconds he confronted Dick, from the next room, with Henk Dienske who had been caught the day before. Rühl then turned to Henk and asked him: "How many times have you visited the van Ommen home?" Dienske answered: "Two or three times."

This threw Dick for a loop. He maintained his disbelief. Rühl tried to bluff Dick with: "I have asked your wife". Henk was then taken back to his cell. Dick stuck to his story. "Someone must have let Dienske into your home; we'd better go and arrest your wife." This prompted Dick to change his story in an attempt to protect me. He then confirmed that he was the one responsible and that indeed Henk Dienske had visited our apartment. After a couple more questions, Dick was told: "Es wird schwer bestrafft!" (This will be severely punished!)

Sponmoelee left Dick's cell on May 1st, he had been such a good companion. This left just Voogd. Two days later Voogd also left the cell and was transferred to Amersfoort, from where he ended up in a German prison camp. He took Dick's hand, on leaving, and wished him: "Mr. van Ommen, God bless you!" He knew several hymns and psalms by heart which they sang together in their cell.

31. Behind Bars

After much thought, prayers and consultations with my parents and brothers and sisters I decided to turn myself in and tell the SD that my husband was not the person they were after. Some of my family members had suggested that I go into hiding.

Our daughter was then nearly ten and the twins were seven. Since they had caught their "de Ridder" as Henk Dienske on April 20, they might have lost their interest in the smaller fries of his organization. I also expected that they would sentence a woman less severely than the men and I was worried about my husband's health; he was not as robust as I am[45].

On April 25th, I knocked on the gates of Weteringschans prison and told them that they had the wrong person. My sister-in-law, Saakje de Vries, had come to collect the twins and their sister Lientje was staying at my parents' home.

An urgent message had been smuggled from Weteringschans prison to the leaders of the LO, the provincial organization of the Resistance, that Henk was being put under enormous pressure by Rühl and his cruel henchmen. If they would manage to break their leader down then the whole organization could be compromised.
The armed annex of the LO, the LKP (Landeljke Knok Ploeg) under the command of Gerrit van der Veen, who also lived and worked in our neighborhood, undertook an attack on the Weteringschans prison on May first in order to free Henk Dienske. We, my husband and the parents of Henk Dienske, were all in the same prison at the time. We could hear the commotion and the rifle fire, but we found out that it ended in total disaster due to the deceit of a couple Dutch traitors.

After Voogd had been transferred on May 3rd from Dick's cell, he found himself alone in his cell for the first time. In the evening the door opened and a young man, of around thirty, became his new cellmate. He turned out to be a member of the same Reformed church affiliation as we are. He had been married recently and had become a father in the last two months. His home was Zaandam. He had come home for a short visit from a forced labor assignment in Berlin. Instead of returning to Berlin he had gone into hiding and was caught in Haarlem.

---

[45]Rennie outlived her husband, who died of heart failure at age 57, by 35 years.

114

Dick did not remember his name. The man had been an active member of his church and they read together from Dick's little Bible. They played a board game that they fabricated on the back of the cell house rules. He had tobacco and matches and they would take turns drawing a puff from their cigarette.

The parents of Henk Dienske, Johan and Jo Dienske, were released from prison on May 3rd.

On May 5th, Dick and his new cellmate were reading the Bible passage where the apostle Peter is led out of his prison by an angel. That very afternoon, around 4 o'clock, Dick's name and cell number were being called out. The cell door was thrown open and the guard announced: "van Ommen, get ready to move". Several possibilities flashed through Dick's head, transfer to another prison or camp or possibly release. Dick said to the guard: "Probably a transfer". The guard answered: "I don't think so, it is too late in the day for a transfer, you will probably be released". And sure enough, though he had difficulty believing it, he ended up getting his personal items back that they had taken from him and he was sent to the Euterpestraat, SD headquarters, to check out.

There Dick stood on the busy Leiden Square, trying to get used again to the bright day light. A month earlier, when he was put behind bars, it was still early spring, cold and the trees were bare. Now the trees were in bloom and tulips bloomed in a park nearby. The first thing he had to do was to find a payphone. The Muizelaars, a few doors down the street from us, had a telephone. The neighbors told him the sad news that I had been arrested in the meantime. His joy turned into concern for me. He had hoped that his confession, and the fact that they had their "de Ridder", they no longer would have any interest in me. Dick's next call was placed to his boss at the branch office of the Amsterdamse Bank. Mijnheer van Velzen was surprised to hear his voice. He assured him of his support and his concerns when he heard of my arrest. He told Dick to take his time and take care of his personal affairs before coming back to work. The third call was made to Siebold, my brother on the Singel 2A. Siebold came right away to find Dick on the Leiden Square.

They went together to the SD headquarters to check out. He presented himself to Rühl in room 33, where he was told: "Your wife will end up in a concentration camp". Siebold had already spread the word to the family that Dick had been released.

They took a taxi to the Singel where Dick met our twins, Jan and Jaap. The boys had never seen their father like this before. Unshaven, his collar unbuttoned and he had lost a lot of weight.

Siebold and Saakje, after Dick had a shave and dinner, accompanied him to my parents who had moved in the beginning of the war from the Keizersgracht to a ground floor apartment on the East side of Amsterdam. The stairs in the beautiful old house on the canals had become too much of an effort for my parents.

Lientje, who had been staying with my parents since my arrest, came running towards Dick with a big bouquet of spring flowers she had gathered from the garden. There was a lot of catching up to do on the events that had happened while Dick was cut off from the outside world. He heard that the old Dienskes had also been released two days earlier. Dick stayed the night with his parents -in-law. He did not sleep well the first night of his newly gained freedom whereas he never had a problem sleeping on his straw mattress in the jail.

The next day, a Saturday, Dick returned to our apartment in the Alblasstraat. He showered and hung his clothes to air out and to get rid of the prison smell. He weighed himself, sixty-two kilos (137 pounds). Afterwards he returned to the Singel.

Dick had promised his young cell companion that he would pay a visit to his wife in Zaandam. He found her home and she was very happy to have news of her husband and to know of the fellowship they had together. That same evening, he met with Johan Dienske and Pastor Kunst of our Waalkerk church at the home of Frits de Die, in the Waalstraat.

Frits was the brother of Henk Dienske's wife and his home was where Henk hid out most of the time before he walked into the trap that led to his death in Gernan captivity. The four men wanted to try come up with a plan on how to smuggle word to me as to how much they knew at the SD about Henk's activities. The next day, Sunday, Dick went to our usual church service again at the Waalkerk.

It was a very emotional moment to be back in the house of the Lord with his brothers and sisters. Many of them came to welcome him back and express their concern and support for me. Jo and Johan Dienske came to see Dick in the afternoon. Jo told Dick that she had found a piece of paper in the prison court yard, where the prisoners were allowed to spend fifteen minutes in the fresh air every day, with a message for her from me: "Keep smiling, Oma Jo, Rennie". Johan Dienske had been in a solitary cell in another wing of the prison.

In the meantime, I had been transferred from Wetering-schans prison to the prison on the Amstelveenseweg. Dick had tried to smuggle a note to me, through several different channels, to let me know what they knew of the facts that the SD had been able to get from their interrogations of Henk Dienske. But this information has never reached me.

On Ascension Day, May 18ᵗʰ, Dick went with Lientje and the boys to visit my youngest brother, Jentje, and his family in Uithoorn, ten miles south of Amsterdam on the Amstel River. The train terminal for the connection to Uithoorn is right in front of Amstelveenseweg prison. Jaap came on his own to the station from the Westlandsgracht where he was now staying with Dick's younger brother and family. Jan was brought from the Singel. Dick and Lientje came earlier from my parent's home and Dick checked in at the prison gate with the excuse that he needed his fountain pen out of my personal belongings. The guard came back with my purse. He removed the fountain pen and while the guard looked the other way, he slipped the same Bible I had smuggled to him into my purse. Dick asked if he could see me. The man, he turned out to be the prison director, answered: "I have not seen my wife in five years".

Dick stopped in the middle of the street, before the four of them walked into the station, and turned around to the massive stone prison building and yelled to the top of his voice: "Rennie, Rennie!!!"

This particular episode of the war has always stayed in the then seven-year-old Jaap's memory. He had to walk past the prison every school day and that day he found out that his mother was locked up somewhere behind those high stone walls.

Once a week, on Friday, prisoners were allowed to receive their clean laundry from their family members. That Friday May 19, the day after Ascension Day, Dick found out that I was transferred that morning to the Vught SS concentration camp. Dick brought the news to my brother and family on the Singel and ran there into my Uncle Jentje who had just heard the same at the SD headquarters. He relayed Rühl's answer to his question as to how long my prison term was for: "For as long as the war lasts".

My Uncle Jentje had made another visit to the Euterpestraat to plead my case before the SD. We had hoped that his impressive Frisian Country Squire image would impress the Germans. And the fact that he was the father of my German cousin, *Rennie*, who had shared her cell with Mrs. Mussert the wife of the head of the Dutch Fascist party, before the German invasion.

Uncle Jentje had also brought along his Iron Cross distinction he had earned for his help to the German war effort in the First World War. On his first visit Emil Rühl, the second in command, told him at the SD headquarters: "this woman must be guilty, she refuses to answer any of our questions".

Rühl could not help him. On the second visit, he managed to get an audience with the top dog, Willy Lages who told him to come back May 19. When my uncle returned on the 19th he was referred back to Emil Rühl in room number 38, where they told uncle Jentje that I had been sent to the Vught concentration camp in the southern part of Holland.

The following day, Saturday, Dick visited Mr. van Proosdij[46], the lawyer who represented Henk Dienske and the others arrested of the same Resistance group. A court hearing for the Dienske group was to have taken place in October. But after Hitler's "Niedermachungsbefehl" (Order to kill) of July 1944, any form of court heaings and "justice" was dispensed by the kangaroo court of the SD. None of my group ever had their day in court.

---

[46]A.C.G. van Proosdij, the father of Jaap van Proosdij who worked with the German-Dutch lawyer Calmeyer. They saved over 600 Jews through a clever system of falsifying their ethnicity.

32. "Das sind die Frommen!"

After hours of interrogations, Emil Rühl, my exasperated interrogator blurted out: "Das sind die Frommen!" (These are the Pious!) He had not managed to get any information out of me.

Are they so special? Yes, they are the ones over whom God stretches out His arms. This may sound awkward, but it is the truth. They are the ones who manage to hang on to their Bible, in spite of the prison rules; the ones who secretly hold religious exercises in the concentration camps and sing softly behind the barracks.

Rühl and his cronies finally realized that they were not going to get any wiser from me. I was transferred to the prison on the Amstelveenseweg.

I shared my cell, meant for one prisoner, with three women in Weteringschans prison. The senior of the four of us slept on a cot and the other three on straw mattresses on the floor. As the new arrival I was told, after the: "Good Night", that we were going to sing a song for our children. This was the children's prayer song that I sang with my children at home before they went to sleep. "Ik ga slapen ik ben Moe, sluit mijn beide oogjes toe, Here houdt ook deze nacht weder over mij de wacht". (I am going to sleep, I am tired, I close my eyes. Lord, please, watch over me again this night). Because it could get us into trouble if the guards heard our singing, we had to sing it softly. But I was unable to join them. I could not handle the thought that my own children that very hour would be praying this song and that I would then tug them in. I tried, but the words stuck in my throat. After a few more days, I was able to join in.

One of my friends in the concentration camp once told me: "Self-pity is the quickest way to lose your grip". She was right, but I need to remind myself, like now when I am here alone in my small room at the rest home.

When one of the inmates came through the prison with her cart to distribute library books, I asked if I could read a Bible.

I knew that they were standard issue for every prison cell. "Oh, no, not a chance!"

The morning of May 19, just before Dick came with the weekly Friday laundry exchange, I was sent with five other prisoners and a guard by train to the SS concentration camp Vught, near the Belgian Border.

I managed to smuggle the following note to Dick, my husband, through a civilian train passenger. It was written on two sheets of toilet paper. I still keep it in my war souvenirs.

Dear Dick,

On transfer to Vught, Friday. Could not believe it.

I will be o.k. Glad you are with the children. Be sure to give them a big hug from me.

Tell my parents not to worry. I can take it well. The Lord is my shepherd. I take refuge in Him. The boys' shoes are at the shoe repair shop behind the RAI. Mine are in the Vechtstraat.

Your bicycle key is under the coat rack. Butter of D. on top of the cupboard in the kitchen and in the flower vase. Greet the relatives and thank them for their thoughts and prayers.

Greetings also to the Dienskes. I heard that Jo was let go. I will write from Vught and I am allowed to receive packages. My dear husband, be well. We hope to see each other again.

A big hug from your wife.

On the train ride, I found a Bible in my purse which was given back to me when I checked out. This was an enormous lift on this otherwise sad day. Now I knew that Dick had been released because it was the same Bible that I had smuggled to him, six weeks ago.

Dick received my message already on the next day. A good patriot delivered my message. He presented himself on the Singel, at my brother's address. He asked our son Jan, who was staying with my brother's family, if his name was van Ommen.

33. Concentration camp Vught

Dick was delighted to have news from me but naturally concerned what the consequences were. Dick received word that he could deliver packages to me at Vught. That same day he got onto a train with a package. He found a trucker there who regularly delivered letters and packages to the prison. Dick walked a few times around the fence of the camp hoping to get a glimpse of me.

Around this time, Uncle Jentje, in Hilversum, received a name of a German who might be able to intervene for me. He was a certain Obersturmführer Behrens with the SD, in the national head quarters of the SD, in The Hague. Dick went with Uncle Jentje, who had brought a file with him with his German papers and distinctions and also those of his daughter Adri, my cousin whose husband had fought and fallen for the Germans near Leningrad. They were told to come back another time and when they did come back were sent away with:

"Sorry, can't help you".

Vught was the only SS concentration camp the Germans operated in the Netherlands. It took nearly a whole day to get through the registration. I stood in line for hours, passing by lines of tables where more forms had to be filled out. At the end, I had to turn in everything I carried on me. They already had taken my wedding ring. I had to undress and all my clothes were bundled and marked with my prison number. There I stood, stark naked, facing a number of total strangers, other female prisoners and Aufseherinnen (female prison guards, who were often recruited from the criminal prison population). This first encounter with this sort of intimidation would become a common occurrence in the coming year of my incarceration. The next stop was at the shower rooms, next we were inspected for cleanliness. In the adjoining room, we received a pair of overalls, a panty, a camisole, a head scarf and wooden shoes. A couple prisoner worked in the clothes sorting room. You could give your prison number to these gals with a list of the items that you would like to get back. This way we managed to retrieve rosaries, corsets, etc. I was able to retrieve my Bible this way. Because the barracks were frequently searched, I needed to hide my Bible very carefully.

We all received a man's sports coat. Obviously taken from the Jews because the darker spot where the Star of David had been sewn was clearly noticeable. I cut the bottom of the inner pocket and dropped the Bible inside the lining.

Morning reveille was at 6 a.m. and then we were marched to the sewing room. There were no Aufseherinnen, we were supervised by fellow prisoners, and we were able to spend time reading our Bible.

We worked ten hours per day, six days a week and the Sunday morning. Sunday afternoon, we organized Bible readings. This had to be done in secret. The moment a guard was spotted the code word: "Dikke Lucht" (Heavy Air) was passed to all corners of the barracks. We managed, at times, to smuggle a written sermon through the barbed wire from the men's section where there were several ministers and priests. This was very risky and a few of us were caught and had to do "bunker" time (solitary confinement in a small cold dark cell).

The safest spot to hold our meetings was in the very back of the Jewish women barracks. These women worked on the night shift in the Philips factory. They slept during the day. We tiptoed through their rows of bunk beds and held our devotions in a storage room in the back of their barrack. We sung our hymns and psalms softly. The Jewish women and their children were rounded up on June 2nd and sent that night to Auschwitz. Of this group of approximately 500 Jewish women that left Vught 382 managed to survive the war. Just like Corrie ten Boom[47], the watchmaker, these women had assembled intricate electronic mechanisms. They came from the Diamond cutting factories of Amsterdam and Antwerp and because of their special skills they were worth more alive than dead to the SS "Corporation", who earned millions from their slave labor. The day after their evacuation, we had to clean their barracks. What a sad assignment! We found a variety of personal items in the straw of their mattresses and pillows, letters, wedding pictures, marriage certificates, children portraits and.... poison pills.

On the 9th of June I was transferred to the satellite camp of Den Bosch to work in the Michelin tire factory. The super vision was not as severe as in the main camp of Vught.

---

[47] Corrie ten Boom, known for her book and movie "The Hiding Place"

The Aufseherinnen and the guards with their dogs slept in the adjoining building. Our group of women was now able to read the Bible together without too much interference.

Dick had been given a contact by his sister-in-law, Mimi van Ommen, where our Jaap was staying. She had the name of an Engineer, Mr. Oudemans, who worked for Philips. Dick took the train to Den Bosch and was well received by the Oudemans.

The working conditions for prisoners in the Philips factory were far better than the other prison work out of Vught. Oudemans promised Dick that he would do his best for me. When he showed him out, he pointed Dick to a group of people who were on their way to the camp. Dick thought that they had come for the day to visit the camp but then discovered that these were prisoners on their way back from a work assignment. He realized too late that he could have smuggled a letter through them to me. It was a beautiful summer day and he decided to go for a quick swim on his way by the lake of the "Iron Man".
He had plenty of time to get back to Amsterdam, he thought. But because the allies had just bombed the rail road bridge across the Waal River, at Zaltbommel, he had to take a long detour and did not make it back to Amsterdam till late in the evening.

The twins had come back to the Alblasstraat after they finished their first year of grade school in late July. Dick had made an arrangement with Jo Dienske, across the street, to cook for the three of them and do some light house work.

One evening that week, when Dick tucked the boys in, Jan had a question: "Eternity, what is that exactly?" "Will we be able to play there with our toys?" Before Dick was able to think of an answer, Jaap blurted out: "Yes, and it will all be pre-war quality!"

Dick knew that the Vught prisoners were punished with an embargo on letters and packages during the month of July. The embargo was extended through August. He tried to surprise me for my 43rd birthday on August 30, through a number of "good" guards, but he never managed to get a package through to me.

Jaap came down with Diphtheria at the end of August. Both boys had to stay out of school because of the threat of contagion.

34. A daring escape

Tiny Boosman[48], Kek IJzerdraat and Nel Hillers arrived in Vught at the end of July, from Amstelveenseweg prison. Now for the first time the three were able to catch up on their individual experiences since their arrest because they had been separated in different cells in their Amsterdam imprisonment. The four men, Dienske, Touw, Stroethoff and de Rooy were not on the same train to Vught, they were sent to the Utrecht prison, as they learned afterward. Dienske showed up in Vught a few weeks later.

Tiny received a smuggled message from her husband that our case was to be heard on October 5th in Utrecht, according to the lawyer for our group, A.C.G. van Proosdij.

The three ladies were put to work in the same detail where I worked in the gas mask factory. Tiny and two other prisoners, Nies Verbeek and Atie Le Mair, had worked out a plan to escape. They had made contact with the local Resistance. There were a couple regular paid staff of the pre-occupation personnel who could be trusted. They smuggled messages in and out of the camp for us. The chief of the department even made a special trip to visit Tiny's family in the den Texstraat. The three ladies waited till after the evening head count so they would not be found missing until the morning formation. They slipped unnoticed into the plant and then had someone lock them in. They then pulled the inside doorknob to gain some time in case there was any attempt to come after them. Because there was a curfew from 9 p.m., they could not wait till the cover of darkness. Anyone caught in the streets after 9 o'clock was arrested. The three women climbed via a roof support through a swivel window into the roof gutter. Fortunately, they had been issued shoes in the factory instead of the wooden shoes we had been given on our arrival in the main camp. The shoes hung around their necks tied with the shoe strings. The few personal things that they still owned were put in a small pouch, they had made for the occasion; they carried the pouch between their teeth.

---

[48] For details on arrest of the three women and four men see Part Three chapter: "The Van Breestraat 155" and "Seven Dienske Group members arrested"

It turned out that the fire escape they had drawn on their map was two roofs further over than they had planned for. This meant that they would be in full view of the guard towers but they got lucky. Next, they had to scale a high wall with barbed wire on top. With a wooden keg put upon a crate, Tiny could just peek over the wall. She went first and except for tearing a thumb on the barbed- wire she landed on the outside. Nies caused them a few anxious moments; she fell back twice before she managed to get across. Atie threw her shoes over the wall, the shoes missed her companions by an inch. Freedom lay ahead of them. They sat there for a minute catching their breath and then stripped off their prison work coveralls. Underneath they were wearing street clothes that they had stolen from the sorting room where the same girls worked who had managed to retrieve my Bible.

They planned to spend the night in a haystack nearby and then get in touch with an address they had of a local Resistance member and obtain new identity cards.

After putting some distance between them and the prison walls they became more confident and exchanged a few words.

This turned out to ruin their well laidwelllaid plans. One of our "Hundenführer" (K-9 guards), hidden near their path in the tall grass, making out with a local floozy, jumped up screaming: "Halt, Halt", while firing a shot in the air with his revolver. He had recognized their voices because he stood guard on the factory floor close to their station on the production line.

We called him "Mickey". He was furious, he appeared to have been thrown off balance and as scared as the escapees were, he stammered: "Gerade Sie...huh...Ich dachte Sie waren eine so anständige Frau. Aber mir ins Unglück stürzen, das wollen Sie!" (You, who would have expected this from you? I always thought that you were such a respected woman. But now you want to ruin my life!")

Meanwhile, the alarms started to go off everywhere. The threesome were marched back to the camp, Mickey seemed to want to skewer the ladies from behind on his pistol barrel. The floozy followed behind, still carrying Mickey's coat over her arm.

When they got closer to the plant, they heard a lot of shouting, the guard on the watch tower could be heard yelling above the noise.

They later heard that he claimed to have seen their escape but knew that Mickey would be there to intercept them.

The three escapees were placed against the barracks wall and we were all dragged from our beds to stand in formation.

The "Kleefclub"[49] thought this was very amusing and they mocked the three women.

The commander tried to save face by telling us that the three women had been caught while still inside the prison walls. We were all sent back into our barracks and the three escapees were taken into a room where everything was taken from them even their underwear. All that they were left to wear were their coveralls.

That night they were made to sit against the wall of the guard station. Later in the night they were allowed to stretch out on the floor, it was cold and drafty in the thin coveralls. At 6 a.m. they were once again placed outside against the factory wall. They stood there until 3 p.m. We managed to secretly pass them a sugar cube, a tomato. Then they were put back on the production line at 6 p.m. Without any sleep and worn out from standing against the wall for nine hours. Under all the emotions it was nearly impossible to drag through the night shift.

In retrospect, they might have had better luck if they would have waited a couple days.

Emil, an Austrian SS guard had helped them with their escape plans. They had learned that he could be trusted. If his superiors had discovered his involvement, it could have cost him his life. They decided to go ahead anyway because Nies had been threatened to be sent to Ravensbrück for a violation she had committed.

---

[49]"Kleefclub": Literally "Glue Club", this was the name given by the rest of the women to the prostitutes. Most of these ladies of the night had been incarcerated because they had infected German soldiers with venereal diseases, there were about from 5 to 10 of them with us on this journey. They stuck together and were, most of the time, unreliable companions for the others.

35. **In the Bunker**

The next morning, they were transferred to the main camp in Vught and locked up in the "Bunker". This was the maximum security lock up in the camp. It was a concrete structure which had become the most feared punishment for the inmates of Vught.

In January of that year the then camp commander, Grünewald, ordered 74 women to be locked up in a cell meant for five prisoners. Ten women suffocated.

Hetty Voûte had been locked up in the bunker a few days before for sabotage in the gas mask factory. Geke Linker also showed up to join them for the same offense as Hetty.

Tiny was put in the same cell with Hetty and Geke, Atie and Nies shared another cell.

They figured out how to communicate with their neighbors. It turned out that they were the only five women in the bunker. To the left of the threesome were Simon and Albert and to their right were four paratroopers, they called them the "Flitsers" (Flashers). Right above the Flashers was Koert, to his right was Frans, and further right Bertus. Right above the three ladies was Manfred and above their neighbors, Simon and Koert, lived Ton, an eighteen-year-old, whose father, a Naval officer, was also locked up elsewhere in the bunker.

As soon as they saw the guard leave through the gate in the evening the whole place came alive, the "intercom" started buzzing. By dragging the small table under the air duct and putting a stool on top of it one could speak right into the duct hole and it could be heard as far as five cells away, in both directions. And it was impossible to hear in the prison corridor.

The ladies entertained and lifted the spirits of the men, on occasion, by singing the "Dona Nobis Pacem" out of Mozart's Requiem mass.

The tension heightened in the prison in the last days of August. If any men were brought into the prison court yard after 5 p.m. the women knew exactly what was in store for them. The men had no idea what fate awaited them. It often was a reprisal for a successful operation the Resistance had just accomplished against the enemy and death sentences also were being carried out.

Frans[50] was the first of their neighbors to be taken away by the guards. The women had expected him as the least likely victim. Frans came from Rotterdam and the Resistance in Rotterdam had just delivered a blow against the enemy. His neighbors felt defeated and saddened; the day before Frans received news from home for the first time in many months. He was filled with joy and gratitude. He offered to give the daily devotional over the "intercom", the previous evening.

One afternoon they heard the eighteen-year-old Ton yell out: "My father, my father!!" "Where, Ton, who is it?": "The tall one with the grey hair!"

Everyone peered through their barred windows on the court yard. When Ton felt that it was safe, he whistled the first stanzas of the midshipmen anthem.

The tall man slowly turned his head to where the sound came from. Ton carefully stuck his fingers through the bars and the man waved his hand slowly over the top of his head as if he was straightening his hair.

Each day more and more men were processed through the courtyard.

---

[50] Most likely Frans Christiaan Fehres, born in 1923 in Rotterdam, executed Sept 3rd 1944

36. August in Vught

At the end of July, we were transferred to another barrack in Den Bosch, now we had even more freedom of movement. Our group of Christian women grew with new arrivals from the main camp in Vught. Somehow, we managed to stick together until the very end of the war. I keep very fond memories of these relationships we built. We started to recite the Profession of Faith together regularly. My Bible was the only complete New and Old Testament in camp Den Bosch. It was being used by many in all the corners of the camp.

One day, we all came back to the barracks for lunch when our entire section was ordered to stand appèl (in formation). Our beds were torn apart, all letters, portraits, bibles and hymn books were cut into small pieces and carried off to the kitchen to be burnt in the ovens. The reason was most likely due to the fact that our "employer" had received another shipment back from Germany because the gas masks had been sabotaged by us. Our standard way of sabotage was to push our thumbnail into the still warm soft rubber. This was not visible at the time of inspection but it rendered the masks useless.

Afterwards, we went searching through the slivers of paper to see if we could reconstruct my Bible. We could not find any parts of it.

But, lo and behold, a couple days later one of the Jehovah Witnesses asked me: "Are you by chance Mrs. van Ommen?" We only knew each other by first names and my last name was written in the Bible. She had found the Bible in her bed. Apparently, someone in the kitchen had been able to save my Bible and thought that it belonged to one of the Jehovah Witnesses. You will understand that we said a special thank you to the Lord.

37. Mad Tuesday[51] in Camp Vught

The excitement grew by the hour. The sound of the artillery of our liberators grew louder and closer and it was sweet music to the prisoner's excited ears. The guards and the despised Aufseherinnen had shrunk away into the back ground. If one of them dared to show themselves in the barracks, it was done with an exaggerated display of courtesy.

No one went to work that day and we were all treated to coffee with sugar from the SS kitchen. Some of the women lit a smoke without any interference. Plans were being formed as to how we would be reunited with our loved ones. We exchanged addresses and assured one another that we would stay in touch after we were free.

A rumor made the rounds that the Red Cross would take over the supervision of the camp and that we would be quartered with farmers in the neighborhood, temporarily. It was certain that the Allied Forces would be there within hours and that the German enemy had been brought to their knees. The guards were packing and would soon be on their retreat.

Riffle fire could be heard from the direction of the male prison camp. We assumed that this had to be close combat with the liberators. But the women who had been here for a longer period knew better. The riffle fire came from the execution range. After the riffle folly, there would be a single shot, the coup de grace.

One-hundred-fourty-two male prisoners were executed in the last three days before the camp was evacuated.

The head executioner in Camp Vught was SS Sturmbannführer-Major Erich Deppner, these murders are still known as the Deppner Executions. His career started under Hans Albin Rauter, the highest SD boss in the Netherlands and Willy Lages of the SD in Amsterdam who worked directly under Rauter.

Heinrich Himmler complimented Deppner personally for his first successful execution of 72 Russian prisoners of war in camp Amersfoort in April 1942.

---

[51] "Mad Tuesday": Tuesday, 5 September 1944. The allies rapidly approached Holland, collaborators and even soldiers made a mad rush for the German border.

Deppner was captured in Berlin in 1945 by the Russians who released him in 1950. Next, he found shelter with the U.S. Armed Forces who managed to make good use of his "way around town".

The Dutch government requested the American Authorities for Deppner's extradition, to stand trial for his atrocities. The Americans refused the Dutch requests. Deppner lived in comfort and peace in Germany until his natural death in 2005.

We, the hundred odd women, in our satellite camp at the Michelin factory in Den Bosch, experienced the same excited atmosphere. We heard from the civilian factory personnel that the British forces were on their way from Belgium. There was a festive mood amongst us; we sang the songs that for the most part were composed here. We used to sing them softly, several of them were a bit rough and mocked our common enemy, but we became bolder by the minute and it seemed that the louder we sang them the more scared our guards reacted. One of the communist women began to sing the "Internatonale" which was promptly followed up by all, with our national anthem, the "Wilhelmus".

We watched with amazement the feverish activity on the factory floor, gasmasks were hurriedly crated up, and complete sets of machinery were disassembled and loaded into boxcars.

When the long train was filled the German production boss and his team also mounted the train, accompanied by our loud jeers. We hoped that we would never see them again.

There was nothing to do for us any longer in the factory. Our guards took us back to our barracks.

Three R.A.F. fighter planes flew low over the camp, that evening. This show of force removed any lingering doubts that freedom was only hours away.

Later in the evening, we were brought in a variety of vehicles to the main camp Vught. It was late and the women there were already asleep. There were no empty beds for us and we had to crawl into any available cot with a sleeping prisoner, to the annoyance of the sleeping woman. But because we had witnessed the exodus from our factory, we had news for them and now everyone was participating in the mounting euphoria. We stayed awake and celebrated for most of the night.

The next day, around noon, we all received a warm meal from the SS kitchen and once more coffee with sugar. The Germans obviously wanted to leave better last impressions for the liberators as to how we had been treated.

But the sound of the artillery from the approaching Allied forces became weaker and our euphoria diminished at the same rate. The riffle fire from the executions had also stopped. "It is probably a pause in the fighting" was suggested. But the hours went by and then we came to the realization that it was a bit unrealistic that the British would go out of their way to liberate a few thousand prisoners in the nearest concentration camp. They probably had a couple more strategic targets to deal with, like the port of Antwerp.

We were back on the same sour bread diet that evening and the coffee was the usual brown tasteless liquid without sugar. The festive mood changed into disappointment and a deep concern as to what was in store for us now.

38. Mad Tuesday in Hilversum

Rennie Arendt-de Vries had lost her source of income when the Wehrmacht had taken over the rest home "Limborg". Most of the guests transferred to her father's nearby rest home "Hoffwerk".

Rennie wore her Swastika insignia with pride. She had become involved in the local NSDAP women's organization. She was sent to the island of Rügen, in the Baltic Sea, for training as a Mütterheim[52] leader. Mütterheim were set up to assist the widows and children of fallen soldiers. *Rennie* took charge of the Mütterheim in Hilversum.

My husband, Dick, tried to have me released with the help of my cousin and her father. Uncle Jentje made at least four visits for me to the Euterpestraat.

In the first week of September, *Rennie* Arendt was told by the German authorities in Hilversum to pack her suitcases and be ready for evacuation to Germany. A special train stopped in Hilversum on September 5, "Mad Tuesday". *Rennie* and her two sons climbed aboard. Georg was then fourteen and Gerard was nine. Uncle Jentje brought them to the station and he had an address for them of an acquaintance in Neumünster, Holstein, not far from where they had lived in Holtenau.

Three railway wagons were painted with red crosses and filled with wounded German soldiers. Just before crossing into Germany, the train was attacked by two American Thunderbolts.

All the windows were broken, there were several casualties, and many injured. *Rennie* was cut by the shattered glass. When Georg, years later, had a tooth pulled the dentist also removed a matchbox full of glass splinters from his cheekbone. Gerard escaped the attack without a scratch.

In Germany, they were confronted with the ravages the allied bombings had afflicted. Everywhere they saw bombed out cities, rail junctions and factories in ruins. After many detours and delays, they arrived in Neumünster at the address of the Dutch acquaintance of her father.

---

[52] Mütterheim=Mother shelter

39. From the Bunker in Vught

On Monday September 4, the five women and their neighbors in the bunker could clearly hear the allied artillery and the drone of aircraft engines. Then already early that afternoon the men were being brought down into the court yard. Koert[53] and Bertus[54] were also in this group, they counted 76[55] men. Barely a sound could be heard, some cried, some stood in prayer but all were calm and resolved. This spectacle has remained with these women for the rest of their lives.

The women were completely powerless other than to convey them their sincerest feelings. They wrote down the addresses that were being whispered through their neighbors barred windows and promised to visit their families if they would manage to regain their freedom. Their last words for their loved ones were nearly always the same: "tell them that I have no regrets…"

The women wanted to console the men with their "Dona Nobis Pacem" but the emotions were too much for them, their vocal cords were paralyzed.

After several hours, the bell rang and the first eleven men were led away to the execution field. A volley of rifle fire rang out followed by a couple of coups de grâce (death blows).

Then came the next group and so it went until the courtyard was emptied out.

The SS butchers returned a little later through the gate talking loud and laughing. After a sleepless night, the noise of the jackbooted SS men filled the hallway again. They stopped at the cell door of the Flashers. The next day the remaining roughly 2800 men were put into cattle cars on transport to German concentration camps.

The five women came back to join us while we were getting ready to be loaded into the same transport train as the men.

---

[53] Koert Bruno Maria van Haaren
[54] Probably Bertus van Noort
[55] 64 men were executed on September 4 according to http://nl.wikipedia.org/wiki/Nederlanders_ge%C3%ABxecuteerd_tijdens_de_Duit se_bezetting

40. From Vught into the unknown

We were ordered to stand in formation on the exercise field of the camp early in the morning of September 6. Everyone was given a blanket and a chunk of bread and we were then marched to the rail depot of the concentration camp. A long line of cattle cars stood stretched out on the tracks. The male prisoners had already been stuffed in the forward cars. My group, of about 100 women from the Michelin factory detail, had grouped our selves together. Most of my group, 82 women, managed to end up in the same cattle car.

These cars were meant to carry a maximum of six cavalry horses....

The heavy wooden doors were shut and we heard a lock and chain being attached. We could only stand up and barely move. There was a latrine barrel in one corner and no water. The first thing we did was, with our wooden shoes, to break the wooden slats from the blinds in the small windows, to give us a little more air. We deposited all our bread rations in one corner as far away as possible from the latrine.

One woman was assigned to distribute the bread. Next, we divided our group in three sections of 27 women to take turns in standing, sitting and stretched out on the floor. Now we had a plan and we felt a little more in control. The train started moving slowly. It felt as if the Lord stretched his arms out over us with a blessing when two young women softly started singing the Dutch version of:

Abide with me, fast falls the even tide.
The darkness deepens; Lord with me abide.
When other helpers fail and comforts flee,
Help of the helpless, oh, abide with me.

And the fourth verse:

I fear no foe with thee at hand to bless;
Ills have no weight, and tears no bitterness.
Where is death's sting? where, grave, they victory?
I triumph still if thou abide with me.

135

More and more women in our car and along the track joined in. The chorus could be heard afar.

In the earlier part of this book, I wrote about my hymn singing mother. Amongst us, we had complimented and enlarged our repertoire of the Psalms and Hymns we had grown up with.

We had no Aufseherinnen in the car with us, so, we could sing as much as we liked. One of the women stood on the lookout at the peephole and relayed to us what she observed. After a couple hours into the journey, we were in Nijmegen, but then it seemed that we were heading south once again. Then someone read: "Den Bosch". Were we going back? Maybe the rail tracks to Germany had already been captured by the allies and they would still be able to come to our rescue.

Night fell and it was very difficult to guess our locations, there was a total black out.

Suddenly the train came to a screeching halt, as if someone had applied the emergency break.

There was a loud commotion outside and we heard gun shots. Maybe a group of partisans would break us out of the train! But after some more running back and forth along the cars it quieted down and the train slowly came in motion again.

The Dutch SS-man, who guarded our train on the outside, climbed inside and told us that three men prisoners had attempted to break out. They were gunned down; their bodies were left along the railroad track.

41. In Germany

That next morning, we were inside Germany, for sure. The same guard told us that we were headed for the infamous concentration camp of Ravensbrück. This was very bad news. We had already heard what we could expect in this hellhole. But it made sense to bring us to the Northern part of Germany, as far away as possible from the approaching Allied Armies.

When will Dick get to hear that I am no longer in Vught and will his mail be forwarded?

We had not had a drop of liquid since we left, 30 hours ago. The guard collected as many cups and bowls from those who had managed to bring them, as he could handle, when the train stopped in a German station. He returned with the help of a couple of the German station personnel.

The women pushed and shoved trying to reclaim their drinking gear. A few arguments broke out. What was going on? What had happened to our resolve of unity and acceptable behavior? A few of the older women intervened with calming words. We looked at each other, we felt ashamed. We had spilled precious water; we were angry with our selves and the enemy who had abused us into this desperate behavior.

The guard opened the doors on a crack, at times during the day, to give us some air. We saw the destruction everywhere from the allied bombardments. It gave us some courage. During the night, we would hear the bombing raid sirens howl. The exploding bombs could be heard, in the distance. Stray shrapnel from the Anti-aircraft guns would clatter on the tin roof of our cattle car.

The whole chain of cars stopped at 3 a.m., the following day, in the Sachsenhausen concentration camp.

The doors in the first cars were opened and we heard the clatter of wooden shoes on the stone platform and the shouting of commands by the guards. This was the destination for the men; their cars were uncoupled from the long train.

A chorus swelled from the remaining eight box cars. Over six hundred women sang a farewell to the men. The men nodded to one another:

"Listen, the women are singing!"

Concentration camps in N.W. Europe   Verzetmuseum

42.   Concentration Camp Ravensbrück

On Friday afternoon, September 8 1944 our train rolled into the station of the town of Fürstenberg, from where we marched to the concentration camp. Ravensbrück is located 60 miles north of Berlin. From its inception in 1939 until the end of the war, 140,000 women went through its gate. Only a third came out alive. Even of those survivors, a portion died prematurely from the inhumane treatment and many remained scarred physically and mentally for the rest of their lives. The majority of the women were political prisoners, some religious objectors like Jehovah Witnesses, Roma and Lesbians. All nationalities from the countries overran by the Germans were represented. Polish women made up about 25% of the total, next were the Russians. A close third, 20%, were Germans, a detail conveniently ignored for a long time, the large number of Germans who were incarcerated for refusing to accept Hitler's ways. Most of the Polish women were removed from their homes for no particular political reason and used as slave labor.

138

To crush the Warsaw Uprising, which commenced August 1st, 1944, the Germans had effectively used Polish hostages as human shields in their counter attack on the revolt. In retaliation, the Germans executed over 40,000 Warsovites and deported large numbers of the men and women, randomly collected, to Ravensbrück and other concentration camps.

Mengele, known as the "Angel of Death" in Auschwitz also practiced his cruel medical experiments in this camp on some of the inmates.

We marched singing through the gate.

It did not take our new masters long to silence our songs. We watched in disbelief how the prisoners here reacted to our arrival. They crowded around the windows to get a look at us. They came through the doors and windows and stared at us through the barbed wire fences. We could not understand their language but we did understand from their gestures and starved faces that they wanted food. We threw the left-over chunks of bread over the fence and they leaped like wild animals on their prey. This scary and senseless scene was soon stopped by Aufseherinnen who clubbed them back into the barrack. "Welcome to Ravensbrück!"

A large canvas roof was to be our shelter for the night. Straw had been spread on the dirt floor. I found personal items in the straw from prisoners who had passed through here already; letters, photos and other small souvenirs that had belonged to real people with a name and address and now were only identified by their prison number or had already been sent to an extermination camp. It was infested with lice and flees and human feces. Many of the women chose the open air and spread their blankets in the coal dust and tried to make themselves as comfortable as the circumstances allowed. It was cold during the night and when they awoke, the next morning, and looked at each other, they were covered with coal dust. We found a water spigot; we used our messbowls as washbasins.

The "locals" watched us, they shook their heads in disbelief at our hygiene. They had long stopped any other functions than what the guards commanded them to do.

Our self respect and resolve was our highest priority, it was our only hope for survival. The registration started that morning but I happened to be with the last of the 650 women and camped out for three nights in the coal dust and occasional rain showers.

Some of the women had arrived with little more than their blanket. They had discarded their soiled clothing on arrival. How do you work your way, without accidents, through 82 women to the latrine can when dysentery strikes? At the end of the registration line waited the same routine as in Vught, through the showers. Every nasty creature you can imagine lived in the shower rooms. The coverall and headscarves were taken from us and instead we were given a dress and a camisole and now with our wooden shoes we looked just like the rest of the prisoners here.

I had given my few belongings ahead of time to a couple older women and this way I managed to hang on to my Bible.

Polish women ruled the coop in the barrack where I was assigned to. Some of these women had to be treated, every morning, for skin diseases in the quarantine barrack. At first, we considered it a bit repulsive, but we discovered that the quarantine barrack was a refuge away from the filth. The floors were scrubbed in this barrack, while we stood for roll call in the early morning. My new companion here was a woman [56] I had met the last day in Vught. We met twenty years earlier when we both were on the national board of the Meisjesbond (YWCA); we shared a bunk in the quarantine barrack. We had no work assignments here and had plenty of time to read the Bible and to discuss many subjects. Kiky Heinsius went exploring our neighborhood one day and wrote about this as follows:

"I discover a pram on the sunny side of one barrack. I carefully bend over to look inside. An old little baby boy looks up at me with big deep hollow eyes. Where is his mother? Suddenly an Aufseherin stands right next to me. Startled, I want to get away as quick as I can. The guard does not seem to take any notice of me. I stop and wonder what she is up to. With her index finger she softly pads the baby's cheek while purring:" Koo, koo, koo…. and Tee, tee, tee….The little fellow manages a short grimass with his toothless face. He laughs, but his eyes show no emotion.

The Aufseherin turns to me with a big grin on her face and says: "Schön was?" A short while later, I see the same Aufseherin. She is driving a group of prisoners ahead of her, cursing and swinging her club."

---

[56] Rennie does not give a name. In all probaility she was the so called "tante Riek" also "Mother of the Dutch Resistance" Mrs. Heleen Kuipers- Rietberg. She was a director of the Gereformeerde Vrouwenbond in Winterswijk. She ended up in Vught a week before the evacuation. She died in Ravensbrück December 28, 1944.

140

Several Belgian women had come with us from Vught. One day one of the Belgian women tapped me on the shoulder: "Rennie, read me something from your Bible". I turned around and thought: "How do I do this?" How much does she already know? Then I remembered how an evangelist once gave a talk at a Christmas celebration for German domestics, years ago. I started with the Creation, the fall of Adam and Eve and continued until Easter and the Resurrection. This way I thought that I had given her a broad outline. "Rennie, and how does it go further?" A few of the women started to mock her: "Do you want to convert to the Protestant church?

I often recall this particular moment with this young woman. How do we use the opportunities given to us? We are the fortunate, the Elect, but how do we use this gift?

A few weeks later, we were transferred from the quarantine barrack into a much larger barrack, number 28. Four bunks wide, three high in rows of ten. The path between them was so narrow that you could not even push a broom through it. It was dark, dinghy and dirty.

We took our clogs with us in the bunks because if you left them on the floor they would be stolen. Wooden shoes and clothing were traded for a slice of bread...

Once the September sun warmed up it was very pleasant, but those poor girls stood shivering hours before the sun came up.

Young girls were going to work early in the morning, in the freezing cold, without footwear and just wearing a thin dress.

I ended up in a detail where we had to remove the sandy top soil.

A young Gypsy girl, with whom I exchanged a few words at times, told me one morning: "Rennie, I dreamt about you last night, you will be safely reunited with your loved ones". Oh, how much I wished to have been able to encourage that sweet little girl in the same way. Very few of the Roma, just like the Jews, survived this hellhole. The limited space between our bunks and the ceiling did not allow us to sit straight up and it was always dark. When we came back from our work details, we would lay on our stomachs, in a circle with the Bible in the center. Then we would sing our Psalms and Hymns. This was an incredible experience to hear that others sang along from all the corners of the barrack. It felt as if we were close to Heaven. God lifted us out of all this misery to Himself.

Removing top soil in Ravensbrück Photo Gedenkstätte Ravensbrück

Next to us bunked a couple of girls of the "Kleefclub"[42]. One of them, "Black Lily", commented the next day: "I know those songs, I worked in a Diaconessenhuis" (A Christian Hospital).

You will no doubt find it hard to believe that there are times that I long back to those moments in this Godforsaken place; when I am reminded of Hosea 2 verse 14:

"I will take her into the wilderness and speak tenderly to her".

Now I often find it difficult to hear this voice, among the many distractions. It is in this wilderness that I learned so clearly some of the Bible passages. Much is said about the Wrath of God, but for me it was the Love of God who brought us into the concentration camps.

Roman 8 verse 33: *"Who will bring any charge against those God has chosen?* And verse 35: *"Who shall separate us from the Love of Christ? Shall trouble or hardship or persecution or famine or nakedness or danger or sword?*

And verse 38: *"For I am convinced that neither death nor life, neither angels nor demons, neither the present or the future, nor any powers, 39: etc. will be able to separate me from the Love of Christ Jesus our Lord.*

I'd like to have verse 38 on my tombstone.

With us were two sisters ten Boom, Corrie and Betsie, from Haarlem, who were accustomed to hold devotionals in Vught and who continued this practice here in Ravensbrück.

They were inexhaustible. At times, they would hold the same Bible study in five different corners of the barracks on the same day, because of the craving for it from the women. Many a face-to-face talk between the sisters and the women resulted from these meetings.

A month after our September 8 arrival in Ravensbrück a call went out to apply for a selection to another labor camp. They were looking for 200 Dutch women, not too old and with reasonably good vision. A similar opportunity was offered to us just days after our arrival, but we had treated it with skepticism and hid in the barracks. But after the one month here, we decided that anything else had to be an improvement over this hellhole. Practically our entire 650 Dutch women contingent applied for the selection.

43. Dick's Diary September-October 1944

September 11: A sad day. I phoned the Red Cross this morning and they told me that all the Vught prisoners have been sent to Germany. This was confirmed to me through the daughter of Mr. Wolfs, she stopped by to tell me this. They are probably sent to Oranienburg, terrible news.

September 13. The pastor, Ds. Ferwerda and the custodian Van der Baan of the Keizersgracht church have been executed in the Kerkstraat.

September 14. I called Mr. van Proosdij, the lawyer for the Dienske group, asking if he would still be able to do anything for them, but he did not give me much hope. Mrs. Parerera told me that the women had been sent to Ravensbrück. The Germans are not allowing a proper burial for Pastor Ferwerda. He has to be cremated.

September 15. Most of the prisoners who were within weeks of having served out their sentences have been released from Vught. One of the free women came to tell me that Rennie is doing well.

September 27: The paratroopers that landed near Arnhem have given up their attempt to secure this bridgehead. The Allied air assault on Arnhem has been defeated and pushed back across the Rhine River. Jaap and Jan went to see their grandparents for a few days. Jan wants to come back tomorrow to make a workbenchworkbench in the attic. The twins came home last week each carrying two long 1 x 8" Spruce boards. They had taken the boards from a pile of construction lumber that was destined for a Wehrmacht project, next to the public swimming pool, het Zuider Amstelbad. The whole pile disappeared in no time flat into our neighborhood.

People came from everywhere and it looked like an army of ants, most of the wood disappeared to fuel the emergency stoves[57].Doctor Lybrant stopped by today to check the boys and he found them to be free of the diphtheria contagion, they can go to school again.

I phoned the SD headquarters and spoke to Rühl. I announced myself: "This is van Ommen". "Ah, Herrn van Ommen". I asked him if he knew where my wife was. He did not know. I asked him to try and get her released.

---

[57]So-called "Noodkachel" Made from a large coffee can. They were used to cook and to a certain extend provide some heat in the harsh winter. The city gas had been cut and there was no coal to heat the standard stoves.

Rühl referred me to the Oberbefehlhaber, Raute, in The Hague; he commented that if I told him that I had to look after three children that he would most likely grant my request. I was surprised by his cooperative attitude.

I immediately called van Proosdij, the lawyer, and will go see him tomorrow.

September 28. I went to see van Proosdij this morning. We composed a letter to the Oberbefehlhaber.

October 1st. We have decided that the boys should stay at their grandparents for now. They will start second grade at the Hoogeweg School, tomorrow. Jo Dienske, our neighbor across the street, cannot handle looking after us three here any longer.

If I find no new arrangement then I will also leave here from the Alblasstraat and go to the Pythagorasstraat. I wished that we could have maintained the arrangement with Jo Dienske until Rennie comes home.

Jaap Dienske[58], Henk's younger brother, was released from Amersfoort prison, yesterday. Several others were freed at the same time.

Jaap lost his first baby tooth. Jan's same tooth is loose as well.

October 3rd. The town of Putten[59] is being burnt to the ground. The entire male population has been sent to Germany as a reprisal action for an attack by the Resistance on a German convoy.

The boys like their new school. Their aunt Mieke has sewn new shirts for them from Rennie's brown dress.

October 4th. It has now been 6 months since I last saw Rennie. I wonder when or if I will ever see her again. The allied advance is making very little progress. The Germans are standing their ground.

---

[58] Jaap Dienske had already been arrested in 1943 for distributing "Trouw", an underground daily newspaper. He was not directly involved with his brother's activities. He was married to Jo Hillers, the sister of Nel Hillers, who worked for Henk Dienske and was arrested with Tiny Boosman and Kek IJzerdraat.

[59] Putten: This was one of the cruelest reprisals the Germans committed in the Netherlands. Very few of the male population survived their captivity at Neuengamme, the same camp where Dienske perished.

I received twenty-two pounds of potatoes, onions and beets from the victory garden the bank operates, which I brought to the Pyhtagorasstraat. Our neighbor, Miss Schraverus, on the first floor is now cooking for me, so, I will stay here for now.

October 6th. The situation is getting worse. The electricity was cut off last Monday. ss

Fuel and food has also become impossible to find. May God help us! It is the last day that we are together in our own home. Jo and Johan Dienske will move back into their apartment, across the street. I am going to the Pythagorasstraat.

Pa[60], without telling me, placed an ad for a housekeeper for me in the "Standaard" newspaper. I happened to find out because I placed a similar add at the same time.

October 9th. It is my birthday. It is under sad circumstances. However, I am grateful that the Lord has protected me and that I can be here with my two sons. My thoughts are with Rennie continuously, but especially on this day. It must be particularly hard for her to be away from us on my birthday.

Jan and Jaap wished me Happy Birthday early this morning and brought me tea in bed. They told me that they thought that it did not feel like a real birthday.

The trams have stopped running because the electricity has been cut and therefore few people made it here to wish me Happy Birthday. But a number of them telephoned. October 19th Jan and Jaap are learning to knit. Oma is teaching them. There is little else to do without electricity and just the weak light of a petroleum lamp. They say their prayers in silence before they turn in. I noted that Jaap seems to take a long time. I asked him if he had a lot of questions for the Lord. He replied: "I pray for mom and the other prisoners, the men at sea, the people in Arnhem and Putten[61]".

---

[60] "Pa", the title Rennie used for her father

[61] The Battle of Arnhem had just been lost and abou 500 men from the village of Putten had been taken as a reprisal by the Germans, most of them never returned.

146

44. Dachau

I was part of the 193 Dutch, 11 Polish, 21 Slovenian, 3 French and 4 Belgian and another 10 women from various nationalities, who marched out of the Ravensbrück gates on October 12.

None of us had any idea where we would end up and thoughts went through my mind as to what would become of the women we left behind, in those miserable circumstances. Will the Gypsy girls on bare feet and in thin dresses be liberated before the winter sets in?[62]

At least, we received some extra clothes on our departure, a pair of pants, a shirt and a vest.

Unfortunately, I lost my little Bible on leaving Ravensbrück. It happened when we had to do the shower routine, in the middle of the night. I begged: "Bitte, Frau Aufseherin!" But she looked at me as if she did not understand what I was asking. Back when I was still in Den Bosch, I found a New Testament in my bunk, one day. Because I had a complete Bible, I gave it to a friend there. She was with us and had managed to hang on to it through the showers. We literally read it to shreds from then on.

We were travelling in a better class of cattle cars this time and fewer of us were stuffed in each car. Straw was spread on the box car floors and we managed, in a fashion, to all be able to stretch out at the same time. A guard and an Aufseherin were assigned to each box car.

It turned into a long and slow journey. The train was often directed to a side track to await the All Clear after an air bombardment. The guards allowed us to go take a pee when we were side tracked.

---

[62] The chances of survival, for the women left behind, tuned out to be far lower than the group that ended up in Dachau. 201 names are known of the 900 Dutch women who entered into Ravensbrück but estimates of the total go as high as 300. Of the 200 women in Rennie's group, 2 died in captivity. The Dutch obviously fared better than the other nationalities since the total Ravensbrück survival rate is estimated between 15 and 25%.

The thought of trying to escape on those stops flashed through our mind but even if we could have managed to get out of the guards' side arm range, we would be in enemy country in our prison garb.

The train was stopped for quite a while on the second night in a darkened rail road station. The SS guard got out of the car and after a while he returned and asked for three of the prisoners to follow him. They returned carrying a great big pot of bean soup. The guard followed them with a bunch of paper cups. That was a treat for us. We asked ourselves what in the world had made the guard do this for us.

Later on, Kiky Heinsius, who had slept close to the guard and the Aufseherin, told us that she had overheard them talk with much scorn of the conditions in Ravensbrück and the cruelty of the guards there and that the two also felt lucky to be going away from that Godforsaken place.

The AGFA camera factory on the Tegernseelandstrasse

45. AGFA-Commando-Dachau[63]

On October 15, after three nights in the cattle cars, we rolled into the station of Munich/Giesing, a suburb of Munich. We were being put to work in the AGFA camera factory. This was a satellite work camp under the supervision of the notorious SS concentration camp Dachau and its SS prison guards and Aufseherinnen.

The main camp was about sixteen miles away. Our new home was an L-shaped block of apartment buildings. It was supposed to have been a U shape, but a bomb destined for the Agfa factory cut the completion of the complex short. A wooden barrack served as the messhall.

Our housing at the Weißenseestraße.
Photo 1947: Stadt Archiv München FS-NK-STR-0043.

The entire complex was surrounded by high barbed wire fences with guard towers on the four corners. Around us were bare tracts intended for additional apartment blocks. Once a Russian prisoner escaped over the barbed wire fence, in the middle of the day. The guards and Aufseherinnen were sent out to search.

The Austrian prisoner doctor, Ella Lingens, wrote in her book "Gefangene der Angst" that, as soon as the Aufseherinnen were around the block and out of sight, they hid out in the local Gasthaus. We had to stand for hours in formation, as punishment, after work.

---

[63] https://en.wikipedia.org/wiki/Agfa-Commando

On the third day, the punishment was lifted and when we entered the mess hall, the escapee was standing on a stool with a sign around her neck: "Ich bin wieder da." (I'm back again). She had not been able to find food, shelter and transportation.

Even though we arrived late in the night at our destination, a warm meal was being served to us in the dining hall. We were seated around real tables, soup was being served, tasty thick soup with vegetables and potatoes and even some meat in it. Bread, coffee! The commander urged us to eat it all, that there would be breakfast again for us in the morning.

Every one of us had only one reaction: "Just, imagine if we would have missed this opportunity." Our new commander was Kurt Konrad Stirnweis, SS Waffen second Lieutenant, a Bavarian.

Stirnweis informed us that this first night we would bed down in the dining room, on the floor because our barracks would not be ready for us until the morning. A group of Polish women was sent back, with the same train we had come in on, to Ravensbrück. That gave us a scare. Could this become our fate as well?

For the twenty odd Polish women who had come with us and for the 250 who remained here, this turned out to be a continuous issue, they considered us a threat. As I wrote already, they were different. Most of them were not here for resisting the occupation; they had been plucked at random from the streets and from remote villages. Most of the Dutch women knew to speak German and had at least a high school education. The Polish women often got into fights with each other, they lacked the unity and resolve of our group.

The commander's priority was to fulfill his production quotas for his superiors in Dachau. We were told that he had earned himself a mean reputation in the main camp, among the male prisoners. He could act as a typical loud SS boss but he did surprise us at times with acts of kindness. As an example, when a few of our women came down with typhoid fever he would collect milk for them from the neighbors. A colony of locals, who had lost their homes in the bombardments, had set up shelters, with what they had been able to salvage on the grounds outside of our fence. They grew some vegetables and tended a couple of goats. Stirnweis filled a bucket with leftovers from the kitchen for the goats to trade for goat milk. We soon all knew him as: "Paps". ("pops")

His next in command was a sadistic Latvian, Alexander Djerin, we nick named him: "Little Brother". The Aufseherinnen did not swing clubs here. They lived in separate quarters next to the apartment blocks. and seldom entered our barracks. "Paps" would stop by when we were in the mess hall. Our quarters were divided into three different "Blocks". The Polish women and the Russians were housed in Block 1 and 2. The sick bay and the air raid shelter were in their building. The Dutch, and the few Belgian and French women were in Block 3. About twenty of us were in one section divided over three rooms. There was one washbasin and a toilet per section. I was appointed Blockälteste (Block Elder), I was the go between for the women in my block and the Aufseherinnen. Sometimes I had to exercise some authority in minor quarrels, but we all were aware that it was a matter of survival to be able to get along.

Most of us managed to move in to these rooms with our closest friends. My roommates were Nel Hillers, Nel Niemantsverdriet, Katrijn Huizinga, Gatha Kuijk-de Groot, Alie Pijper, Jozien Koomans, Jo Schilpzand and Jet Eding.

1954 At our apartment entrance Alblasstraat 41 with most of my AGFA roommates. Photo: Jan-Egbert Baalbergen

We shared our worries and our joys. We laughed together, but there were also times when we sat and cried together. Friendships that have lasted for the rest of our lives were formed in this room.

Reveille was at 5 a.m. In contrast to the hours of standing in the cold, in Ravensbrück, here we were counted when marching out the gate on our twenty-minute walk to the factory.

Armed SS guards and Aufseherinnen accompanied us.

We now found out the reason for some of the tasks we had to be able to perform in our selection process. They had us thread a needle, as an example. We were to assemble timing devices for explosive ignitions in bombs and artillery shells.

German civilian worker on the assembly line on each side of us showed us the process. The factory floor was well heated with large coal stoves because the instruments were temperature sensitive. The German women next to me were very kind and they would at times bring me something extra to eat. We had to come up with a way to sabotage the products, just like we had done in Den Bosch.

The factory was closed Saturday afternoon and Sunday. The Aufseherinnen made sure that we did not run away out of boredom. They came up with all kind of chores for us. Some of us had to dig out the potatoes, which were stored in the ground as a way to preserve them, to be used in the coming week in the kitchen. When the weather turned colder, we had to go and gather firewood outside the gate, under a guard's watchful eye.

46. Sundays in Dachau

On Sundays and also on Tuesdays, Thursdays and Fridays, we invited any one in our block for devotions. We read from my New Testament, prayed and sang together. Several women joined us who had not set foot in a church for a long time. They still remembered the hymns they had learned in Sunday school or elsewhere.

One of the young women made up hymn books for us. She wrote these in beautiful script on the back of discarded factory correspondence, which she had retrieved from the factory trash cans. She named the collection: "Hymnal for the Scattered Sisters in the Munich Diaspora".

We distributed these at our meetings and now we had a much greater choice than just the ones most knew by heart. I managed to hold on to my copy of the "Hymnal" and I still leaf through it at times now and it reminds me of those wonderful moments we shared under those difficult circumstances. I was very fortunate that I had learned so many of these songs by heart from my hymn singing mother. One of the women in our room was a religious education teacher. We called her our Pastor. She regularly "preached" a sermon for our services, and we invited others to give the homily. I have taken turns as well.

About a third of the Dutch women took part in our services.

The Roman Catholics held their service separately, but at times we would have them together. They borrowed my New Testament for their services. It was a great feeling to be able to sing with them together: "The Church's One Foundation".

One woman joined our group who was raised in a Christian home but had not set foot in a church for many years. She was married to a non-practicing Jew and her family had distanced themselves from her. Her participation, to me, was a clear sign of God's Love.

Dachau's main camp had a much greater access to "preachers". During the 12 years of its existence, Dachau housed the largest religious community ever assembled in one location. 2,771 "men of the cloth" were interned by the Nazis in Dachau. Of this number, the majority were 2,579 Catholic priests and seminarians and of those the Polish priests were, by far, the majority.

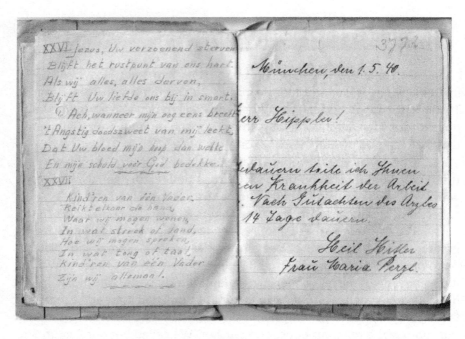

On left third verse of the hymns "Diep, o God, in't stof gebogen" sung in America as "Comfort, comfort oh my people" On Right is the front of the correspondence out of the factory trashcan. Note the "Heil Hitler". The letter is dated May 1, 1940, just days before the Fascists invaded Holland.

The others were 109 Protestant Pastors, 30 Eastern Orthodox priests and 2 Muslim Imams.

More than a third of these lost their lives in Dachau.

On August 24th, two weeks before we left Vught, our mail privileges had been taken away. We had not been able to get any news from, or to, home since then. By now, most of them would know that we ended up in Ravensbrück, but no one knew that we had been sent here to Munich.

47. From Dick's Diary, November-December 1944

November 9. Roosevelt has been re-elected.

November 10. I visited today with Ate (Dick's younger brother) and Mimi on the Westlandgracht. Afterwards, I went to see Jaap[64] and Jo Dienske who also live on the Westlandgracht. I was hoping that they would have some news from Nel Hillers[65], Jaap's sister -in-law, but they had not had any news either since before their transport to Ravensbrück.

November 20. The youngest of the Henk Dienske children is very seriously ill with Diphtheria. Many children have already died from Diphtheria. Fopma's youngest child has died from the same sickness. A persistent rumor makes the rounds here that there are razzias (round ups) planned for Amsterdam as well. Are we going to have a repeat of what happened ten days ago in Rotterdam where they rounded up about 50,000 men between the ages of 17 and 40 for forced labor in the Arbeitseinsatz?

November 22. The little boy of Henk and Bep Dienske died last night. Johan Dienske came to bring me the sad news. The boy has barely known his father.

Good progress, especially for the French. They are at the Rhine; Metz, Belfort and Eschweiler have been liberated.

The Hague had their Razzias yesterday, all men between 17 and 40 have been rounded up

November 23. Today is Bep's (Dick's sister) birthday. I brought her a bar of soap, 1 candle light and a box of matches. November 26. This afternoon, we heard very low flying bomber planes. Bombs exploded. There was intense anti-aircraft fire. I could see the planes dive and rise. None were hit, a beautiful sight. Shortly after, we heard that they had turned the headquarters of the SD on the Euterpestraat in a pile of rubble.

---

[64] Jaap is the brother of Henk and he had then just been released from the prison in Amersfoort where the prison commander released a number of men in turn for their promise that they would support his pleas when his day of reckoning came at the imminent capitulation of the Germans.

[65] Nel Hillers, also worked for Henk Dienske and was arrested on May 22nd, she was one of Rennie's eight room mates in Dachau.

November 27. I took a look at the Euterpestraat mess. The ruins were still burning. Gurbe (van Brug, mast maker, who started to work for Opoe de Vries before 1913) sent five pounds of lamb meat from De Lemmer. It cost us 4.50 guilders per pound.

We had a fabulous meal this evening, kale hash with lamb.

December 5. Saint Nicholas Eve. The twins have been excited for days. In their Dr. de Moorschool, they had been visited by two Black Petes (the traditional helpers accompanying St. Nicholas), but Saint Nick himself could not make it all the way from Spain. We managed to put a surprise together for them, with a candy cane in it. Jan said: "I will save it for Aunt Rientje". (Rientje is Rennie's youngest sister who was being cared for in a revalidation center in Harderwijk.) Jaap wanted to save it for his mother.

December 8. The shortage of food is getting worse by the day. Butter costs 57.50 guilders per pound. The city people are searching for food on rickety bicycles, on foot, pushing baby buggies deep into the country side. Some of them die along the side of the roads.

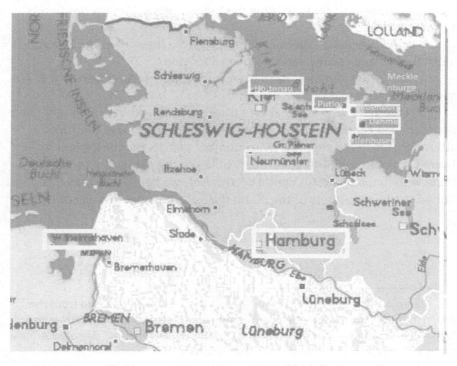

Locations where the Arendts were scattered in the next chapter

48. Winter in Schleswig-Holstein

Neumünster, where *Rennie* and her sons had taken refuge in early September, came under a heavy bombardment, by British Halifax bombers, on October 25. The entire neighborhood where they were staying was flattened and burned to the ground. Georg sustained phosphorus burns on his legs. On a visit to Rome in 1968, he had the ugly scar covered with a transplant off his derrière. He still has a small bombshell fragment lodged in his back.

With the few belongings that they managed to recover they moved to Dahme on the Baltic Sea, on the Mecklenburger Sound. Georg followed a teacher training course in Ratzeburg, near Lübeck. The German fighting force ran critically short of manpower and at the age of fourteen Georg was drafted into a flak battery in Putlos. His unit shot down several allied aircraft. Georg remembers seeing the family pictures the crew members carried on them when their bodies were removed from the wrecks.

Towards the end of the year, Georg met a man who claimed to know his father. My nephews knew no better than what their mother had told them years ago, that their dad had been killed in a civilian air plane crash in 1935.

Georg had a short telephone conversation with his father who was working then in Rathenow, just west of Berlin, in an aircraft factory where they built the Arado AR-196, a float plane that was launched by catapult from heavy cruisers. Georg confronted his mother with his discovery and she had to fess up to her deception.

August, the father, sent a wedding present from Berlin in 1956, but father and son never managed to see each other. The iron curtain was drawn shut between the two parts of the country.

49. The beginning of winter in Dachau

We were able to piece together, from the bits and pieces of news that we heard through the Germans on our assembly line, that the Allied troops were on their way. The Third Reich was being brought to its knees. More and more often, we would be running into the bomb shelters when the air raid sirens roared, either from the factory floor into the basement or, if we were in our barracks, to the bomb shelter under block two. At times, the bombs hit a nearby target. Those were anxious moments. Imagine that we would survive the imprisonment but end up home as invalids for the rest of our lives. When the bombs impacted nearby, someone would start praying the "Our Father" and most would join in.

As soon as the "All Clear" was given, we climbed out of the shelter and back to our block. From the third floor, we stood watching the spectacle of the destruction. We saw the black silhouettes, against the inferno of the blood red sky, of familiar landmarks in the city of Munich, the twin towers of the Frauenkirche, the Saint Lukas-Lehel church, the Alte Peter, etc. The wind carried the smell of the burning wood and the sound of the roaring flames all the way to our suburb.

We did not give much thought to the pain and loss this destruction brought upon the civilian population. For us it was a sign that our liberators had not forgotten us.

On our way to the factory in the morning, we saw more bombed out homes after the raids. It was always a relief to discover that the "Maria Clemens" home, an orphanage/boarding school on the Spixstrasse 14, had not been hit. The children played, supervised by the nuns, on the school grounds.

The AGFA factory escaped unscathed, to our disappointment.

We were all given an overcoat in November. None of them fit. We pulled the coats around our famished frames with a piece of rope. They were pulled from the piles of discarded clothing from deceased prisoners and exterminated Jews. At times, we were also given a change of clothing, also discards often infested with lice. But it was better than no clothes at all. After the distribution of these garments, we organized a fashion show.

Several of the women showed off their men's under-pants. Another would swing her hips, like a professional model, to show her undergarment with front and rear flaps and lace borders.

Somehow, we managed to make the clothes fit, but footwear was a much bigger problem. The shoes hardly ever fit. It was not uncommon to have either two left or two right hand clogs.

In the last months, I managed to get a pair of men shoes. They were at least three sizes too big, but it was such an improvement over my uncomfortable clogs that I remember skipping up the stairs into the factory like a little girl again with new shoes on my first day of school.

In Ravensbrück, ending up in the sick bay meant for most the equivalent of a death sentence. The situation here was better but we did not have a doctor. Two Polish women worked in the infirmary, but they paid little attention to anyone other than their own. After work, we would spend time with our sick comrades to help them and to keep them company. When typhus struck our barracks, we had to carry the sick to the toilets because we had no bedpans. We had one thermometer for our entire block.

The moment that "Paps" received the news of the typhus outbreak, he became very concerned. He had the entire guard squad inoculated and we were given pills. Stirnweis went immediately to the Dachau hospital. He returned with a bed pan under one arm, a thermometer and a real doctor. The doctor, Ella Lingens[66], also a political prisoner, from Vienna, received the assistance from two of our Dutch women, Hans and Erna[67], who had nursing experience.

When our sick ended up staying too long in the infirmary, they stood the chance that they would be transferred to the Dachau main camp hospital and that was comparable to the Russian Roulette in Ravensbrück. Lingens turned out to be too energetic for "Paps" and he had her sent back to hospital in Dachau.

---

[66] Ella Lingens, wrote her story of the war years and imprisonment as "Gefangene der Angst"

[67] Erna Tisch

159

In her place, he appointed a Polish woman, Ilse, supposed to be a doctor, but we did not trust her pretended credentials for one second. She feasted on the supplementary rations that were meant for the sick and she could not stand us, the Dutch women.

Germany commenced their counter offensive in the Ardennes on December 16. The Allied Forces were stopped cold in their fast track from Normandy through France, Belgium and the south of Holland. We were given the impression, from what our German colleagues in the plant told us, that the Germans would be able to push our liberators back into the North Sea. Suddenly, our euphoria for a quick end to this senseless war was dashed. We were depressed and wondered how long we would be able to hang on.

Our one slice of bread with the morning's break was discontinued and the soup for our lunch break was watered down a little more each the day. The air raids increased in frequency and lasted longer and we were now often spending the entire night in the ice-cold underground shelters; with just a couple hours of sleep we were sent on our way to the factory in the early morning. The tension, fear and fatigue took its toll on our physical and mental state. Typhus and scarlet fever put a number of our women into the sick bay.

A Danish and a French prisoner received a Red Cross package from their countries. We looked with great anticipation for a similar recognition from the Red Cross in Holland; not only to receive some extra food but to know that our country and families had not forgotten us since we left Holland in early September. But our people must have written us off.

50. Christmas 1944 in Dachau [68]

With Christmas approaching, our thoughts went out to our loved ones from whom we had not heard anything for four months. We tried to lift each other's spirits but that was not an easy task when everyone is preoccupied with the same concerns. Has Holland been liberated? Have any of our family members been harmed in the liberation offensive?

Commander Stirnweis decided that this Christmas would not go by unnoticed under his command. Mrs. Stirnweis had come to visit for Christmas and "Paps"[69] had sent his mistress away for the next few days. But his well intended plans were almost called off all together.

Paps had managed to procure a large sausage, as a surprise for his wife. But the wurst disappeared from the kitchen. The commander was furious. A search through our quarters turned up nothing. So, in his desperation, he tried the standard method, putting us in formation. There we stood for hours in the cold, in the snow, for a sausage.

No one came forward. He called it off, by then he realized that whoever had stolen the prize had consumed it by now. The preparations for the festivity resumed after this incident. Paps had a Spruce tree cut in the forest and the Christmas tree stood with a few silver stars and candles on the table in the middle of the mess hall.

Frau Stirnweis had brought colored crepe paper with which the Polish women were busy decorating the hall. We smelled the baking of cookies and we were told that we would be served coffee with sugar and cream and a Frankfurter sausage.

A spirited discussion ensued among the women in our block whether we should just ignore the commander's invitation, particularly after the standing in formation and just out of principle. We polled our neighbors and they shared our resolve. But when we heard the Polish women sing their beautiful Christmas songs, we got suckered into Paps' program.

---

[68] Note: This chapter is for the most part a verbatim translation of Kiky Heinsius' memoirs

One by one, we tripped into the mess hall to check it out. It did not take long for us to overcome our reluctance after seeing all those delicacies on the festively decorated tables. Paps sat in the center between the tables and the Christmas tree. The candles were lit. He was obviously pleased in his function as host; he encouraged us with a wide grin on his face. We took our places at the tables. Coffee with sugar, milk, a cookie and the sausage were served.

It was starting to feel like Christmas. With some hesitation at first, several of our women started singing "Holy Night Silent Night" followed, with a little more conviction, by "De Herdertjes lagen bij Nachten" and "Oh, Tannebaum".

As our way of a peace demonstration we ended our repertoire with extra emphasis on the "Vrede op Aarde" ("Peace on Earth") refrain from the popular Christmas hymn "Ere zij God".

To every one's astonishment, we saw the commander stand up, take his hat off, and join our song in the German version. He kept standing and gave us a speech in which he wished us a safe return to our families. Was this for real?

When we walked back to our barrack one of the women remarked: "He is and will always be a Nazi. He is just in a sentimental mood for Christmas".

The next day, Christmas day, there was another celebration in the mess hall. The Polish women had put together a Christmas pageant. All the tables had been lined up against the walls, and the benches were lined up as in a theater. The Three Kings and the Shepherds had been dressed in blankets and tinsel.

Mary wore a long black skirt and a white blouse. Joseph was dressed in men's trousers and a dress shirt. Mary and Joseph's clothes had been borrowed from Stirnweis. The commander had invited his bosses from the main camp in Dachau. He wanted to make an impression on them how well behaved his subjects were, to show them the contrast to the mess they had to put up with in Dachau.

Two women from our group, Mary Vaders and Riekie Heiligers, mounted the "stage" and sang the popular Dutch tear jerker sea shanty "Ketelbinkie".

Mary recited one of her many poems she composed and sang for us in English "A Love is So Sweet in the Spring Time".

The SS men enthusiastically stamped their boots and with shouts of "Bis, Bis!" demanded encores. The Dutch women closed their part of the entertainment by all singing "Waar de blanke top der duinen" and "Ik heb U lief mijn Nederland", both very melancholic patriotic songs. Several of the Dutch women wore orange crepe paper bows in their hair, made out of the paper brought by Frau Stirnweis. Orange is the Dutch national color.

The small group of Slovenian women could often be heard singing a beautiful melody. The commander assumed that it was their national anthem. He asked the women to sing it for his guests. They were more than happy to oblige. Because this happened to be their Partisan song:

"Po šumama i gorama" ending with:

"Mi ne damo zemlje naše Da je gaze fašisti"

which translates to: "We don't allow our lands to be trampled by Fascists!" They sang it with gusto!! The visiting officers applauded enthusiastically with "Bravo, Bravo!" It took an enormous effort, for those of us who knew the real meaning, to keep a straight face.

That very night, Mary and Joseph scaled the barbed wire fence in their borrowed civilian disguise, never to be seen again. Stirnweis became enraged. His kindness to lend them his clothes had made him a fool. Their freedom cost us, the following days, many hours of standing in the cold in formation, as a communal punishment. A small price for us to pay for Mary and Joseph.

51. A Decoration

To prevent another break out under his command, Stirnweis called for a fresh paint job on the red crosses that were painted on our clothes. The red paint had worn off and we had helped the process by rubbing it off. None of us liked the idea of standing out even more like a bunch of zombies.

But our reluctance changed when we found out that this time instead of using red, we were being repainted with orange paint; the Dutch national color. One of the women, on discovering the new color, yelled: "Attention! Everyone stand at attention, we are being decorated with the Cross of Orange!" We stood obediently straight and proud at attention while we were being decorated.

And after we had our turn, we clicked our heels and acknowledged the honor with: "Danke Schön, Frau Aufseherin!" The guards discovered much later what our theatrics had been all about but by then the paint had dried.

photo: Swedish Red Cross

52. New Year

January 1st 1945. It had been exactly 8 months and 3 days since I had been arrested and more than 4 months since I had any news from home. The Red Cross apparently had not been able to locate us here. Jaap and Jan were now in second grade and Lientje in 5th grade. Had Holland been liberated yet?

Our situation worsened by the day in all aspects. The already pitiful food rations were cut back even further. We were given two thin slices of bread in the evening which were meant for dinner and breakfast the next morning. It took enormous self control to hang on to that one slice of bread until the morning. Lunch at the factory consisted of a small bowl of lukewarm water with a couple of slivers of cabbage and carrots.

From the time we arrived here out of Ravensbrück, we were given a little extra food every Saturday evening, in the form of two boiled potatoes, a spoonful of cottage cheese, jam and margarine. But the potatoes, through the colder weather, were now often frozen or rotten. If you were lucky and quick enough, you could exchange a bad potato but often there were none left and many a tear was shed in disillusion and hunger pains.

Hunger was with us all through the day and plagued us in our attempts to sleep. It became increasingly more difficult to keep up our spirits and resolve with which we came here last October. I and many of my companions were having dizzy spells through our weakness and the majority of our women suffered digestive problems.

Coal for the stoves in our quarters and the mess hall was no longer available. Paps would take a detail of the prisoners from the factory out to gather firewood in the nearby forest. This way, we managed to have some heat in our barracks when we came home from the ten-hour workday.

But this was discontinued when Stirnweis was told that the factory could not afford to have any of the workers off the assembly lines.

The lights went out on a more regular basis when the electricity was cut through the air raids. We had little other choice then than to crawl under our blankets. We would lay there in the dark and sing a few songs and then we lulled ourselves asleep by thinking up all sorts of recipes of delicacies we hoped to taste again sometime soon.

The winter was harsh. The thermometer would drop to 25 and sometimes 30 degrees Centigrade below Freezing (-13 to -22 Fahrenheit). With all our clothes on under our thin blankets, we'd still shiver and it was very hard to fall asleep. Often, we were rudely awakened by the loud explosions of the bombing raids and the repetitive volleys of the anti-aircraft guns.

It was a sad looking bunch that set off on our two km march for work at five a.m. in the morning after a sleepless night on empty stomachs. Our wooden shoes would accumulate thick clumps of snow to their soles, after a fresh snowfall, and it was a hazardous trek especially for the older women. At times, the snow was so deep that some of the women, after having fallen several times, would not be able to get up and laid crying in desperation. The Aufseherinnen would pull them up and cuss them out. "Schneller, Schneller!!" The bitches with their spiked boots had little sympathy for our struggles.

The German factory personnel would be ready for us with clean industrial rags to brush the snow off and wipe away the occasional tears and to rub our frozen feet back to life. How would we ever be able to harbor any hatred against these Germans?

53. Slave Driven

The AGFA management was unhappy with our performance. A rumor made the rounds that the masters wanted to institute a bonus system; more food for a higher output. But that posed serious conflicts of conscience for us. Why would we want to aid the enemy with their war efforts? Right now, we were performing forced labor but if we accepted their bonus system, we'd be collaborators. The supervision had been increased and sabotage became harder to hide. If any one of us were to accept this bonus offer then we would lose our unity and that had to be avoided at all costs because it was our last formidable weapon.

Fortunately, we managed to all agree on this after consultations through the entire Dutch block. The bonus system remained a rumor but we wanted to have an answer ready, just in case, so that we could present our complaints over our reduced food rations.

Dr. Ella Lingens, the Austrian political prisoner doctor who had been temporarily with us from the main Dachau camp during the Typhus epidemic, had calculated that at the rate we were being fed we had only a few more months left to live.

Commander Stirnweis was caught between two fires. He had tried to improve our meals but it had fallen on deaf ears at the AGFA management. We decided to commence with passive resistance. More of the women reported to the sick bay with ailments that were hard to diagnose, stomach problems, dizziness, headaches, etc. They were then prescribed to stay in bed for the next days. The rest of the crew worked as slowly as possible and when we were ordered to work harder, we all had the same answer:

"I cannot work harder. I am worn out and have nothing to eat".

Stirnweis was completely frustrated. He spent more time on the factory floor to try getting us to work harder. He pulled women out of the sick bay he suspected to be faking their illness. None of us was impressed by his frustrations. But we still had nothing more than the miserable thin slices of bread and the bowl of dishwater.

Our lunch "Soup..." was starting to show up later and later, from the kitchen in our compound, in the factory. At times, it arrived only minutes before the end of the lunch break at 1 p.m.

You can imagine what that meant to us when we had existed, since the evening before, on two thin slices of bread.

If an air raid took place during our lunch break, we had to flee into the cellar and then a number of us came down there with an empty bowl. After the "all clear" had sounded the unlucky ones with their empty bowls would find their "soup" ice cold.

One day, the factory management decided to send the soup back to the mess hall when the air raid had lasted until more than a half hour after the end of the lunch break. But that started a near riot. Even the Poles did not put up with that. In the end, the slave drivers gave in and distributed the "Soup" after all.

54. The Strike

Until this day, no one seems to know how it started and who gave the signal. There had never been any discussion among us to lay down our work

It started in the front of the factory, on January 12, 1945; just shortly after the lunch break. Women stopped their work, and like a row of falling dominoes, in a matter of minutes, all of the Dutch women sat still with both arms crossed over their chests. The small group of Yugoslav women followed suit. The Polish women kept working. Our German "colleagues" were in shock. Yes, we knew all too well how strikes had been dealt with in the Netherlands in 1941.

The factory management sent for commander Stirnweis. We had started singing defiant protest songs. Stirnweis was in a rage. He called us names and cursed. He ran back and forth from the front to the back of the factory floor. "Why aren't you working?" and he'd get the same reply: "We don't want to work any longer. We are starving". When he pleaded in the back, he'd be drowned out by the singing of the women in the front and when he moved to the front, the rear guard would take over the singing. The German workers were taking this all in with great fear. But we became bolder by the minute. We had had it. You just cannot buy us, starve us to death and have us do your dirty work.

Everyone was sent home. It was still early in the afternoon when we walked back to the barracks, our heads held high.

It came as no surprise to us that this was not going to be the last of it. We had to stand in formation for hours in the bitter January cold. The Yugoslavs who had not been ordered for the same punishment stood with us in solidarity.

We did resume our work the next morning but the formation punishment continued. They wanted to know the names of the instigators, but we did not know them. Then they tried a new trick. The guards drew, at random, three women out of the formation. We were then threatened that if the real instigators did not come forward these three women would receive severe punishment. When the women were out of Stirnweis's sight for a split moment, they motioned to the group: "No!" This preserved our solidarity, once again.

Next, a delegation came out of the main camp in Dachau, led by Willy Bach[70], Gestapo agent and specialist in interrogations. They asked us again for the names of the instigators we answered that we all stopped our work together.

One of our women presented the delegation with a bowl of our daily lunch "soup" and asked how we were expected to perform to do a day's work on this. This way she hoped to aid Stirnweis' arguments in the conflict between him and the factory slave drivers. And it worked. The two factions almost got into a running fight. Bach stood by speechless, in disbelief.

He promised to make a report to Berlin. A strike by prisoners would be severely punished. This had never happened. Bach and his entourage climbed back into the black limousine and sped back to Dachau. Stirnweis was hoping that this whole affair would just go away.

In the end, he managed to get one of the non-Dutch prisoners to finger Mary Vaders.[71] She was punished with seven weeks of solitary confinement in the infamous Dachau Bunker. We welcomed her back with great joy and relief from her ordeal. She was sick but her spirit was unbroken. We had achieved a small victory; the soup contained a little more nourishment. No more talk of bonuses and the production pressure had eased as well.

---

[70] Willy Bach was infamous for his interrogation techniques. He made his victims stand up straight for days in a bunker cell, hung them from a bar and clubbed them senseless. He received a six-year prison term.

[71] Mary Vaders composed a number of beautiful poems while imprisoned. She published these as: "Kruis Driehoek en Nummers" (Cross, Triangle and Numbers = these were the insignias used to identify the prisoners)

55. After the Strike

We found that our relationship with the German workers in the plant had actually improved. This could have forced them to higher performances if they would have ended up taking us away. I think that we gained some more admiration from them. And it became more and more apparent through our whispered conversations that they were getting tired of this war as well. They had their worries for their husbands, fathers, sons who were fighting on the different fronts.

At times, they let us smuggle a newspaper out of the plant and reading through the propaganda we determined how close the allied forces were from here. We concluded that at least the South and the West of Holland had been liberated. But in late January, on the way to our factory, we ran into a group of Dutch forced laborers and they told us that they had been rounded up in Rotterdam in the previous weeks. That put a damper on our spirits.

We no longer used the mess hall because there was no more fuel for the stove.

We brought our slices of bread with us to our rooms. We had started to breakdown our wooden stools to burn in our wood stoves. Next, we took part of our bed boards out. The wood wool out of our mattresses was used to start the fire. Then one of the smart women among us suggested that since we were not using the mess hall any longer, we should go and get the stools out of there. The guards became less and less noticeable and the Aufseherinnen turned a blind eye when we were on our fuel forays. Many of the windows had broken panes because of the concussions caused by the bombardments. Since we did not pay rent there was no maintenance performed. We hung blankets over the broken windows.

On Sunday, February 25th it was my turn to give the "sermon" in the morning's devotion. I preached on the text of the Last Supper from Luke 22.

56. Dick's Diary February 1945

February 6. This morning on my way to work, I ran into Pastor Kunst. He was on his way to talk to a barge skipper. Kunst had found a way to place 150 children from the church families on farms in the Wieringermeer[72]. I told him that I would like our boys to go there as well. He would look into that. They needed to be on the dock the next morning at 5 a.m. I had quite a job making the arrangements on such a short notice. Jaap and Jan had to be picked up from their grandparents and then I brought them to Siebold on the Singel, for the night, which was just a short walk to the dock. They had to get up at 4 a.m. In the Damrak, near the Central Station, lay a large Tjalk[73]. Straw had been spread on the cargo hold's floor.

The children were all stretched out on the straw.

The nurse for our neighborhood, Mrs.Goede, came along with Pastor Kunst and another two men from our church. The children are in good hands. They are headed for the towns of Middenmeer and Slootdorp. The mood was good and our boys enjoyed the adventure as well. They recognized many of their Dr. de Moorschool friends who they had not seen since July. Jan was a bit concerned that he would not be home for his 8th birthday. One of the children managed to fall into the ice-cold water while trying to board. The father jumped right in and both of them stood soaking wet back on the quay.

The barge took off at 6.30. A tugboat took the sailing barge in tow. I miss them but they'll have much better chances to get the food that has become so scarce here in the city. It also became a bit too busy for Pa and Ma. It has become eerily quiet around here now. February 13. We have received a letter from the temporary foster parents of the boys. They are staying with a farmer family Dekens. There are five children on the farm in ages from four to eighteen. They are very happy there. I may come and visit on their birthday.

---

[72] Wieringermeer was one of the very first "polders", reclaimed land from the Zuider Zee. About 30 miles north of Amsterdam.

[73] Tjalk is a traditional Dutch flat bottom, lee boards, sailing barge.

Jan and Jaap also added their letters. From Jan a very short message, Jaap wrote in more detail. They were locked in the hold for five to six hours. On arrival that night, the children were all quartered in a hotel in Middenmeer. They get to walk one of the horses, there are chickens, pigs and rabbits. They can stay until the end of the war. The boys had brought each a couple of sandwiches for the trip and since several of the children had nothing to eat, they shared them. Jaap wrote that this prompted one of the older Mulder boys to conclude that our parents were NSB members (the Dutch Nazi party) because they were the only ones who would have access to bread.

There were eleven hungry mouths to feed at the Mulder family who live about five doors up the street from us. Yesterday, I came upon a young boy, I guessed him to be about nine years old, who stood there crying. I asked him: "What's the matter, young man?" He replied: "I am hungry!" That just breaks your heart. People are coming through the neighborhood begging for bread or something to eat.

I read in the news paper that the death count for the week from January 26 to February 4th is 506. The same week last year was 169.

February 19. I helped unload a barge with a load of tulip bulbs[74], I received a little extra for my efforts and came home with 50 kilos.

February 21. Mrs. Heringa (Anna Heringa-Jongbloed**)** has died in Ravensbrück. One of the women in Ravensbrück has been released.[75] I hope to be able to get in touch with her.

February 23. I am busy cleaning the tulip bulbs; the flower stem has to be removed otherwise they continue sprouting. It is a good starch substitute, mashed like potatoes with a few carrots; tastes o.k. Aunt Gepke sent us a letter. She likes where she is in De Hommerts near Woudsend[76], with her niece. She wrote that she had a dream that Rennie was back.

---

[74] Tulip bulbs became a sought-after substitute for potatoes.

[75] Most likely this was Corrie ten Boom, who was released on January 1st. Or Hebe Kohlbrugge released January 1945. At this time Dick van Ommen still does not know any better than that his wife is still in Ravensbrück.

[76] Woudsend-Ypecolsga, where the aunt she was named after, Gerbrigje de Vries-Tromp, was born, see the first chapters of this book.

She wrote that her great-great grandfather, Rinze [77]Claasesz Platte, born in 1767, a sea captain had been taken prisoner by the English during the war with England, around 1800[78]. Two years later, he suddenly showed up again in De Lemmer.

Pastor Kunst brought me a letter he had received from the church commission in Middenmeer.

In this letter, they point out that the twins did not have it all that bad with their grandparents in Amsterdam and did not lack anything. I am going to see the farmer family this Thursday for Jaap and Jan's birthday and I will try to clear this up. It is really too bad that this had to happen.

February 27. I left at 7.30 a.m. for Middenmeer. Siebold lent me his bicycle. Mine has given up the ghost. The weather was good, a stiff breeze, via Zaandam, Purmerend. I reached Hoorn at noon where I ate a sandwich. At 3.30 p.m. I arrived in Middenmeer. It is a beautiful modern farm. The boys had gone to Kolhoorn with the horse-drawn wagon. They came home at 6 p.m. They looked fine.

They have found a very good home. Very kind people, they came to the Wieringermeer from Groningen. The children also treat the boys very well. Jan spends the whole day with the farm hands on the land. He has learned the names of all the animals.

I managed to clear up the farmer's complaint, that had been reported in the letter to Pastor Kunst, to his satisfaction. The next day was their birthday. The boys had dressed in their Sunday clothes. Mrs. Dekens had baked a cake for their birthday.

Later that day, I went to find Catharina Geel[79]and Hannie Broers, neighbor girls in our street, to bring them the regards from their parents. They are also staying in Middenmeer with foster families. March 1st. I took off again at 8.30 a.m. The whole farm crew waved me farewell and told me that I could come back any time.

---

[77] Rinze was the name sake for Rennie (baptismal name Rinsje) and her grandmother Rinsje/Reesje de Vries-Ages.

[78] This was most likely the 4th Anglo-Dutch war 1780-1784 British reprisal for the Dutch choosing the side of the American War for Independence.

[79]Aunt of Jacobine Geel a well-known Dutch T.V. evangelist.

174

Mrs. Dekens gave me six ham and cheese sandwiches for the road and two pears, which I have saved for Rientje[80] and Moe.

They also gave me a seventeen-pound sack of wheat. I enjoyed the couple of days I had with them. The wind was strong on the way back, rain showers; I made it back home by 4.30 p.m. Just before Hoorn there was a German road block, but I managed to find a way around it. There is hardly a child left in the Alblasstraat after the transport to the Wieringermeer.

March 29. Early this morning, Saakje showed up at my office to tell me that Jan and Jaap had been dropped off at their house on the Singel at 11.30 p.m. by a cop. The farmer had received other children and then sent our boys away.

I thought that their concerns about the twins' behavior had been addressed during my recent visit.

It seems like a very strange way of doing things. Apparently, the driver, who took them back to Amsterdam, had a letter on him for Pastor Kunst. The boys looked o.k. but unkempt. They arrived in tears on the Singel, dragging their blankets over the wet streets. They had one piece of luggage with them with wet laundry. They had put them under a tarp in the back of an open pick-up truck but they had not had enough cover from the rain and the cold night.

They had left in the evening in a hurry. The driver had dropped them off at the Police Station on the Adelaarsweg in Amsterdam North.

One of the Policemen had accompanied them to the Police Station near the Koepelkerk where the twins recognized that they were near the Singel and then had the policeman ring the bell at nearly midnight at their aunt and uncle on the Singel.

March 30. Good Friday. Went to see Pastor Kunst. He had received the letter from Wieringermeer and was not very happy with the way this was handled. He had already had other unpleasant experiences with his contacts in the Wieringermeer. Kunst has given them a piece of his mind and accused them of committing an unpatriotic act towards the van Ommen family.

---

[80] Rientje is Rennie's youngest sister and had chronic health problems in that period.

175

ACCOUNTANTSKANTOOR R. J. RIDDER

SPECIAAL AFDELING
LANDBOUWBOEKHOUDEN

BEËDIGD MAKELAAR IN
ONROERENDE GOEDEREN

Bankrelatie's:
Coöp.Boerenleenbank, Middenmeer
R. K. Boerenleenbank, Middenmeer

GIRO 287814 — TELEF. 4
K 1915

Middenmeer, ..22...Februari... 1945.
Brugstraat 32

Den .eledelzeergeleerde Heer
Dr.P.G. Kunst,
A M S T E R D A M — C .

Hooggeachte Dr.Kunst,

Namens de diaconie kom ik U het volgende ge-
val meedelen van de kinderen van Ommen, Jan en
Jacob, ondergebracht bij dhr.K.Dekens, Schagerweg
Middenmeer.

Deze beide kinderen bevonden zich bij hun
grootmoeder, voor ze hier geplaatst werden. Uit
hun opmerkingen is overduidelijk gebleken, dat
deze beide jongens in geen enkel opzicht gebrek
leden, doch gewend waren aan wat men in deze
tijd feestmalen zou noemen; bij Oma was wittebrood
geregeld op tafel, elke dag groente. Wanneer
bij de pleegouders zo nu en dan meelkost wordt
gegeten met ham n.b. er bij, wensen de beide
jongens bovendien nog groente, omdat ze dit bij
Oma gewend waren. Zo is hun hele gedrag, zodat
de pleegouders deze jongens niet langer wensen
te houden. Trouwens zulke kinderen behoren ook
niet uitgezonden te worden. Dan gaan duizenden
kinderen vóór. U zult ongetwijfeld dezelfde mening
zijn toegedaan. De fam.Dekens krijgt straks weer
andere kinderen uit Haarlem in plaats van de
van Ommens, zodat gelukkig geen kinderen door
deze debacle er de dupe van zullen worden.
Wilt U zich z.v.p. in verbinding stellen met
de ouders of grootmoeder, dat zij naar hier iemand
laten komen om Jan en Jacob op te halen? Gelukkig
hebben zich niet meer van deze gevallen voorge-
daan. Hopende, dat U voor deze aangelegenheid
zorg zult dragen, teken ik

met vr.groeten,

Uw dv.

176

The letter:
R.J. Ridder Accountants
Middenmeer, February 22, 1945

The very reverend Mr. Dr. P.G. Kunst,

Dear Dr. Kunst,

As spokesperson for the church commission, I wish to advise you of the following incident with the van Ommen children, Jan and Jacob, who have been given a home with Mr. K. Dekens, Schagerweg, Middenmeer.

These two children were living with their grandparents before they were assigned a home here. From their remarks, it has been clearly established that both boys did not lack anything, but instead were accustomed to what, we would call in these times, festive meals; at their grandmother white bread was regularly served, they had vegetables with every dinner.

When they are served potatoes with ham, they insist on having vegetables with it, because that is what they are used to at their grandmother. This is their general attitude and the reason that their foster parents do not wish to keep them any longer.

As a matter of fact, this sort of boys should never have been sent to us. There are thousands of children who have better reasons to be sent here.

No doubt, you will share our conclusions. The Dekens family will shortly be receiving other children from Haarlem in the place of the van Ommens so that fortunately no children will become the victims of this problem.

Would you, please, get in touch with the parents or grandmother to have them send someone to come and get Jan and Jacob?

Fortunately, we have not had any other similar cases to report.

In anticipation that you will look after this matter, I am,
with kind regards,

Your dv.

Later on, I heard from the boys that they had been a little too inquisitive. With the aid of the five-year-old son, Klaas, they had, for instance, discovered a secret tunnel from the farm that led underneath the road the farm fronted on to the canal that ran parallel with the road. This way the farm workers, who were hiding on the farm from the German forced labor service, could escape to a rowboat that was moored at the end of the tunnel in the canal. They also found an ambulance that was buried in the hay stack to keep it out of the hands of the Nazis.

Sunday April 8. Henk Dienske has died in Beëndorf by Helmstedt in February from the abuse and undernourishment in the concentration camps. His wife, Bep Dienske, was notified in person by a German. Official cause of death was, as usual, heart failure.

It is difficult to comprehend. Here we stand before one of the mysteries of God's ways. All the reformed churches in Amsterdam read the announcement of Henk Dienske's death.

April 12. President Roosevelt died unexpectedly.

This afternoon, I visited with Bep *(Dick's sister)* and Jo Schijfelen. We have decided that from Monday, the 23rd they will come and move in here in the Alblasstraat. Their children are all with farm families in Friesland. I will have to get the stove organized. The majority of the people now insert a small stove, so called "Kookbus", made out of a coffee can into the standard wood stove This uses much less firewood.

April 14. Buchenwald Concentration Camp has been liberated and 25,000 political prisoners are now freed. Dick Alberts[81] has helped me replace the living room heating stove with the salamander stove. This will now also be our cooking stove.

April 15 Sunday. Pastor Berkhouwer's sermon was on Psalm 27: "Trust in the Lord and be strong". The sermon was all about the soon anticipated end of the war. As the entrance song, the organist played the funeral march of Guilmant to commemorate President Roosevelt's death.

---

[81]Longtime friends who lived in the adjoining street the Griftstraat.

Arnhem, Groningen, Beilen and other towns have been liberated. Battles are raging in Zwolle and Apeldoorn.

April 17. This afternoon, I found a postcard from a Mrs. Visch from Rotterdam.

She reported that as of the middle of February, Rennie was well in body and spirit. What a relief! After not having heard anything in the last seven months. I am very worried though, notwithstanding the successes. There are so many horror stories reaching us now from the concentration camps that have been liberated.

On that same day, three weeks before war's end, the Germans blew large holes in the dike that protected the Wieringermeer polder. No lives were lost but this senseless act of a defeated enemy brought the water level to the roof lines and caused extensive damage and loss to the much-needed food crops and livestock. The 150 odd children that had come to the Wieringermeer with Jan and Jaap had to be evacuated and new homes had to be found for them.

57. Easter in Dachau

April 1st. Easter Sunday.

It was Joukje Grandia-Smits'[82] turn to lead our Easter service.

The entrance song was Hymn 221 verses 1 and 2.

Hail to You first of the days
Dawn of the Resurrection
Through Whose light the power of hell has been conquered
And death has been eliminated

The text for the sermon was taken from Matthew 25, 1-22, the story of the Resurrection. Our recessional song was "A Mighty Fortress is Our God"

Later in the day, we all joined the Roman Catholic women at their Easter Service. They used my New Testament. We appropriately sang together "The Church's One Foundation is Jesus Christ the Lord".

On April 12, we heard in the factory of the death of President Roosevelt. This caused us some concerns. Would this slow the American advance down now that their leader had suddenly passed away? But we did not have much time to contemplate this thought because an air raid alarm chased us into the shelter. This time, it appeared to be directed on the factory. Bombs exploded all around us. Thick dust clouds darkened the view from the small windows. But just as before, no direct hits on the factory.

---

[82] Joukje Grandia-Smit know under her code name "Clara" is known as the very first courier for the Dutch Resistance the LO-LKP.

58. Red Cross Parcels

Later in the week after the heavy bombardment, we saw Paps march into the factory, unexpectedly. He stopped at the work-stations and was excitedly waving a couple documents. What was going on? It turned out that Dachau had received Red Cross parcels for us. One of our women, Emmy, did not trust this at all. She shrugged her shoulders. He showed her the papers that showed:

225 Belgian R.C. parcels
300 Polish R.C. parcels
10 French R.C. parcels

When we arrived back in the camp, we took our turn to enter the mess hall where Stirnweis stood proud as a peacock behind a large table with the parcels.

The roommates of Emmy each received one of the Belgian parcels, but when it was Emmy's turn the commander said: "Sie nicht, Sie haben mir nicht geglaubt" (Not you, you did not believe me) and then directed her to stand with her face turned to the wall.

We felt really bad for her and already planned to share our treasures with her. But when all was said and done and we were busy going through our treasures, Emmy came in with a huge smile on her face. Stirnweis had given her one of the French parcels which was four times bigger than our Belgian treat. It contained sugar cubes, Ovomaltine, biscuits, cigarettes and a slab of dried fruit.

A very lively trading scene developed in the barracks. Cigarettes were exchanged for sugar cubes, and so on. One woman showed us how she could make candy from the sugar cubes and the dried fruit. She boiled the mix in water and then spread the thick sweet goo on bed boards, which were first wetted down, after it had dried out enough, she cut it in strips and cubes. More of our bed boards had to be sacrificed as well as what was left of the stools to fire the cooking stove. We had a feast!

59. Change of the Guard

Little by little, our SS guards had been replaced by older men, because things were not going well for the Third Reich and they were reaching the bottom of the barrel to replace the many battle casualties. About twelve of them kept guard in shifts; they stood guard on the outside of the fence and manned the four watch towers. They would trot along on our march from the barracks to the factory and then stood guard outside the factory. We never ever exchanged words.

But even the older SS guards were sent to the Eastern battle front. In their place, we ended up with a strange rag tag group of older Bavarians, armed with hunting shotguns, dressed in civilian clothes with their typical dark green Bavarian felt heads. That first morning when we marched out of the gate they, in unison, dipped their hats and in Bavarian style greeted us with: "Guten Morgen" and "Grüss Gott".

On the second day of their presence, we chanced to send one of the women to the barbed wire fence; with: "Wache, was gibt es noch Neues?" (Guard, what is happening?) She received the latest news from the war situation with a couple encouraging remarks that the war was not going to last much longer. Our spy would then give the guards a couple of our cigarettes from our Red Cross parcels and quickly return to bring us the latest news.

60. Dorry

Her full name was Dorothea Irene de Vries. The SD had taken her away from her home in Amsterdam leaving her young daughter behind. It was a case of mistaken identity. Dorry had nothing to do with the Resistance.

She was cut down by a double-edged sword. First of all, the frustration of her impotence to prove her innocence and secondly, the fact that she felt as an outsider among the rest of the women who had played a role in resisting the common enemy.

The following is a verbatim translation of the (thus far unpublished) memoirs of Kiky Heinsius[83]:

"Dorry passed away last night; we heard the sad news when we awoke this morning. She developed scarlet fever and ended up in the sick bay with an ear infection. No one had expected that this could spell the end for Dorry.

We are all very sad to lose this sweet modest woman who quietly went about her business among us.

When we ended up in the bomb shelter during day light hours, I would look at her with admiration. She would stand there, the image of peace, while she'd be making trinkets as souvenirs to take home, as if the bombardments did not concern her in the least bit. She'd craft the most beautiful items from the bits and pieces she picked up from the factory waste. When I would compliment her on her creations, she would respond with a shy smile.

She is gone now and it is the bitter reality that this could have been prevented with just a little more medical attention. Our volunteer nurses have done all they could but their efforts were doomed from the start without the aid of a medical doctor.

The factory has been shut down a few days ago and we all know that the end of the war is near. And just now this, it should not have been allowed to happen.

---

[83]Kiky Heinsius memoirs written of her imprisonment in the same concentrations camps as Rennie van Ommen-de Vries.

We said our good byes this afternoon to our deceased. She lay so still in the coffin, in her beautiful white robe, three flowers tugged in her hand. The flowers were probably cut from the neighboring victory garden; I have no idea where the white robe had come from."

April 26, 1945
Dorry was buried today in Munich.

A real hearse came to bring her to the cemetery and a couple of her friends were permitted by the commander to accompany the casket, so that they could report to her family after the war had ended where Dorry had been laid to rest.

The guards saluted when the hearse started to move away.
All of us watched from behind the barbed wire fence, overcome by a deep feeling of loss and defeat."

I visited Dorry's mother after the war to express my sympathy to her and to tell her what I knew about Dorry of her time with us. It was impossible for me to console her mother. She harbored an intense hatred for the ones who had brought this loss and sorrow upon her.

61. Dick's Diary. The last days of the war

April 21st 1945. This afternoon, I left with the boys from the Pythagorasstraat. We have been there since October 7th, with my parents - in-law. It worked well, but our presence and the recent addition of their youngest daughter Rientje, upon her discharge from her Tuberculosis treatment, became too much for Pa and Moe. It is very difficult to find a housekeeper under the present circumstances.

April 23rd. Lientje also came home today from Alphen. Our family is almost complete. Jaap and Jan have gone back to the second grade at the Dr. de Moorschool. Lien went back to her 5th grade class at the Bugenhagenschool. The children at her school receive a meal from the municipal kitchens every afternoon. It usually consists of pea soup made from the skins peeled from the potatoes in which float a few peas, completely tasteless.

The Hillers family in the Van Breestraat also received news through Mrs. Visch in Rotterdam about Nel Hillers. The Russians are close to the center of Berlin, they have liberated the concentration camp "Oranienburg".

April 25. It is a year ago, today, that Rennie was locked up. Maybe she has already been liberated. The Russians are not far away.

April 30. I received a letter from Jaap Denecht, from Rotterdam. He lives in the same neighborhood as Visch and he went to see Visch to get more details. It turns out that Visch is a man. I had been under the impression that it was a woman who had been discharged and I assumed that Rennie was still in Ravensbrück. I am glad that she is in Munich instead of Ravensbrück. We heard, today, that Munich has been taken by the American 7th Army without any Resistance.

The first food air drops were made yesterday, by bombers of the Allied Forces near The Hague, Leiden and Rotterdam. Everyone came out to wave with flags and cheer the low flying aircraft.

62. The Death March

The AGFA factory was shut down on April 23rd. The entire distribution chain was destroyed, whatever we produced could no longer be transported to its destination.

On April 26, commander Stirnweis informed us that for our safety he would accompany us on a foot march to the South.
On that same day, four of our companions dropped their disguise they had managed to maintain since their arrests, all five turned out to be Jews. They then told us their real names. We never had any idea of their real identity. If the Germans would have found out it would have been their death sentence. It was an emotional discovery for all of us to know that they would soon be free together with us and that they had been able to hide in our midst.
Hans Canneheuvel, one of Tiny Boosman's roommates, turned out to be Johanna Frankfort-Israels[84]. Corry Parijs and her mother, Bertha (Bep) Leegwater-Hammel, managed to hide among the gentiles without even changing their names. Corry gave me her address as Waalstraat 152, which is just a few blocks from where we live.

Gonda van der Laan went back to Betty Trompetter. She had worked for one of the Dutch top Resistance leaders, Johannes Post, under the code name Tineke. She was the one who kept an eye on the hostage, the mother of the Dutch SS prison guard Jan Boogaard[85] who turned out to have betrayed the second attempt, on July 14, 1944, to break into Weteringschans prison. Betty, alias Gonda/Tineke, was arrested and sent to Vught. Post was executed with fourteen others on July 16 in the sand dunes of Overveen.

Trompetter's sister, Henny[86], is the only other one of her family who survived the Holocaust. Their parents were both murdered in Auschwitz and their two brothers were also victims of the holocaust. The S.S. had run out of poison gas and bullets.

We have since learned of the sinister plan that Himmler had intended for us and all the Dachau and surrounding prison camps.

---

[84] Johanna remarried Henry F. Cunningham Jr and passed away in 2002 in Charleston S.C.

[85] Jan Boogaard, received the death sentence, executed March 1, 1947

[86] Henny Trompetter moved to the U.S. and worked for the United Nations where she met her husband A.H. Dantas de Brito, they lived in Rye, N.Y.

He issued an order that all the camps were to be evacuated in order to leave the least possible evidence of the crimes the Third Reich had committed and to be able to be rid of the few remaining witnesses before the advancing allied armies. Seven thousand male prisoners left the main Dachau camp on this same Death March.

Thousands of prisoners perished on these Death Marches, in locked box cars that stalled on a track to nowhere and in the Baltic Sea in the infamous Mecklenburger Sound disaster. We were, so we found out months after war's end, destined for the Tegern Lake in the Bavarian Alps.

Stirnweis gave us a choice to stay behind in the camp, which reduced some of our fears as to what might lay in store for us. Twenty-two of our Dutch women stayed behind, they were either too weak to leave or still did not trust our destiny. A Dutch nurse stayed with these 22 women. Another ten Dutch prisoners were left in the hospital of the main Dachau camp. This group was freed on April 29 when the American 7th Army liberated the Dachau concentration camp.

The remainder, about 170 Dutch women plus a larger group of Polish women marched out of the München-Giesingcamp on April 27th. We used our bed sheets to make a sling in which we carried the few belongings we had, the handcrafted souvenirs, the addresses we had exchanged, etc.

On that last evening, before the Death March, when we had our standard soup bowl dinner, we were all given a small sausage and a piece of bread. The majority of the women ate it right then and there.
The long line started to move out around 6 a.m. The women who stayed behind waved us out until the long line disappeared around the bend of the road. That first day we marched about 30 kilometers, making an occasional rest stop. "Paps" tried to avoid us being spotted from the air for fear of air attacks and he took us over back roads. But on a couple occasions we had to quickly dive in the ditch along the road to avoid the low flying allied fighter planes.
That first night we slept on a large farm, in the feeding troughs, on the stable floor and some slept outside. It rained on the second day and we were soaking wet. The blankets we carried were drenched and weighed heavy on our tired and frail frames, our feet were covered with blisters and we had not had anything to eat.

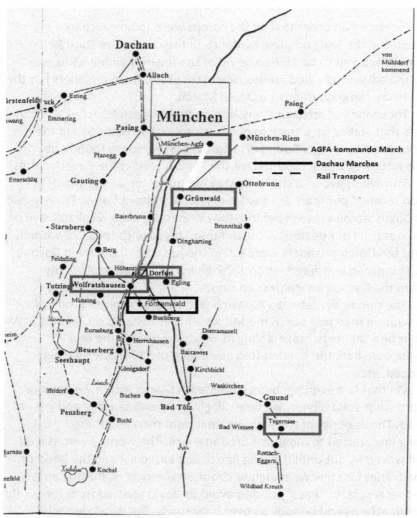

Routes of the Death Marches from Dachau and Satelite Camps   Photo: Gedenkstätte Dachau

We were starving. The commander was in a hurry that day and pressed us on. He would not let us stop to relieve ourselves, so, we had to just try and do this while moving in the formation. By the end of that morning, we were fed up. Why the hurry? We started to wonder if this was not some sinister plan after all. Why did we have these real S.S. guards again instead of the old game wardens?

The Death March April 28 through the village of Perchau. Photo Benno Gantner

189

We spotted a large shed in a meadow and we all ran into it, but there was not enough room for all of us. Stirnweis reacted in fear to our rebellion. Screaming "HerrGottsakramentnocheinmal" at us trying to get us back on the road. He tried convincing us that this was not a good place to take a break and that he knew of a bigger farm down the road.

The barn leaked like a sieve, which helped the arguments of our leader to get our 450 odd women back in some form of control again. We were totally exhausted and when it did not go fast enough for Aufseherin, Hanna Zimmermann, who spoke fluent Dutch, she called us "Schweinhunde" while she made herself a ham sandwich.

The rain had stopped in the meantime.

When we reached the road again, out of the meadow, an SS man stood there together with a couple of young farmers and women observing the 450 women. The SS man pulled Kiky Heinsius by her sleeve and said: "Hören Sie mal, verstehen Sie Deutsch?" ("Listen do you understand German?") And when she nodded: "Machen Sie sich Mut, der Krieg wird bald vorbei sein, der Befehlshaber von Bayern hat kapituliert." (Hang in there, the war will soon be over. The Bavarian governor has capitulated).

A while later, a young woman rode her bicycle along our sorry looking contingent and tried to raise our spirits by shouting:

"Krieg bald aus, Krieg bald aus!" (War soon over!) We all nodded and replied: "Danke schön!"

When we walked into the small town of Wolfrats-hausen, the Polish women decided to stop for a while at the Roman Catholic Sankt Andreas church. The villagers came to take a look at this strange procession. When the guards did not chase them away, they whispered the latest developments of the war in our ears. Several of the village women came back and distributed bread throughout our crowd.

Another mile further, south of Wolfratshausen, we stopped at a large farmhouse, the Walser-Hof, where we were given shelter for the night. Stirnweis gave us a short speech and told us that this was the end of the march and that he was going to await the arrival of the Americans with us here.

A loud "Hoorah" went out from us. As tired and worn out as we were, we still managed to gather the little left in us to laugh and cry and embrace each other.

I and many others, I am sure, thanked the Lord. This was truly the beginning of the end, at last.

We spread straw on the barn floor and fell quickly asleep under our wet blankets. Shortly afterwards, the farmer's wife came to wake us up to tell us that she had soup ready for us.

Walser, the farmer, welcomed us all in his Bavarian dialect before the soup was served and welcomed us. He told us that we were welcome to stay until the liberation; he apologized that he could not offer us bread but that there would be enough soup to go around. We broke in loud applause to his kind words.

It is hard to imagine how this farmer and his wife managed to feed nearly 450 women for over a week mostly out of their own pockets.

The Red Cross distributed Ovomaltine in cans and we used the empty cans to eat our soup. Not far from the farm was an abandoned forced labor camp, Föhrenwald, where our host, farmer Walser, managed to obtain two fattened pigs. Frau Walser, with her maid, cooked up a great soup from the pigs but the fat caused our unaccustomed digestive system to revolt.

The Walser Hof in 2012   photo taken by the Boosmans

Sunday, April 29. Where are the Americans?

We desperately needed some sort of starch to go with the soup. We formed a couple of small groups to go search for bread or potatoes. This was the first time that we could go on our way without having to be in a formation with armed guards.

It was a beautiful spring day. We hop scotched hand in hand like a bunch of grade school girls through the meadows towards Wolfratshausen. The newborn lambs appeared to be infected by our frolicking and followed us along in a similar fashion from a safe distance. The fruit trees were in bloom, white and pink. To the south, we could see the snow-capped Alps. At the intersections of the country roads stood the traditional shrines displaying a statue of the Virgin Mary or a Crucifix, many with fresh flowers.

The towers of the Roman Catholic Saint Andreas Church and of the Evangelical Saint Michael Church stood high over Wolfratshausen on our approach. It all looked so peaceful and harmonious. This had to be a place where God dwells. We had gotten to know a compassionate Samaritan in farmer Walser; and yesterday also townspeople along the road. But I could not help wonder how Hitler managed to pull the wool over so many eyes. How was it possible to ignore the atrocities that took place just fifty miles to the North of this peaceful and harmonious setting? Small groups of German soldiers passed us, deserters on the run. We also observed long files of male prisoners still being driven south.

The guards had no pity on these staggering skeletons. An occasional rifle shot could be heard and that meant one less body to worry about for the SS guards. There were also clusters of male Dachau prisoners of many different nationalities who had escaped or been abandoned by their guards. They still wore the striped prison garbs. We managed to find some bread in the village with the help of a couple Russian prisoners from the Dachau camp. When we got back to the farm, we found it in a great uproar. The aufseherinnen and the guards had taken off with the approval of the commander.

Stirnweis' sidekick, sergeant Djerin[87] left with one of the prisoners we detested.

The 21 Slovenian women, decided to find their way home on their own and left in small groups that morning.

In the meantime, an SS officer from Dachau had come on his motorcycle to tell Stirnweis that if he did not get his 450 women back on the Death March by the next day he'd be executed.

Stirnweis managed to stall him to the next afternoon.

"Paps" assured us that we would remain here and that he was certain that the area would be liberated the next day by the Americans.

Monday, April 30, 1945.

The church custodian, Ignaz Leeb, together with the widow of the former custodian, Karolina Engelhardt, raised the white flag on the St. Andreas Catholic church steeple. The villagers followed his lead. But a couple hours later, the white flags were lowered again, when the SS commanding officer threatened to shoot the offenders. They came looking for the custodian who was hiding in a closet in the sacristy.

Major Dr. Karl Luber, the commander of the local civil guard came to the rescue and took the twosome into custody in his headquarters. The SS officer demanded that they be turned over for execution. Luber refused and told them that this would require a sentence from a military tribunal. The SS retreated. Shortly after, the mayor received a call that the SS was getting ready to explode the 300 kilograms of Nitrate Pentahydrate under the Andreas Bridge. The approaching American tank assault could be heard from afar. The vice mayor Ettenhuber ran as fast as he could to the bridge and with the assistance of Luber's, next in command, Lieutenant Kollmeier, managed to cut the fuse wire.

Our leader would not allow us off the farm. When would the SS officer be back here from Dachau to enforce yesterday's ultimatum? We were all highly charged awaiting the events to follow.

---

[87] The Polish women had the Americans lock Djerin up, he was sentenced to six years prison.

63. *Rennie* Arendt-de Vries at war's end

Towards the end of the war, the three Arendts lived in Oldenburg, near Lübeck.

After the capitulation, *Rennie* and her boys moved once again, this time to Kellenhusen on the shores of the Baltic Sea. Georg witnessed on these shores one of the grimmest parts of the war history. He remembers seeing the shoreline littered with corpses.

At the end of April, Himmler ordered all the concentration camps to be evacuated and the camp administration records to be destroyed to hide the evidence. He sent the remaining survivors on Death Marches like the one our group of women were on from Dachau. Buchenwald had already been liberated by the 7th Army. Ravensbrück and Sachsenhausen were taken by the Russians. This left Bergen Belsen and Neuengamme and their satellite camps which had already become overpopulated by prisoners that had been driven West ahead of the approaching Russian army from camps further East. Many of those prisoners had died along the road. On Himmler's orders, they were driven north to ports on the Baltic Sea; by foot, squeezed into boxcars. Again, many of them were left dying along the side of the road. About ten thousand reached the Baltic Sea shore. They were loaded into several ships anchored in the Mecklen-burgerMecklenburger sound, the majority, about 4,200, aboard the luxury cruise ship s/s "Cap Arcona". On the early morning of May 4th nearly the entire number of the 2,800 prisoners aboard the freighter m/v "Tielbek" jumped overboard into the icy waters and attempted to swim to the nearby shore.

But of the few who managed to reach the shore most were gunned down by the "Volkssturm" on orders of the SS. That same afternoon, the "Cap Arcona" and the rest of the anchored ships were bombed and sunk by English bombers thinking that the German military were trying to escape. Of the 10,000 aboard the ships, less than 2,000 survived, that one day before the war ended

Two weeks earlier American Thunderbolts strafed a column of the white busses with red crosses of the Swedish Red Cross evacuating the survivors of the Ravensbrück concentration camp to Sweden.

64. Liberated

Suddenly, we heard bombs exploding near us, while we were at lunch. We ran outside and waved wildly our white bed sheets and pillow covers. We quickly raised a white sheet on the farm's tall flagpole. We watched the bombs drop slowly from the airplanes. It was the first time that we could actually see the individual bombs come down. The fighter planes flew low over us and we could see the pilots and we just waved with all the enthusiasm we could gather.

Later in the afternoon, we heard a low rumbling engine noise in the distance, getting louder and louder. More bombers? The noise grew louder and then we recognized the clatter and clanging of tank treads. A tank column appeared over the bump in the road and then, one by one, they disappeared again in among the trees to reappear again on their way into Wolfratshausen.

We wanted to go and greet our liberators and wanted to run down to the town. But Stirnweis did not let us go. He wanted us to wait another day because he expected that there would still be some pockets of resistance in the area. It dampened our excitement but we had to agree with his judgment.

Shortly after, we saw Stirnweis take the road, dressed in civilian clothes, to the town to report to the Americans and to advise them of our whereabouts and situation.

Stirnweis[88] had kept his promise he made to us on Christmas Eve. He looked relieved when he returned, two hours later.

The Americans had instructed him to stay with us until they would be able to find us a new temporary shelter.

That evening, we sat around and speculated as to how soon we would be repatriated. Maybe as soon as tomorrow?

---

[88] The Lagerälteste, the spokes person at the time for our Dutch women prisoners, and a few more of our ex-prisoners, testified at his trial. They brought up his occasional attempts of compassion and his help to avoid further harm on the death march. All charges were dropped.

195

The Polish women began singing their national anthem, the Mazurka. It started with just a few voices that swelled to a chorus of the nearly 250 Polish women in the barn. And atAt the end you could hear from all corners the shouts of *"Niech żyje Polska", "Long Live Poland", "Lang Leve Polen!", "Vive Pologne!"*

Next were the Yugoslavs with their Freedom Fighter's battle song. The half dozen Belgian women sang the "Brabançonne" in French and Flemish. We then sang the "Wilhelmus". The one Française, Marcelle[89], sang with gusto her "Marseillaise". Quiet fell over the barn, but with all the excitement of the day, most us stayed awake contemplating what might be in store for us in our newfound freedom.

May 1st. Tuesday morning, a number of us set out for Wolfratshausen. An overnight snowfall had left a thin cover of snow on the countryside. The white flag still fluttered from the steeple of the St. Andreas church. *We were free!*

All over the town, we ran into small groups of men prisoners from Dachau. A few of our women told us of running into a couple of French prisoners of war who offered to trade their bread for sex. We succeeded to obtain MP guards from the American command, to be posted at the Walser Hof. The Americans initiated a curfew to give us some more protection after dark.

Our liberators were the 12th infantry regiment of the 4th Infantry Division of the U.S. 7th Army.[90] One of the first things the Americans did for us was to order food and shoes for us from the local middle class.

All 450 of us women were resettled from the Walser Hof near Wolfratshausen to the nearby former forced labor camp "Föhrenwald" on May 4th. The camp had served as quarters for laborers in nearby IG Farben ammunition plants. It consisted of individual wooden buildings with a dormitory for fourteen persons and a dayroom, showers and the buildings were heated with a large wood stove.

---

[90] Just a few days later the 12th Infantry Regiment was relieved by the 101st Airborne Division commanded by Major General Maxwell Taylor.

On Sunday, May 6th, we had our first opportunity to attend a regular church service again, since we were taken prisoners. We went as a group into the Evangelical Christian St. Michaels Church. The reverend Georg Weber officiated. He thanked God that his church had escaped the damages of the war. The charges that had been laid by the retreating Germans under the old stone bridge across the Loisach River, next to the church, had not harmed the church. The bridge on the other side of town, over the Isar River, had been completely destroyed.

Pastor Weber, in his sermon that Sunday, talked about "Ankunft der feindlichen Panzerspitzen". (Arrival of the enemy forward tank column). So, here we were, in a church with our brothers and sisters of the same Faith, but with a distinct difference of opinion of who our enemy happened to be.
Pastor Weber announced that Sunday that there would be Holy Communion on Ascension Day. The next Thursday, May 10. We asked him if we would be able to receive communion with them.
I will never forget that day. The church bells were allowed to be rung again after a five-year silence. One freed Dachau prisoner, still in his striped prison garb, a walking skeleton, moved unsteadily to the communion table with us.
An American army chaplain, William R. Van Slyke, from Hamilton N.Y., came regularly to the Walser Hof to conduct a service with us. With his assistant, they carried a portable organ in a foot locker. We were told that this instrument had travelled with them in the same Jeep from North Africa along their hazardous journey. Our Roman Catholic sisters were visited and brought communion by a Roman Catholic Polish-American chaplain.

65. Dick's Diary. Free at Last!

May 1st. I had expected that the war would be over by now, this has not happened yet, but it cannot be far away. As it turns out Rennie has been liberated[91] before we are, I feel a lot better about her having been liberated by the Americans than the Russians.

May 2nd. Hitler is dead. This has been announced officially. His successor is General Donitz. We are not sure what this means.

Today food drops were made by allied planes over Schiphol. The population came out from everywhere to see this. Schools emptied out. The boys with their school class and Lien also came to see it from atop the dike that surrounds the south of Amsterdam. They waved with bed sheets and flags. Many were filled with emotion and tears of joy and relief ran down their faces.

May 5th A day we will never forget. Yesterday evening the news reached us that the German army had capitulated here in the Western part of Holland. Dick Alberts was one of the first to hear it on his radio. He opened the windows in the back of his 4th floor apartment that faces the back of our block and yelled to the top of his voice:

"We are Free!"

Windows started opening up everywhere and the Dutch flags were brought out.

This morning it became official.

The milkman, de Ridder, gave out American and English flags along his door to door delivery route.

I went to work as usual. It was very emotional. The whole city is celebrating. It is difficult to realize that the war is now over and that we will no longer be trampled on. When I rode past the Weteringschans fresh flowers lay on the spot where just a few weeks a number of men were executed, the tears welled up in my eyes; and so it went all day. There was little to do in the office, not a single customer showed up.

This will always be a special date from now on; I was liberated a year ago from Weteringschans prison.

---

[91] Dick van Ommen still thinks his wife is in Ravensbrück, which has then been liberated by the Russians.

This evening we went to listen to Radio Orange in the Rijnstraat, a radio was placed in an open window and a large crowd had gathered around; suddenly everyone started running; a German army truck came down the street and chased everyone away, all in panic but no one was hurt.

May 7th. At 12.30 this afternoon we heard: "There are the Canadians". We all ran out to watch this. And sure enough, there were the first tanks, a small forward contingent. They were greeted with enormous enthusiasm; they were being showered with flowers.

The Dam square had filled with a jubilant crowd in the afternoon, all of a sudden, shots were fired by Germans into the crowd, people panicked and a number of people were killed.

The NBS[92] (Netherland Home Guard) got into the fight. It is incredible how many NBS men have come out of nowhere and all are well armed.

The shooting on the Dam Square May 7th

---

[92] The Germans were provoked by the Dutch auxiliary, who were armed against strict orders to wait for the Canadians to disarm the Germans. 22 persons were killed and 119 wounded.

May 8th. Jan rode on one of the Canadian Army vehicles on their way into the city.

It is a slow long parade and the route from the Berlage Bridge, across the Amstel is lined with people welcoming the troops and handing them flowers. What a great bunch of men these soldiers are.

May 10th. It is exactly twelve years ago that I married Schützhaftlinge (prisoner) Rennie de Vries. I am sure that this day will also stir up many emotions with her.

What a contrast on this day between now and then. Fortunately, the future is not as bleak as it was until just very recently and we will be able to be reunited with our loved one.

I can hardly wait. We have had twelve wonderful years together and now I realize this even more after the fourteen-month separation. May the Lord grant us that we will be able to celebrate our 12 ½ year wedding anniversary this year together.

Today is Ascension Day. I did not go to church. I have been baking pancakes on the emergency stove. There is no bread. The food supply is still very critical.

I attended a special thanksgiving service at the Luther Chapel. The minister used a text from Isaiah 14 verse 16:

Is this the man that made the earth to tremble, that did shake kingdoms?
The Dutch and English anthems were played and later the organist played the American and Canadian national anthems.

May 23rd. This is a day with Good News: "Thank God, Rennie has been freed".

Hinke (sister-in-law) came to bring this news to me from Beverwijk. A woman, Kek IJzerdraat, who lives in IJmuiden stopped by at Hinke and Jan's home in Beverwijk to tell them how they had been liberated by the Americans on April 28. Rennie looked well and she had joined up, with a couple other women, with the Americans, in order to arrive home faster. Good idea. I can just imagine seeing her show up in the next days dressed in an American uniform.... This woman did not look very well, as far as her clothing goes. She had a very bad trip here from Germany.

What wonderful news!

66. Grünwald

An American Army Jeep stopped by. Sergeant Nathan Asch and his driver Claude Farmer attached to the American War Press were looking for two women who would be willing to work in the kitchen for the war press Headquarters in nearby Grünwald. They were looking for women who knew English.

Suzy van Hall[93] suggested they talk to me since I had some experience as Blockälteste with the operation of feeding the women in the mess hall. Nel Niemantsverdriet also liked the idea. Nel and I had been friends for a while.

We have remained friends over the years and see each other regularly. Nel grew up on a truck farm and still lives in Barendrecht, south of Rotterdam.

We worked ten days for the Americans and then were flown from Munich to Holland in the war press plane. We arrived close to the same day as the rest of our companions who had been repatriated through Switzerland by train.

We worked with two young Latvian women in the kitchen. There was now plenty of food for us to eat. In those ten days we gained back much of what we had lost in weight and strength in captivity.

The War Press had taken over the large home of the Erik Lindner family in Grünwald, the rear garden bordered on the Isar River. The twenty-two men of the War Press contingent were under the command of Colonel Max Boyd, his next in command was Major (later Lieutenant Colonel) Jay Vessels, Air Corps Public Relations Officer. Claude Farmer was the driver and Don Jordan the cook. The names I remember of some of the journalists were Nathan Asch, whose father is Sholem Asch author of "The Nazarene", Harry Cowe, Charley Green, Art Everett (Bay City, Mi.) and Paul Zimmer (Oakland, Ca.). Their task was to photograph and document the horrors of the Holocaust in Dachau and surroundings.

---

[93] Suzy van Hall was a close friend of Gerrit van der Veen and was arrested with him after the botched-up attempt to free Henk Dienske from the Weteringschans Prison on May 2nd, 1944.

They also accompanied visiting V.I.P.'s from America and elsewhere who came to take a look for themselves at the still fresh tracks of the Holocaust. The visitors were usually from the U.S. military, Government representatives and a number of Hollywood movie personalities. One of them was Willy Wyler, the director of "Ben Hur", "Roman Holiday" and "Funny Girl".

Our son Jack immigrated to the United States in 1957 and met Harry Cowe in Seattle in the nineties. Harry was eighteen when I knew him in Grünwald.

Harry still remembered our short stay and they exchanged photos that each had of Nel and me. Jack also corresponded and talked on the phone with Charley Green in St. Paul.

Harry Cowe worked for many years as a reporter for the Seattle Times. Jay Vessels became the City Editor for the Minneapolis Star Tribune, after the war.

Major Vessels third from left, Rennie and Nel and three journalists

Most of these men had come up together from North Africa through Italy. Ernie Pyle, the wellknown war correspondent, and Bill Mauldin the cartoonist of "Willie and Joe", often were part of this war press contingent.

202

L.R. Nel, Harry Cowe, Rennie, Nathan Asch

The first thing we did was to get rid of the prison rags, the coats with the large orange cross painted on it and our prison numbers sewn on them. We found a sewing machine in the basement and used checkered tablecloths and curtain material to sew blouses and skirts. For the very first time, since we left our homes, we got to sleep in a real bed with clean sheets.

A group of the war correspondents had gone to take a look at Himmler's estate in Schönau, not far from Hitler's "Eagles Nest" in Berchtesgaden. They came back with souvenirs taken from Himmler's home. They shared a few items out of their booty with us. I brought back to Holland two Delft Blue candlesticks and for each of the twins a boy's navy uniform and for Lientje a Dirndl dress.

Because the roads were still impassable in many stretches because of bomb craters and blown up bridges, the men used a single engine plane for the longer distances.

On their return, they would make a few low passes over the house to alert Don Farmer to come and get them with the jeep from the nearby airport.

On one occasion, they passed over just a little too low and pruned the crown off one of our Spruce trees.

Nel and I got permission to go see our left behind comrades in Dachau. It was a beautiful spring day. We borrowed two men's bicycles from the soldiers, which they probably had also "borrowed" as victory spoils from the locals.

Major Jay Vessels in the cockpit

We had a lot to catch up on with the ten that were still in the Dachau camp hospital. They were liberated by the Americans on April 29

One of the ten had always been known to us as Gonda but on that last day in the AGFA Kommando she was one of the five who revealed to us the fact that she was a Jewess.
I had to get used to calling her Betty Trompetter. Betty was still very weak, and Jo Goos had stayed with her to look after her.

We brought them up to date as to what had transpired since they waved us out on April 27 and about the repatriation of the other women. When we got back to our bicycles one of the bikes was gone. Nel tried to carry me on the back of her bike but that did not go too well. Just after we had switched places, a U.S. military vehicle stopped to ask us how they could find the American War Press headquarters. I offered to ride along with them and this way I managed to get back in time to cook dinner for the troops.

Flying home from Munich with the War Press plane

67. Going Home

The 22nd of May was the long-expected date. We had completed our "contract" and the Americans had managed to find a couple more Russian women to take our places.

They wanted us to stay longer but they also understood that we were anxious to get back home to our families. We were paid in Dollars.

Nathan Asch accompanied us in the War Press single engine plane together with the two pilots.

Nel and I had never flown in an airplane. It all looked so peaceful from the air, the Alps, the Black Forest then we followed the Rhine for a while. The German cities lay in ruins. We crossed the German border over Belgium and soon Nel was calling out in her Rotterdam dialect: "I see Dordrecht" and next her home "I see Barendrecht!"

The airport closest to Rotterdam, Waalhaven, turned out to be plowed under by the Germans and we were then directed to land at Ockenburg, near The Hague. Our plane damaged its tail wheel on the rough landing strip.

The Canadians lent our pilots one of their planes to fly to Paris and had the American plane repaired when the three some returned the next day.

After we had said goodbye to Nathan Asch and the pilots, we were interrogated by a couple of young men in blue overalls and BS (civil guard) armbands. They suspected that we had worked for the Germans. After many dumb and demeaning questions and a long wait they finally let us alone after they stole our cigarettes and chocolates, the Americans had given us. After all the insults and shameful treatment, we had suffered at the hands of our Nazi enemy, we were totally unprepared for what awaited us here on our arrival. They then turned us over to the Canadians in The Hague. There we had to tell our story again to Dutchmen from the Irene Brigade[94]. We came very close to spending the night once again in a Dutch prison but, in the end, they brought us to a Roman Catholic hospital to sleep on the floor again, with the nuns as our hosts.

The public transportation system was still in shambles and Nel decided to first come with me to Amsterdam before going south to her home in Barendrecht.

My husband had just received word of my expected home coming that morning, on May 23rd. Kek IJzerdraat had delivered the news on her way home to IJmuiden at my brother's home in Beverwijk.

---

[94] Irene Brigade was a military unit formed in England of Dutchmen who had fled from Holland.

68. The journey home of my camp companions

On My 7th a group of our American heroes and a small group of Frenchmen from General Leclerc's division came to celebrate the official end of the Second World War, the Germans had capitulated. We had little to offer our guests other than the few things that we had received the day before in our Swiss Red Cross parcels. The G.I.'s brought wine they had taken from Hitler's "Eagles Nest" in Berchtesgaden and all sorts of delicious snacks. Our stomachs were not accustomed to these delicacies any longer and we suffered for it the next day.

The Dutch women sang their national anthem the "Wilhelmus" and the Americans sang their "Stars and Stripes". It was very emotional. So much had happened in the last few days and now it was now official that they all had survived but both the soldiers and the liberated had lost comrades and loved ones.

Nel and I left in the next days for Grünwald.

Everyone was anxious to return home. Once again, they went through another registration and this time a doctor checked their condition. The doctor shared with the women the horrible discoveries he had made in the last days. Not far from the camp, they had found a stalled freight train convoy. The doors had been nailed shut, when breaking the doors open, they found the wagons filled with corpses of prisoners. The surrounding woods were full of abandoned Death March victims. Many were close to dying, for many their freedom had come too late.

On May 14[th,] a long line of white trucks from the Swiss Red Cross showed up to take the Dutch, Belgian and French women on their first part of the long-awaited return to their homes. The trucks took them to Sankt Margarethen, just across the German Swiss border where they were transferred into passenger trains. They were greeted all along the way in the stations where the train stopped.

On May 19, they reached Brussels, via Bern, Geneva, Lyon and Metz. Here they were met by a representative of the Dutch Red Cross and given some spending money to go into town. But the ladies discovered that the Belgian shop keepers did not want to take any money when they found out that the women were returning political prisoners.

The Belgians and the Dutch representatives treated them as returning heroes for two days.

They learned that the situation in the West of Holland was only slowly recovering from the German occupation. Food was still very scarce and public transportation was still in shambles. Officially the Western provinces were still not open for travelers to come into from the eastern provinces.

On May 21, the women arrived by train in Oudenbosch just over the Belgian-Dutch border.

In sharp contrast to the reception the women had in Switzerland, France and Belgium, they were confronted in their home country with sneers like:

"Another train load of NAZI whores!"

So, their welcome back in Holland was no better than the experience Nel and I had. We had become used to be called all kinds of names by the Aufseherinnen. But to hear it in our own language was a new low.

A few of the brave defied the travel restrictions to the Western provinces and hitch-hiked home from Oudenbosch. The three companions who had also worked for my boss, Henk Dienske, made it home in different fashions. Kek IJzerdraat hitchhiked back to IJmuiden on May 22nd and stopped, to announce my imminent arrival, in Beverwijk, at my brother's home. Nel Hillers stayed with a family in Oudenbosch until May 31 and made her way home to arrive in de Van Breestraat on June 2nd. Tiny Boosman caught a ride in a Canadian army truck to Apeldoorn, which had already been liberated in early April. She had developed pulmonary edema and tuberculous arthritis in the concentration camps. Tiny had managed to hide her condition through the health checkpoint for fear that she would be kept for treatment along the evacuation route. Her uncle in Apeldoorn, the director of a local hospital, arranged for transport back to Amsterdam. Tiny stayed until the end of 1947 in a Swiss sanatorium where she was nursed back from the abuses of her twelve-month imprisonment.

69. Home at last

Dick was not back from work yet when Nel and I arrived in the Alblasstraat.

We went to get Lientje from her school; I was a day late for her 11th birthday. Next, we walked to the Dr. de Moorschool to pick up Jaap and Jan from their second-grade class.

I'll never forget this day. How grateful I was to be reunited with them.

The news of my return ran from house to house in our neighborhood. Flags were flown all through our street and the Griftstraat neighbors, which we faced from the back of our apartment, flew their flags from the rear of their homes towards our side. They came to bring flowers and "welcome back" greetings from everywhere. The neighborhood association "de Pomp" delivered a beautiful basket with Hydrangeas.

I had contemplated this moment for thirteen months and had attempted to imagine what it would be like.

The first call I made was on the neighbors across the streets, Johan and Jo Dienske, the parents of my boss, Henk Dienske. The last day I saw them was April 4th of the previous year when they were arrested together with Dick.

They shared with me the sad news that Henk had lost his life in a satellite camp of the notorious Neuengamme concentration camp.

They were happy for me that I had survived but I found it very difficult to find the right words of comfort to offer them. Henk was a deeply religious man and we know that he has earned the crown of the Promise. He gave his all, in saving others from the hands of the Nazis. The American government awarded him with the Medal of Freedom with the Bronze Palm. On June 2nd, 1971, Yad Vashem bestowed on him the title of "Righteous Among The Nations".

After all the block parties and memorial services, we slowly settled back to our pre-war lives.

The nightmares of our ordeal came to visit us for many years. For some more than others. At the reunions, we held regularly, particularly in the first years after our return, we could share our experiences with one another.

In the world, outside of the survivors, it was nearly impossible to share what we had experienced, the horrors and the camaraderie.

The old routines came back. The milkman made his daily rounds through our neighborhood. From far away I heard the approaching garbage truck by the sound of the wooden rattle of the front man marching ahead of the garbage truck to make sure everyone had placed the garbage can on the curb[95]. The one-armed trumpet player came again every Wednesday through the streets. He had a limited repertoire; he played it well, like Jeremiah Clarke's "Trumpet Voluntary" and the Triumph March from Verdi's Aïda. Here and there windows were raised and the one-armed musician would catch a couple coins folded in a piece of news paper.

Our Pastor from the Waalkerk, Dr. Kunst, asked me to participate in a special thanksgiving service commemorating the end of the war, on June 6[th,] 1945. I chose as the title of my contribution: "The Bible in the Concentration Camp". I was pleased and honored that I was given the opportunity to share how my companions and I had so clearly experienced the power of God's love and protection.

The school board of the Dr. de Moorschool, the Christian elementary school the twins attended, asked me to become a board member. I enjoyed this function for the next ten years.

Otto Frank, Anne Frank's father, was a regular customer of the bank branch where Dick worked. Frank's business was a few blocks away from the Amsterdamsche Bank branch on the Damrak, in the center of Amsterdam. Otto Frank gave Dick one of the very first copies, in 1947, of the "The Diary of Anne Frank" with Frank's dedication written in it.

Pa passed away on April 21, 1947 at age 70. This was a great loss for me and our family and his friends. I lost a very dear father from whom I had learned so much and to whom I had always looked up. My praying father. It was a great comfort for all to know that he had carefully plotted and stayed his course to reach the safe Harbor that is promised to him.

---

[95] The Stuyvesant Dutch used this same wooden rattle P.A. system in New Amsterdam as a firealarm.

70. The three Arendts in occupied Germany

Rennie, Georg and Gerard were living in Kellenhusen at war's end.

The entire infrastructure lay in ruins. *Rennie* had very little food to put on the table for the boys and herself. The shops were empty the entire water distribution system had to be rebuilt. They did not escape the feared infectious diseases that ran rampant, like typhus, dysentery.

They received a letter from *Rennie*'s father. The letter had taken months to get to them. He wrote that he knew a Dutchman who worked for the British Intelligence in Wilhelmshaven and that he should be able to be of assistance to them.

Georg had already found a job working as a "Dispatch Rider" for the British on an army bicycle. Besides the pay he received he was also able to get some decent meals in their mess them halls.

The Dutchman in Wilhelmshaven arranged papers that classified them as DP's (Displaced Persons).

On December 3rd, 1945, they packed their few belongings together and locked the door on the apartment in Kellenhusen and got on their way to Wilhelmshaven; a distance of about hundred miles. Little did they know that this journey would take them nearly two months. They hitched rides on British military vehicles, rode in cattle cars. They reached Hamburg, about 50 miles from where they started, just before Christmas. They found temporary shelter in a still standing apartment house, a "Hochbunker", in the Arnoldstrasse in Hamburg-Altona. This is where the three Arendts celebrated their Christmas. *Rennie* made daily trips to the Hamburg train station trying to buy tickets for a train to Wilhelmshaven.

After several weeks of coming back empty handed, they finally boarded a train to Bremen. There was no heat in the train, every seat was taken, the boys had to stand in the corridors. Because of the heavily damaged tracks, the train often had to slow to a crawl.

Uncle Jentje and nephew Georg Arendt at "Hoffwerk" in 1951

71. Starting a new life in Wilhelmshaven

There was no teacher training course available, like the one Georg had interrupted in Holstein. He chose to attend a liberal arts college and studied visual arts; taking courses in drawing, painting and art history for the next four years.

He found employment as a stage designer in Wilhelms-haven. He received praise in the arts critic columns of local newspapers like the Nordwestdeutsche Rundschau for his contributions to theater performances with titles like ""die Tolle Lola", "Rumpelstilchen" and "der Fussbalkönig".

Inszenierung.   Bühnenbild:

Otto Payer

Georg Arendt de Vries

1949

BÜHNENSCHAFFENDE KÜNSTLER
Wilhelmshaven
Geschäftsstelle Mellumstr. 12

Gerard started high school in 1947 at the "Humanistisches Gymnasium".

The reconstruction of war torn Germany was getting in full swing.

A large part of the male population, especially in *Rennie*'s age group, was killed off in the war or had come back from the battlefields or out of bombing raids crippled for life.

Women were left with little to choose from. *Rennie* Arendt has never remarried. With the help of her father and her record that she had never been guilty of helping the enemy in the persecution of Dutchmen, she managed to get documents to enter the Netherlands and to visit her parents in Hilversum.

Her mother, my Aunt Grada, passed away from the damage done by diabetes in February 1951. She was buried in the family crypt on the Noorder cemetery.

Adri, *Rennie*'s younger sister who had committed suicide in 1943, was reburied in the same family grave after the war from the one she had been buried in by the SS.

I saw my cousin *Rennie* at this funeral for the first time since before the war. The contacts between the family of Pa's brothers and sisters had never been very close; in comparison to the closer relationships with the families from Moe's side. This might have had to do with the fact that we were the only ones from Pa's side who belonged to the Reformed Church. Uncle Jentje and his family were Dutch Reformed like his mother and all Pa's sisters. His sisters, Gepke and Jantje both lived nearby in Utrecht.

Georg was confirmed in the Heppenser Evangelical Church in Wilhelmshaven in 1948. Georg moved to Düsseldorf in 1952 where he had found work in his trade.

Rennie and Gerard moved shortly after to nearby Cologne.

Uncle Jentje sold his rest home "Hoffwerk" on Bosweg 13 in Hilversum for Fl. 26,020 in 1953. A good part of his large antiques collection was sold in auction. *Rennie* took a part of it and had it stored for years in a warehouse in Cologne.

Jentje died in 1954 of throat cancer, just short of his 76th birthday. He had been cared for in his last year in the revalidation center operated by his niece Hanna van der Meer in "Huize Klimop" in Oegstgeest. Georg was then twenty-four and Gerard was nineteen. I saw them again on the occasion of the funeral of their grandfather. Georg had become, just like his father, a handsome young man.

72. What have I learned from it?

The following thoughts I put down in most part shortly after the end of the war.

It is now many years since that time but the question keeps coming back why is it that I so often long for those moments in the Dachau period. In the place where we were living in this cold room where it was nearly impossible to keep the floors clean because there was no water or cleaning materials.

Where our bed consisted of a wooden frame with a paper sack filled with wood shavings that would always end up in hard clumps, with two cotton blankets that gave hardly any protection against the harsh winters cold, where your wooden shoes served to elevate your mattress for a headrest.

I know why: it was that special feeling…. Because we were a Community of Saints. But there must be more to it. Because why could we not have a Community of Saints here, right now, in Amsterdam. We are a Christian family, we go to church every Sunday, and we go to Communion.

I know that we are missing something. But what exactly? Is it because we are in a rut? Is it because we don't just reach for the Bible, like we did in the concentration camps, because of a need? I think that here lies the answer. We do not have enough time. We do not hunger for God's Word. We do not know what is in store for us and our children.

One thing is for sure, he will never forsake us.

My attention was once caught on Revelations 3 verse 8, where the apostle John writes to the church in Philadelphia:

"I know thy works: behold, I have set before thee an open door, and no man can shut it: for thou hast a little strength, and hast kept my word, and hast not denied my name".

See, if God listens to you in this way then there is nothing and no one to stand between us.

For this reason, I would like to suggest to you to read your Bible and have your children attend their Bible classes. This might sound too pretentious to you but I have learned that whatever you learned by heart not even the cruelest oppressor can take away from you.

Between the young women amongst us we have been able to reconstruct many parts of the Heidelberg catechism from what they had learned by heart.

Since we only had my one New Testament, our German co-workers in the AGFA plant lent us a Bible and we translated and transcribed many parts of the Old Testament, like the Psalms and the book of Isaiah. This way we had an opportunity to use these parts of the Old Testament in our Sunday services besides just the ones from my New Testament.

I am writing this in 1950, in Holy Week, and I would like to conclude these thoughts with the closing words in my "sermon" in Dachau, just days before our liberation, on Good Friday:

"The risen Lord Jesus Christ was first seen by women,
by women who had knelt at the foot of the Cross".

73. **Widowed**

Dick passed away in March 1956 from heart failure. He was fifty-seven. All three children were still living at home, the boys had just turned nineteen and Karolien was twenty-one.

Dick van Ommen

Shortly after his death I wrote the following:

"It was later than we thought....

I married a committed Christian. This meant that all his evenings were spent on church and political committees, with the occasional exception when there was a birthday party.

When the children were young we would spend the Saturday evenings together and Sunday afternoons we all would go for a long walk. But when the children grew up they went their own way and Dick started using the Saturday evenings to attend more meetings and the Sunday afternoon to rest from a busy week.

Late in the evening I would search for his hand and then he was all mine. We talked about later....when he would retire!

Then suddenly, on his way to another meeting, came the first warning. But his work ethic did not allow him to take the next day off. The following evening, again on his way to a meeting, it happened again. He reminded me the next day in the hospital: "remember to telephone, there is a commission meeting this evening".

Those three weeks in the hospital we acted as if we were engaged again.

Then he died, unexpectedly.

I received the grace to be able to accept it and I was even a little relieved for <u>him</u> that it happened so suddenly. He was just simply a child of God.

All that I now have to look forward to is my "old age". When I mention their father, the children avoid the subject. Father is in Heaven, Finished. On the surface, little appears to have changed. Except that I can no longer find his hand.

Now our first child got married.

Her husband is not that "committed".

And then I think: maybe just as well......"

74. My German cousin in the post war years

The post war years were hard for *Rennie.*
Georg married Margit in 1956. They had a daughter Christina in 1957, son Hubert Matthias in 1959 and Cornelius Christoph in 1963. Georg was working as a film technician in the Apollo Theater, one of Europe's largest cinemas with seated 3,600 and another theater in Düsseldorf, the Schadow Theater. Later, he started his own business. He called it "Kino-Speziell". He travelled in his van with his projection gear to company functions, garden parties and to camping grounds to project his movies.
Rennie took in boarding guests in two rooms of her apartment in Cologne, to make ends meet. Her boarders came mostly from the local art academy. She continued to have problems keeping the rooms rented and she complained frequently about the problems she encountered with the students. She also complained about the way Gerard treats her and about her desperate financial situation in her letters to Georg.
Gerard studied at the "Freie Universität" in Berlin and in the end earned a PhD in philosophy and language. After he earned his BA he came back to Cologne and according to the letters, made his mother's life miserable. *Rennie* had always favored Gerard because Georg reminded her too much of the man who had deserted her.
In one of her long letters to Georg, his mother explains that she cannot send the letter to him yet because she does not have money for the stamp.
On November 11, 1961, the feast day of Saint Martin, she writes six pages. She tells Georg and Margit that she has sent them a package without postage and hopes that they don't object to having to pay the postage. "I have to use thirty pfennig for the package that I promised and I could have made two phone calls for this amount to respond to two people who were looking for a room".
Rennie had been looking for part time work all week. She had to walk, with her cane, to the potential job openings because she could not afford to use her telephone. She applied for a cashier job at a local movie theater, an opening at a Woolworth store and she applied at an umbrella factory.

In several of her letters she brings up that she had to wash Gerard's sheets every day because he wet his bed until he was sixteen. Now he has the audacity to blame her for having neglected him.

She continued in her melancholic mood to write Georg about his grandfather, that he had told her, on his deathbed, that he had hardened his heart over the years and that he felt remorse for having smothered Beppe[96]'s spontaneity and that he had lost the trust of his family for his despotism.

In this same letter, she writes: "I am just as lonely as I was back on Christmas day in 1934, with just you, on the Dalweg in Hilversum. If I would still have the same revolver nothing would hold me back from it". She was then pregnant with Gerard who was born in May 1935.

She goes on: "Can you imagine Beppe going out looking for a job, or having to haul coals up from the basement? Even less so my father. I am deeply ashamed. But there is nothing I can do about it".

Rennie heard of a phone number for people in need: "SOS Menschenfreund" (People Friend) and she was givng it a try.

She made a visit to the local court to see if they can locate her ex husband to try and get support money. She is going to try and find his brothers, Paul who last lived in Krefeld and Bruno in Reidt.

In the last part of the letter she related a more positive experience. *Rennie* described what she saw on the feast day of Saint Martin. She saw mothers push their small children with their jack o' lanterns into stores while they stood outside ready with the bags for the treats the kids were to bring out. She overheard a mother ask her little boy: "Mehr het er disch nit jejouwe?" (Cologne dialect: "That's all he gave you?"). One mother stopped at the horse butcher with her child carrying a jack o'lantern in the shape of a pig. Only after the butcher's daughter got her to sing a St. Martin song did she get a slice of sausage. *Rennie* shows that somewhere she still has a sense of humor when she comments:

"Das war nett. He, ich wollt ich hätt'n Schluck Bier".

("That was fun, hey, I just wished I could have a drink of beer".)

---

[96] Frisian for grandmother

Medizin habe ich garnicht erst geholt.Muß ich ja doch nur selber be
zahlen.Laß sie sich doch kaputthusten,das alte Weib.bin doch nur zu
Last.Hatte Gerd auf einer Briefrückseite die ich ihm weiterschickte
geschrieben ich müsse ins Bett und bat ihn mir Kohlen zu holen....
Abends spät kam er und hat geschnissen mit den Schüttern und geflu

Muß mir also trotz Fieber meine Kohlen selber aus dem Keller schlep
pen.Wo ist denn da noch der Sinn für mein Dasein??????
Der Rhein ist mir zu kalt.Dreh ich Gas auf,explodiert der Ofen evtl
und ich reiß etliche mit.So geht das auf keinen Fall weiter.

Warte nun jede Minute auf Rausschmiß von Becker.Und hab so'n Durst.
Kann nichts mehr abnehmen für mich.

Wenn ich rausgeschmissen werde,habe keine Tauschwohnung mehr.

January 8, 1962, letter from *Rennie* Arendt- de Vries to her son Georg.

In a lamentation, she addressed to Georg in January 1962, she tells of how
she used the envelope cover of a letter that had come for Gerard to ask
him if he would bring up coals for her stove from the basement because
she is too sick to get up from her bed. Gerard came down cursing and
scolding her and she, still running a fever, had to drag herself down and
back from the basement with the coal scuttle. She asks herself what sense
there is in going on living this way: "The Rhine River is too cold, if I open
the gas stove, I risk an explosion that may take others down with me. I
cannot imagine that God will consider my suicide sinful. It is too much!"
She continues: "Gerd is so close by but he does not pay any attention to
me".

There were a couple of ads in the paper from people looking for a room
but: "if I go outside, I will be coughing even more and then I will hear Gerd
reacting with "Mein Gott!" and I have no money for a telephone call or a
stamp. It is useless. Poor and alone is bad enough but now also being
deserted while I lay sick in bed. But I must go out, I have to get dog food
for Isi. Gerd does not bring me anything he is afraid that I will ask him to fill
the coal bucket.

221

I do not want to go on like this anymore. Fever and heart ache. I am waiting for Becker (landlord) to throw me out at any minute. I cannot take this any longer. If I could have ever known this, that I would end up abandoned in this way".

Gerard Arendt published his thesis in 1965 with the title: *"Die satirische Struktur des mittelniederländischen Tierepos 'Van den vos Reynaerde'"*. (The satirical structure of the old Dutch animal fable „Reynard the fox".). Dr. Arendt became a professor at the Free University in Berlin, lecturing in the Dutch section of the language faculties. He did well. He married and had a son Ger(ar)d and a daughter Charlotte.

The two brothers Gerard and Georg had very little contact with each other. The professor lived in a nice large old home in Berlin South and he wanted to furnish the home with the antique furniture, from his grandfather, which his mother had put in storage in a garage in Cologne. *Rennie* had other plans for them.

One night the garage was broken into and emptied. She confronted Gerard with it but he denied it and broke off all contact with his Rhineland relatives. Georg, years later, had a reason to visit his brother in Berlin but Gerard would not let him in but he did recognize some of the missing antiques in the hallway.

Rennie Arendt-de Vries passed away at age 85 on February 2nd 1990, she was buried in Düsseldorf. As soon as Gerard heard about his mother's death he showed up from Berlin and wanted to get the rest of the antiques his mother had in her apartment. He talked his nephews in to let him have, amongst others, an old seamen's chest and a Louis XIV desk. He paid for their car rental to deliver them to him and promised them: "When I die it will all be yours anyway...."

The boys discovered one large room in their uncle's house that remained locked but they could peek through the key hole and see a room filled with antiques.

Was it a pure coincidence that the sly professor received his doctorate on a story about a Fox?

75. **In my later years**

Moe died in 1964 at 89.

Six of her seven (Ina died in 1950) children attended the funeral. She had then twenty-two grand children and already twelve great grandchildren. My dear Psalm singing mother joined the Angels choir.

We had held regular reunions with our old ex-political prisoner group until the early eighties but our ranks were rapidly depleting. I joined organized tours with the survivors to Ravensbrück, Dachau and even to the farm where we spent our first days of freedom, the Walser Hof in Wolfratshausen. The AGFA-Kommando ladies still have a yearly meeting in the Promenade Hotel in The Hague.

The last week of every January, we used to go to the commemoration service for the Auschwitz victims on the Oosterbegraafplaats (East Side Cemetery). In February was the annual laying of the wreath at the foot of the Longshoremen monument to commemorate the 1944 February general strike. In May, the annual Dachau day was held in Amersfoort.

My last official function was when I was one of the six women to lay the wreath at the dedication of the Ravensbrück monument in 1975 on the Museum Square in Amsterdam.

76. Have I done enough?

Have I done enough to promote God's Kingdom?
My neighbor down the street, Riek Brandenburg, was much more outspoken.
She would engage the Roman Catholic fishmonger in a discussion over the restricted use of the Bible in his Church. Mr. Hermans[97] Senior, a very religious man, organized meetings in the Albert Cuypstraat. I was asked to attend on one occasion, I do not recall exactly the reason, but I do remember that I went with some reluctance.
I could have done much more. Did I ever share my Faith with my neighbors? Sure, in the concentration camp, I did. There we had a wonderful community we closed the evening with a short discussion, bible texts, prayers and singing. At lunch break I would pull out my pocket size New Testament.
Our church, the Waalkerk, which had been consecrated a year before the twins were born, in 1936, was the second largest in Amsterdam with seating for 1,500. This soon turned out insufficient for the neighborhood and a second Sunday morning service was added.
I can remember that at times there was not even enough standing room left and boys and girls would find a spot to sit on the stairs leading up to the pulpit. Every Sunday morning just about everyone from our neighborhoods would stream in a long procession to their churches.
Across from us in the Alblasstraat and in the Bernissetraat our Roman Catholic neighbors also lived in a church cooperative building society apartment complex. We saw them walking to mass every Sunday to their Thomas van Aquino[98] church in de Rijnstraat.
The Waalkerk was imploded in 1989.
Do we have to be in the wilderness to hear God's voice? As I wrote earlier: *"Therefore, behold I will allure her, and will lead her into the wilderness and I will speak to her heart"*, Hosea 2:14.

---

[97]Jac. Hermans started his first self service market in our neighborhood, which grew to one of the largest supermarket chains in the Netherlands.
[98] The Roman Catholic Thomas van Aquino church was closed in 2002

This morning my thoughts drifted back to the winter in Dachau when I had managed to trade a pair of men shoes for the old shoes that were too small and hurting my feet.

I nearly danced down the factory steps while thinking: "I am a child of God, there is nothing to be afraid of!"

Occasionally doubts confront me. Just the other day a friend said to me: "I wished I could be sure that it is all for real".

I wanted to bring up a cliché. Am I really that convinced?

But then why did I sing this morning the familiar psalm 89 "Blessed are the people who know the joyful sound"?

Is this just because of the way I was raised? No, I don't think so: "I cannot live without you Lord, hold on to me"

It's time to draw the curtains, it is getting late. Another day went by and not much has happened but that is just fine with me.

Part Three:
Discoveries of the Mastmaker's Grandson

By Jack van Ommen

Jack van Ommen in 2009 at Alblasstraat 41

Mother died just after Christmas 1993. Then the questions, which I should have asked her earlier, started to crop up. The long search answered many questions but they also posed new ones, for which I hope to find more answers from readers. I maintain a web site for this: www.TheMastmakersDaughters.us

Many of the answers I found would have been of interest to our parents as well. Information has become more accessible through electronic information storage. Certain personal archives have only recently become available for viewing after the individuals in question have passed away.

226

77. Liberated, but peace is elusive for some

Most of the women, like Mother, returned to an existing home and family. But for many, after the long train ride, there was a new reality to deal with. Their fiancée, husband or father, who were also often in the Resistance, had not survived the war. Home-coming for many of her companions contrasted in many ways to those who found their families, relationships and homes as they had left them.

A few found that their men had betrayed their trust and entered into another relationship.

Free but widowed, separated or orphaned.

Many homes were destroyed in the southern and eastern parts of Holland where the invasion forces had faced strong German resistance.

Elli Scharp-Halberstad, for example, returned to find their stately old villa "Vogelsangh" in Groesbeek, near Arnhem, in ruins.

The groundwork was already laid in the last months of the war for an organization to assist the survivors of the political prisoners. It was known as the "Stichting 1940-1945" ("1940-1945 Foundation"). This became the organization through which most of the approximately 650 women, who were evacuated in September '44 from Vught to Ravensbrück, stayed in contact.

Through this foundation and the Dutch and German governments they, at last, were able to receive some financial compensations for the slave labor they were forced to perform. For the women with chronic physical and psychological disabilities, resulting from their ordeals, the foundation was able to obtain professional support.

The "Comité van Vrouwen uit Concentratiekampen en Gevangenissen" (Committee of Women survivors of Concentration Camps and Prisons) became an offshoot from this foundation.

The Cold War raged also among the ranks of their foundation members. The Dutch communist women had played a major role in the Resistance against the Nazi occupation. During the war, they had a common enemy but after the war their political objectives frequently clashed.

The communist members tried to use the meetings and functions for their pro Russian political propaganda. This caused many non-communist members to stop their support and reunion attendance.

Ravensbrück was part of the DDR, East Germany, until the fall of the Berlin wall in 1989, and any commemorations became platforms for Communists propaganda.

Mother and several others of the older members have tried to continue to keep the different political sections to work together, just as they had always done when they depended on each other's support. But in 1978 a group of the non-communists formed a new association, headed by Hettty Voûte, which became known as the "Nieuwe Kerk Meetings". This development caused another number of defections from the common bond they had behind the barbed wire.

78. What kind of women were they?

Looking at the photos of the reunions, you are looking at a very ordinary cross section of society. About half of the women in the AGFA Kommando were homemakers, like Mother. The rest earned a living as teachers, office clerks, waitresses, etc.

And just as they ended up in the Resistance without any fanfare, they also slipped back into their former roles in their neighborhoods or workplaces.

I do not recognize any Amazons in these pictures.

At war's end their ages ranged from eighteen to fifty-four, Mother was fourty-three, the average was slightly above thirty. Let us not forget the six or so members of "The Glue Club", of which Susy Tielemans and "Blond Tony" each managed to find passage to the United States by marrying GI's.

Reunion 1947   **Rennie van Ommen #20**

NR	NAME	NR	NAME	NR	NAME
1	Elly Scharp-Halbertsadt	19		37	
2	Mary Vaders	20	Renny van Ommen-de Vries	38	Annie Rijken-van Nierop
3	Tiny Boosman	21	Erna Tisch	39	la van Santen-Jensen
4	Ada van Keulen	22	Leni Leuvenberg	40	
5		23		41	
6	Grada Reiners-van Horen	24		42	
7	Aat Buys	25	Betty van der Horst Trompetter	43	
8	Elsje Groen-Grit	26	Adt Marbus-de Niet	44	
9		27		45	
10	Jo Vinke	28	J. Belkmeer-Wessel (Tante Han?)	46	
11		29		47	
12		30		48	Corry van Mook-Parijs
13	Lies Bueninck	31		49	Joukje Grandia-Smits
14	Mientje Houtman-Proost	32		50	Anje G. van Buuren
15	Leonie van Rooij-Overgoor	33		51	
16	Corrie Langelaan-Besseling	34	Nel Niemantsverdriet	52	
17	A.L. Koppert-Buma (Pommetje)	35		53	
18	Bertha Leegwater	36	J.N. (Jops) van Laar?	54	

There are a few women whose names you might recognize, as for example:

Corrie ten Boom

The evangelist from Haarlem who became well known, particularly in the United States, through her books and the movie "The Hiding Place".
She was one of the very few who were released before the war's end. Her older sister, Betsie, passed away in Ravensbrück just prior to her release. Mother told of watching these two sisters tirelessly spread the Good News from the time they arrived in Vught untill she left Ravensbrück in October 1944. They used mother's Old and New Testament Bible until she left Ravensbrück. Mother visited Corrie, after the war, in the rest home "Schapenduinen" she operated in Bloemendaal, near Haarlem. There are a number of <u>inaccuracies</u> in her book <u>"The Hiding Place".</u> It is possible that when the book was published, in 1971, these facts were not as easily verified as with today's access to the information. In the book's epilogue, the American ghost writers quote Corrie ten Boom that <u>all</u> the women of her age in Ravensbrück were gassed a week after her release on New Year's Eve 1944. The gas chambers at Ravensbrück were installed in February 1945.

Of the approximately 900 Dutch women who were imprisoned in Ravensbrück there are records of 136 women who died in the camp, of which 75 are known to have been Jews.
The unofficial estimates vary between a total of 162 and 200 Dutch women who died in the camp or on the Death March out of the camp at the end of April 1945. The vast majority of these women died from disease, physical abuse and malnutrition, not in the gas chambers.
Thousands of (non-Jewish) Dutch men have been executed, but very few Dutch female political prisoners.
Until shortly before war's end, it still took a quasi official sentence and the approval from Berlin for women to be sentenced to death.

Hitler's "Niedermachungsbefehl" (Order to kill) of July 1944 did away with any sentencing procedures for male "terrorists" and "saboteurs". They all became fair game for the Nazi executioners.
I only know of eleven[99] Dutch female political prisoners who were executed.

---

[99] Besides the four victims named: Grietje Dekker 5/1/'43, Cornelia van den Berg- van der Vlis 8/9/44, Mathilda (Tilly) Klingen 9/24/'44, Anda Kerkhoven 3/19/'45, Dinie Aikema 3/24/'45, Jonetta Terbborg-Elfrink 3/31/'45, Annick van Hardeveld 5/04/'45

The best known of these is Hannie Schaft who was gunned down by Maarten Kuiper, the Dutch traitor who arrested my father on April 4 1944 and he was also in the party that arrested the Anne Frank family on August 4, 1944.

The other three well known martyrs are Truus van Lier, Reina Prinsen Geerligs and Nel Hissink-van de Brink. Just like Hannie Schaft these three had done a man's job, and each had killed a number of the enemy. A female turncoat of their own communist CS-6 Resistance group betrayed them.

These three courageous women were sentenced to death and executed in camp Sachsenhausen, near Ravensbrück, on November 24, 1943. The parents of Reina Prinsen Geerligs visited Mother right after the war to know if she might have had some information of their last days. There are many more Dutch Resistance women who lost their lives in the concentration camps but they are not considered to have been executed. The other inaccuracy in Corrie ten Boom's book is where she reports that the day before the evacuation of Camp Vught, <u>700</u> of the male prisoners were executed.

The correct number is much lower. In the three days before the evacuation, <u>142</u> men were killed by the firing squads in Vught.

During its one-and-a-half-year existence there have been 329 men executed in this SS Concentration camp.

The total death toll of this camp stands at 749, including the executions. The majority of the remainder are Jews, men, women and children who died from disease, malnutrition and the abuse of the guards.

<u>Brecht van den Muijzenberg-Willemse</u>
Her stand on faith and politics had about as much in common with Mother as night and day. Yet they had a very good relationship and respect for each other. Brecht was an imposing personality and among her accomplishments were the leadership of our "Comité" of ex prisoners. She was elected to the Dutch House of Representatives as a member of the CPN (Dutch Communist Party) and held the post of minister of Education, Health and Public Welfare.

When the Russians brutally put down the Hungarian revolution in 1956 at a cost of 3,000 Hungarian lives, she stepped out of the CPN. Brecht used to tell Mother of this American who would come to visit her and offer her outrageous sums for a painting she owned.

In the end, she sold it in 1960 to the Amsterdam Municipal Museum which allowed her to buy a home in the countryside and live in comfort off an annuity she purchased with the rest of the proceeds.

Piet Mondriaan, whose paintings now are commanding prices of over ten million dollars, moved to the United States in 1941 and passed away in Manhattan in 1944. The painting was a wedding present for her 1922 marriage with another Dutch painter, Peter Alma, a friend of Mondriaan. Brecht became the owner of the painting in 1938 when she divorced Peter Alma.

When a number of voices went up for Brecht to step down as the head of our "Comité" because of her left leanings, Mother was one of her supporters who signed a "manifesto" to keep her as their spokeswoman. Some of the others who signed this act of support as well were Dr. Hebe Kohlbrugge, Jo Goos, Bep van der Kieft, Thea Boissevain and Geert van der Molen.

The wedding present from Piet Mondriaan, 20 x 24"
Photo: Stedelijk Museum.

Dr. Hebe Kohlbrugge

Known for her relentless efforts to breach the Iron Curtain to bring the Word of the Lord and assistance from the free European churches to the isolated East Bloc Christians. She undertook several very dangerous missions during the war, under the code name Christine Doorman, to bring critical information through the enemy lines to the British Intelligence.

She was caught, sentenced to ten-month prison time and transported to Ravensbrück with Mother from Vught and released there in January 1945.

Suzy van Hall

She was arrested in the aftermath of the first failed attempt to break into Weteringschans prison, on May 1st, 1944. The break in was led by Gerrit van der Veen one of the Amsterdam leaders of the armed section of the Resistance. This was the attempt to free, for one, Mother's boss Henk Dienske. My parents were both locked up in different wings of this prison on that fateful night and they remember the shooting, guard dogs barking and men running through the hallways.

Van der Veen was shot in the back on his escape but managed to reach a hideout on the Prinsengracht. Suzy van Hall who had worked closely with van der Veen treated his wounds at the hideout.

A Dutch traitor led the SD to the Prinsengracht address. Both Gerrit and Suzy were arrested on May 12.

In passing each other in a Weteringschans prison corridor Gerrit slipped his wedding band to Suzy. He was being led to his execution on June 10 with six other prisoners. Suzy went to look up Gerrit van der Veen's widow, on her return to Holland. Mrs. van der Veen noticed the ring on Suzy's hand; without saying a word, she laid her hand next to Suzy's hand with the matching wedding band. On her return to Holland from Dachau, Suzy learned of the death of her brother, Frits. He was murdered in Gleiwitz as a political prisoner on a Death March from Auschwitz, while being driven westward ahead of the advancing Russian troops. She had always been very close to him. Frits was a longtime friend of Gerrit van der Veen, both were sculptors. Their uncle Walraven van Hall set up an ingenious financing scheme to support the Resistance and earned the title: "Banker of the Resistance".

His brother, Gijs(bert), served as the mayor of Amsterdam in the late fifties.

In a letter to Mother, Suzy wrote shortly after the war:
"I wish that I had never come back".

Joukje Grandia-Smits

Joukje was the one who led the 1945 Easter Sunday service in Dachau. She was a committed Christian. Known under her code name "Clara". She was the first courier for the LO-LKP.

She was one of the first to realize the dangers of National Socialism and decided to resist it with all that she could bring to the fight.

She received a number of recognitions for her courage amongst them: Verzetsherdenkingskruis, Kruis van Erkentelijkheid van Nationaal Verbond, Belgische Oorlogskruis, Croix du Combattant de l'Europe and the War Medal of General Dwight D. Eisenhower.

This is but a small sampling of the women who gained a degree of recognition. Many of the women have, again, after their return from captivity, performed extra ordinary service to society.

79. Heroes and Traitors

Following is a background of the events that led to the arrests of my parents, Henk Dienske, three additional men and three women of the Dienske group. Many of these facts have only recently been uncovered, and it is reasonable to assume that our mother was never aware of them.

My search was particularly focused on the question of who the other players were from our neighborhood who had worked with Mother for Henk Dienske.

Henk Dienske, as leader of the Resistance in the province of Noord Holland, was working with hundreds of members in his particular group. It seems logical that, besides our mother, Dienske would have recruited others from the Waalkerk into his organization. However, other than the association with Pastor Kunst, Henk's brother-in-law Frits de Die, and Henk's parents, my search has not turned up any other members of the Waalkerk community who might have worked with him.

In September 2003, there was a reunion of my elementary school. The Dr. de Moorschool was closely associated with the Waalkerk. All of Henk's children attended this school, one daughter was in my class. I posed this question to his oldest daughter. She did not know any additional names, but she did tell me about the Dutch traitor, Sonja van Hesteren, and the trap she set for her father on April 20, 1944. In 2010 I searched the court documents of Sonja van Hesteren's trial for treason, hoping to find answers to my questions. No new names emerged from my search.

But I did learn some astonishing facts that shed some light on the circumstances surrounding the arrests of my mother and other members of her group. This new information, in all likelihood, has never been shared with those who survived the experience.

What information had prompted Friederich Viebahn, of the infamous SD in Amsterdam, to come and arrest our father on April 4, 1944?

Emil Rühl, second in command at the SD, while awaiting trial in Dutch custody, provided written testimony in July 1946 in the case against Sonja van Hesteren:

"I still recall some details of the following cases. Dienske under the name de Ridder was arrested on the Spui in Amsterdam around April 44. The home of the elder Dienskes had been pointed out for some time by arrestees where they had picked up large quantities of food ration cards, falsified identity cards, etc. I am unable to give you the names of the people who pointed us to the home of the (elder) Dienskes. The parents of Dienske were arrested because they apparently did not want to know who the person was who had been identified as de Ridder by the arrestees."

Rühl claims that they apparently came to the Alblasstraat with information from a person (or persons) arrested earlier. He makes it sound as if he or she might have been a courier. This is possible, but the source remains questionable.

How did they find out our last name, yet not know our street address?

Who was this 'van der Most' from the Deurlostraat, who was at the elder Dienskes home on April 4? He was locked up at the Weteringschans with our father and the parents of Henk Dienske, but then, strangely, he was never heard from again. Was he a stool pigeon?

Rühl also details in his van Hesteren written testimonies how, and from whom, he obtained the <u>identity of "de Ridder"</u>. This revelation came as a total shock to me. We all knew this person. None of my parents' contemporaries, knew how the SD had managed to identify "De Ridder". Rühl's source has, most likely, never shared its secret with anyone else, and has had to carry the millstone around the neck, of Henk's resulting death, to the grave.

The Rühl source still remains somewhat questionable, but I am unable to come up with a reason how revealing his source for obtaining Henk's identity could have benefitted him at the time. This person was still very much alive at the time Rühl recorded this.

Besides Rühl's testimony regarding the Dienske arrest his testimony contained also many details and names of other so-called "V-Männer" (Vertrauens=Confidence Men) and "V-Frauen", who collaborated with the enemy; a disgusting detail of the occupation that the Dutch would rather not be reminded of.

Once the SD knew that "de Ridder" was Henk Dienske, they enlisted Sonja van Hesteren who worked as a twenty-three-year-old SD translator/typist on the Euterpestraat. She engaged in undercover activities to help her bosses track down their prey. Dienske was hiding at his brother-in-law's address in the Waalstraat.

Sonja telephoned the Dienske home in the Dintelstraat on or around April 15, 1944. She identified herself as Corrie Wagenaar, the daughter of Gerben Wagenaar who was locked up in Amstelveenseweg prison. Gerben Wagenaar was the head of the Communist Party Resistance in Holland, with whom Henk Dienske's group frequently cooperated.

Sonja/Corrie told Mrs. Dienske that she had found a note in the dirty laundry from her dad, and that she needed to speak to Henk about it, urgently. Mrs. Dienske told Corrie (Sonja) that she would relay the message to her husband and to call back in a few days.

Henk knew that Gerben had a daughter named Corrie. When Sonja called back, an arrangement was made for them to meet on the twentieth at 2 p.m., on the Spui Square between two public telephone booths. Henk would be wearing a camel hair colored coat.

When Henk showed up at the meeting place, Emil Rühl, Friederich Viermann and two soldiers arrested him on the spot. Much has been written about the circumstances of his arrest.

Curiously, Henk arrived on his bicycle, his saddlebags loaded with contraband. Why did he not check with the Wagenaar home first? Why didn't he reconnoiter the meeting location beforehand?

One theory is that after remaining undiscovered for a length of time, some people develop a feeling of invincibility, a sense that "nothing can happen to me".

Henk Dienske ended up, via the Weteringschans, Amstelveenseweg, and Vught, in the notorious hellhole of Neuengamme concentration camp. He died from abuse, starvation and illness on February 16th, 1945 in the Helmstedt/Beëndorf satellite camp of Neuengamme. He was 38 years old.

One of the most detailed publications about the Dutch Resistance in the Second World War is titled: "Het Grote Gebod"[100]. ("The Great Commandment")

In "Het Grote Gebod" Dienske is described in this way:

"He was the steadfast Calvinist with unequalled energy as man and father. We saw him for the last time the day before he was arrested; his children were jumping up and down holding their dad's hands, happy, that they got to see their dad that day. They were on their way to the pancake house on the Weteringschans; on that very same street where the cell doors closed behind him a few days later.

A lone surviving Frenchman from Beëndorf recounted that they would often gather and read a Bible that the civilian salt mine workers had given to them. Together they had fought under the same flag, they suffered together, they prayed together and they read together of the Promise that is reserved for those who remain faithful to the end."

---

[100] Het Grote Gebod" author H. van Riesen

80. The SD headquarters in Amsterdam

There are several individuals associated with the SD (Sicherheits Dienst) who recur throughout the rest of this war story. In order to better understand the parts they played, I include a brief summary and explanation of the SD's role in Holland and who the chief players were in its Amsterdam district headquarters.

The Sicherheits Dienst was an amalgamation of the Nazi Secret Service and the Gestapo. Its national headquarters was in The Hague, and its operations extended to some five or six district offices in the major Dutch cities.

Amsterdam accounted for the lion's share of the SD's activities. The organization's primary function was to search out and arrest Jews, Resistance members, "political undesirables" and any other individuals deemed to be opponents of the Nazi regime.

Until the last eight months of the war, arrests of suspects were routinely followed by their imprisonment, interrogation, and eventually, by a summary court hearing during which the defendant's crimes were examined by the court. At the end of these proceedings, the defendants were sentenced by the presiding judge, or, in rare cases, they were acquitted.

These are the major players in the SD pertaining to this story:

Hans Albin Rauter, head of the SD Holland in The Hague.
The SD Headquarters in the Euterpestraat, Amsterdam:
Willy Lages, Kriminalrat, head of the Amsterdam HQ.
Emil Paul Franz Rühl, Sturmscharführer
Friederich Christian Viebahn, Staffelsturmscharführer
Hans Bruckmüller, Untersturmführer
Friederich Carl Ferdinand Viermann, Untersturmführer
Ernst Wehner, Untersturmführer
Herbert Ölschlägel, Untersturmführer
Maarten Kuiper, Sturmscharführer

Hans Albin Rauter was sentenced to death in the Nürnberg trials and executed after the war.

Willy Lages, known as one of the "Four of Breda", was sentenced to life, but set free in 1966.

Emil Rühl, second in charge under Lages, sentenced to eighteen years. He was convicted for, amongst others, three "Silbertanne" murders. He subjected many of his prisoners to extreme inhuman physical abuse.

Friederich Viebahn, also sentenced to eighteen years, found guilty of four Silbertanne murders and for his participation in nine executions. Dick van Ommen described him as "Fatso". Other victims described him as "Pig".

Hans Bruckmüller. Not much is known about him, he did participate in several of this book's arrests.

Friederich Viermann, sentenced to seven years, also took part in the random "Silbertanne" executions. He was a regular member of the posses that arrested NAZI 'enemies'. He frequently commanded executions.

Ernst Wehner, was killed by the Resistance in a firefight in March 1945. In retaliation, the SD executed 36 political prisoners.

Herbert Ölschlägel, was gunned down by the Resistance in October 1944. In retaliation, 29 Dutchmen were randomly executed on the same spot by the SD.

Maarten Kuiper, sentenced to death and executed on August 10, 1948. A Dutch traitor and vicious persecutor of his compatriots, Kuiper took part in the arrest of Dick van Ommen and the (Anne) Frank family. Kuiper is the same man who executed Hannie Schaft, a legendary heroine of the Dutch Resistance.

81. The Van Breestraat 155

This chapter is further background to the events that surrounded the arrest of Rennie van Ommen and Henk Dienske. My sources for this section of the narrative are primarily from Tiny Boosman, Bep Hillers (sister-in-law to Nel Hillers) and from the NIOD (Dutch Institute for War Documentation).

The Hillers family lived in the Van Breestraat 155, Amsterdam, "Old South", between the Vondelpark and the Concertgebouw. Jo Hillers, one of the daughters, was married to Jaap Dienske, the brother of Henk Dienske.

Jaap had already been arrested in 1943 when he was caught distributing the underground edition of "Trouw"[101] ("Faithful"). He spent most of his prison time in Amersfoort prison. His sister-in-law, Nel Hillers, worked as a courier for Henk Dienske.

On May 22nd and totally by coincidence, Nel walked into a trap while stopping in at the Barndesteeg. This was the address of the "Heil des Volks", a Christian organization that provided shelter and education to orphans and the homeless. The director of this organization was Frans Stroethoff. He was also involved in providing shelter and material support to the "onderduikers", Jews and men hiding from forced labor for the enemy.

The SD had arrested Stroethoff an hour before Nel walked through the door. They had left a couple of heavies behind to collect any additional Resistance members that might show up. Luck was on their side once again, when an unsuspecting Nel walked in. Next, they sent a posse to Nel's home in the Van Breestraat where they discovered a stash of falsified ID's, bogus ration coupons, and other contraband. Kek IJzerdraat, a young courier from IJmuiden, had made an appointment at this address to deliver two pistols to Jacobus Frencken and Albert Reulen, two LKP[102]men who had come from Limburg in the southeastern corner of Holland. One by one, all three were ushered in with loaded guns by the SD laying in wait at the Hillers' residence.

---

[101] "Trouw" started as a clandestine daily newspaper in the 2nd WW., still going strong today as a Protestant Christian national daily newspaper.

[102] LKP: Landelijke Knok Ploeg. The armed auxiliary of the LO, the national Resistance organization.

Kek IJzerdraat made a daring attempt to regain her freedom by pulling one of the two handguns she had strapped onin her bodypurse. The young Dutch Police collaborator, Evert Broenland, jumped across the table and knocked the pistol away.

Later in the day, Jan Eusman rang the doorbell. The twenty-four-year-old was working for "Trouw", the underground newspaper and he was also a member of the LO. When the door opened, Jan immediately sensed that something was wrong and ran from the scene.

Broenland and Ramaker, another Dutch traitor, chased after him and Broenland managed to put three bullets in his back. With his empty pistol, he attempted to knock him out. They then dragged him back into the Hillers' home. A neighbor, Sister Huisman, a nurse, bandaged his gunshot wounds, an ambulance drove him to the Wilhelmina Gasthuis hospital. Meanwhile, Kek IJzerdraat, the two Limburgers, Nel's parents, with her twenty-year-old brother Kees and her fourteen-year-old brother Loek were all taken to the Euterpestraat. The parents were held for two weeks and Kees for six weeks.

Afterwards, Nel's little brother, Loek, wrote about the experience. He had never witnessed so much action in a single day during his life: a total stranger pulling a gun, the Dutch traitor jumping across their table, the pursuit of Eusman and witnessing the sadistic abuse which followed. Loek wrote: "Eusman lay squirming and crying for his Tinie (wife's name), whom he'll never see again".

His account went on to identify an interpreter by the name Sonja (van Hesteren) who translated his interrogation for a "fat German" (Friederich Christian Viebahn, Staffelsturmscharführer). Loek was taken home later that evening where several SD men were still posted, waiting to intercept any additional unwary visitors.

Meanwhile, at the hospital, doctors managed to remove two of the three bullets from Jan Eusman's back. The third remains to this day in the back of his head. As it turned out, Jan's father had recently done some upholstery work in the hospital and knew his way around the building. Together with Johannes Post[103], disguised in borrowed white coats and stethoscopes they went to the bedside. A guard was stationed outside the door. Jan recognized his father's voice when he quietly asked him if he was able to walk. Jan nodded.

---

[103] Johannes Post. See page 186. Remembered as the leader of the Dutch resistance. Hearings after the second failed attempt to break into the Weteringschans prsion

Later that evening, they returned to the hospital wearing their doctor's disguise. Luckily, the guard had just left Jan's room for a smoke break, after the duty nurse had assured him that Eusman could not walk. Eusman senior helped his son up, and the two of them snuck out of the hospital through a back door.

They and the rest of the Eusman family disappeared into various safe houses provided by the Resistance. All of them managed to stay out of the enemy's clutches until war's end.

Jan Petrus Eusman February 10 2013[104] at 92 years

Later, Tiny Boosman received a phone call from an unidentified caller with the message: "Stroethoff is ill, pass the word". Tiny did not know that Nel Hillers, with whom she worked in the Dienske group, had already been arrested. She decided to stop by the Hillers home, on the 23rd, to check on her and, unfortunately for her, the SD reception committee was waiting.

Arie Touw was also arrested at the same address on the 23rd. He lived in de Van Alphenstraat. His daughter, Petra, told me that regular meetings were also held at their home with several Resistance members of the Henk Dienske group. She remembered these names: Eendebak, Jaap Dienske, Wim Speelman, Willy Pleijter, Jan de Pous and Greetje Itterzon. These last two were married in 1951A. De Pous was one of the early employees of the underground daily newspaper "Trouw". He and his, then, fiancée travelled to Chicago in 1947 where Jan studied economics under professor C.D. Edwards at Northwestern University. He became one of the youngest Dutch finance ministers at age 39, in 1959, and held a number of important government and labor relations posts.

---

[104] Born April 20, 1920 † March 14 2014

Arie Touw was released from Utrecht prison in August 1944.

The two Limburgers were executed on June 10, 1944 together with Gerrit van der Veen and his companions who was caught in the botched-up attempt to break in into the Weteringschans prison.[105]

Kek IJzerdraat and Nel Hillers both ended up in the same prisons and concentration camps as our mother.

The Dutch policeman and collaborator, Evert Broenland, was sentenced after the war to eighteen years in prison but released after serving only eleven years.

Since you will be reading more about Tiny Boosman and have already read about her since she arrived in Vught, the following is a brief history of her involvement. She was married as Ettina van Delft to Dick Boosman, a family practitioner. They had two sons, Paul who was fifteen at the time of her arrest, Dick was nine, and two daughters, Bep thirteen and Dieneke who turned seven, five days after her arrest. Because their home stood in the defense zone along the North Sea coast in Velzen, the Boosmans had to evacuate the area. They moved into a large, 19th century home in the den Texstraat. Their neighbors on both sides and across the street were Jews. At the request of these neighbors, the Boosmans hid several of the ceremonial vessels used in the Lekstraat synagogue until the war's end.

Tiny was responsible for the distribution of ration cards and false ID's in the eastern section of the city. She had been arrested earlier that month through the deceit of "Uncle Kees", but after lengthy interrogations, she was released. The week prior to her arrest, and with the help of Nel Hillers and Cor de Rooy, Tiny had managed to transport 10,000 ration coupons from the Alkmaar railway station to her home.

She accomplished this by sewing individual pouches to carry the coupons and using female couriers to transport them. The women tied the pouches to their thighs and with a strap around the waist they carried one pouch in the front and one in back. This way, they were able to carry the coupons under loose fitting clothing without attracting suspicion.

---

[105] Albert Reulen born in Maaswiel 1916 and Jacobus.P.B. Frencken from Roermond

82. Six Dienske Group members arrested

Tiny believed she had a good alibi for her visit to the Hillers' home. She told the SD that she had come to borrow a particular book from Nel. When the agents asked for the title, she told them, and they were able to find it on the bookshelf.

She was taken to a room in the Euterpestraat SD headquarters where Emil Rühl was waiting for her. He sat behind an imposing mahogany desk with his secretary, Sonja van Hesteren, at his side. In order to confirm Tiny's alibi, he called the prison and the authorities questioned Nel Hillers.

She told them that she had never heard of Tiny Boosman. Under most circumstances, this would have been the proper response; however, given Tiny's story, Rühl knew she was lying. He told her, "Also Sie lügen, Ich wusste Bescheid, Sie wissen bestimmt viel mehr, wir reden noch mit Ihnen". ("So, you are lying, I knew it all along, you surely know more, we'll talk some more")

Tiny was sent to Amstelveenseweg prison as well.

Two weeks later, on her way to another interrogation, Tiny passed Cor de Rooy, handcuffed, on the prison stairs. They both made sure to display no signs of recognizing each other.

Cor had been trapped by a phone call, probably made by one of the female traitors in the Euterpestraat secretarial pool. He was told that he needed to meet with Jan Eusman's father, in the Sportstraat. It was there that the SD arrested him.

With Henk Dienske and a substantial part of his organization behind bars, de Rooy, with the help of Wil Pleiter (alias 'Marian'), had stepped into the leadership vacuum.

Unfortunately, De Rooy was to suffer the same fate as Dienske. He managed to survive until his liberation from the camps, but died shortly after his return, a victim of the terrible physical and emotional abuse he suffered in the concentration camps.

In the meantime, Tiny Boosman had endured many interrogation sessions with Emil Rühl. But her interrogator was not getting anywhere. In frustration, he stuffed her in a small, dark closet for several hours, but she persisted in remaining silent. His next step was to lock her inside a small iron cage, in an isolation cell within the catacombs of the prison.

She was just barely able to stand upright. At night, a straw mattress was stuffed inside by the guard, but she found it impossible to sleep. The only convenience in the cage was a toilet bucket.

Now it was Viebahn (AKA "Fatso")'s turn to try out his skills on her. But he did not get anything out of her either.

Rühl came to fetch Tiny from her cell. On her way to the interrogation room, she told Rühl that she would not say a word unless they removed the Dutch typist. The woman's self-satisfied expressions while she was recording the interrogations drove Tiny nuts. Her statement took Rühl off guard, but he decided to take her to a different interrogation room, to be on the safe side. Apparently, Rühl had learned by now not to mess with her.

Tiny went on to explain to him why the woman had been getting on her nerves: "You (Rühl) are a German, and you are fighting for Germany. I am Dutch and I fight for Holland, so we are enemies. But this bitch is a traitor. I understand why you are using her, but I have a problem in understanding how a German officer can have any respect for these traitors."

At this point, Rühl got into a long tirade about Germany and the Führer, apparently forgetting why he had brought her here in the first place; also, that there were still a number of unresolved matters between them. He now became very polite, and when he had refocused on the business at hand, he soon discovered that she still refused to answer a number of his important questions. He shrugged his shoulders in frustration and told her that the court would have to deal with her from that point on.

Rühl did his best to cast himself in a friendlier light. They returned to the office where another of the typists recorded her testimony, or the lack of it. Tiny signed the report. This accomplished, Rühl rewarded her by telling her she could receive her husband or mother as a visitor. Tiny was told that the SD had already arrested the other members of her family, and Rühl's miscue was proof that this was a lie. She chose to see her husband, Dick. Rühl made good on his promise.

The following Saturday, before morning reveille, the cell door was thrown open: "Boosman, aufstehen und fertig machen, Sie haben Viertelstunde!" ("Boosman, get up and get ready, you have fifteen minutes").

Then, the door was slammed shut again. An hour later Tiny was led down the hallway.

When she entered the prison office, she saw Nel Hillers, Kek IJzerdraat, Stroethoff, Cor de Rooy and Arie Touw lined up against the wall. All of them were loaded into a paddy wagon with a few other prisoners. The driver then proceeded to Weteringschans prison and picked up two more handcuffed inmates before reaching his final destination at the Euterpestraat. Here, the prisoners were put into individual jail cells. The small barred cell door windows remained open while an SS guard paced back and forth in the prison corridor with his automatic rifle. When the guard would occasionally step out to chat with one of his fellow guards, the inmates made good use of the time, whispering messages down the line between cells.

After a short time, the prisoners were all rounded up again in the hallway. The men were chained to one another, and the entire group was marched to the Adema van Scheltema Square by an impressive security detail.

There, in a room on the upper floor of the police station, the entire group was ordered to face the wall. Two of the men along with Kek were led into a second room, but Kek returned after only a short while. The other two men remained there for some time, and the rest of the group could hear the thundering voices of the interrogators inside. Even though they were heavily guarded, members of the group managed to exchange messages with one another while the interrogation was going on.

After a long wait, they[106] were returned the way they had come, save for the two handcuffed men who had been interrogated. They learned later that the men had been taken away to be shot. That was the "Standgericht" (a kangaroo court).

From that day on, everyone expected that they would be next to stand before the "Standgericht". But nothing happened, and during the second week of July, the women were sent to the Vught concentration camp in the south of Holland, near the Belgian border; where Rennie van Ommen had already been sent in early June.

---

[106] These were the two Limburgers arrested in the van Breestraat.

83. Sonja van Hesteren

The State's Prosecutor in the case against Sonja van Hesteren called two witnesses on December 18, 1946. They were Mrs. Dienske, the widow of Henk Dienske, and Clary Smeenk, a victim of Sonja's collaborative efforts with the SD.

The prosecutor had access to a number of written statements from people who had known Sonja. One of these statements had been obtained from her former boss, Emil Rühl of the Amsterdam SD. At the time of his statement, Rühl was in custody awaiting sentencing. He was the same man who had interrogated my father and mother, Tiny Boosman and her two partners in crime.

The <u>first witness</u> against van Hesteren was Clary (Geertruida Jantina) Smeenk.

She became one of Sonja's unfortunate victims while a nurse at the Wilhelmina Gasthuis hospital in Amsterdam. She was twenty-five at the time. Smeenk was raised on a farm in De Krim in the Eastern part of Holland. Clary was married after the war to Bill Jongkind. Bill was born in Mexico to a Dutch father and American mother. Jongkind senior worked in Cuba and Mexico in the sugar cane industry in the thirties. The family moved back to Europe before the war and settled in Belgium where his son, Bill, joined the Resistance and eventually also became a political prisoner.

Clary had a cousin, Klarie Berghuis-Smeenk, who was also active in the Resistance. In 1943, Clary had been part of an unsuccessful attempt, to free several prisoners from Amstelveenseweg prison. Her involvement became known to the SD. They considered it too risky to barge into the hospital and arrest her because of the many exits and her familiarity with the building. They decided to set a trap for her instead. Clary did not take the bait on the SD's first attempt. She received a note in March 1944 from a certain Poldervaart who had been released from Amstelveenseweg prison. Supposedly, the note was given to him by a prisoner named Joep Heijdra. Clary had worked with Heijdra in a Resistance groupcell near Zaandam. A drawing of the prison floor plan accompanied the note along with a request to help him escape. Clary had a strange feeling about the request.

She knew that it was virtually impossible to penetrate the prison, and even more difficult to escape

As it turned out, Poldervaart was a traitor, he was later taken out by the Resistance in the Albert Cuypstraat.
The SD had been waiting at the prison for Clary to take the bait for a couple of weeks. Joep Heijdra was executed on February 23rd.

Viebahn ("Fatso") then devised a new plan. He had Sonja van Hesteren telephone the hospital. A nurse, Dora, took the message for Clary. It stated that a woman had called her, because she'd been given Clary's name by a young man she had met on the train who suggested that Clary might be able to help her. The young woman would be waiting for her that evening at 7.30 in de Eerste Helmerstraat, behind the hospital. She would be holding a bunch of daffodils. This time, Clary took the bait.

When they met, Sonja explained that she was looking for someone who could obtain a falsified identity card for her fiancée who had recently gone into hiding from the Germans. She asked Clary if she would identify herself, which she did. Convinced she had the right person, Sonja gave an agreed-upon signal, and Viebahn and Bruckmüller came out of their nearby hiding place and arrested them both. The next day, when Clary was brought in for her first interrogation, she realized the role Sonja had played, when she discovered her sitting in the room with a smirking grin on her face, recording the interrogation.

Clary Smeenk went through the same hell as our mother; interrogations, confinement, abuse, humiliation, and all at the same prisons and concentration camps. Thank God, she was able to survive Ravensbrück where she was finally liberated by the heroic efforts of the Swedish Red Cross in those last weeks before the war's end. This dangerous rescue mission was headed by Swedish Count Folke Bernadotte.[107]

Clary Jongkind- Smeenk passed away in 2008.
The second witness was Mrs. E.C. Dienske-de Die, the widow of Henk Dienske. The prosecutor demanded the death sentence for Sonja van Hesteren on December 30, 1946. She was sentenced on January 13, 1947 to twelve years. This was reduced to nine years by a royal pardon and ultimately, she served only eight years of her sentence.

---

[107] http://en.wikipedia.org/wiki/White_Buses

84. Sonja van Hesteren, the life of a traitor

She was twenty-four years old at the time of her trial. Blonde-, blue eyed, rosy cheeked, she could have been the perfect Dutch Arian poster child for Joseph Goebbels, the Third Reich's minister of propaganda.

Sonja was born in 1921 in Hengelo, a town in the east central part of Holland, shortly after the marriage of her parents Suze Hogendijk and Martinus van Hesteren. Her father had been married in 1908 to Maaike Blom and divorced her in 1920. Her mother was born in Surabaya, in the Dutch East Indies. Sonja's grandmother left her husband in Surabaya and returned to Holland with her daughter. Martinus was a con artist, and he was also suspected of bigamy. When Sonja was three years old, Martinus was on trial in Almelo court for a civil offense.

While pleading his case, he addressed the court as follows: "Your honorable judges and gentlemen of the court, I had a child that I loved as the apple of my eye. When I came home the other day she was waiting for me on the balcony, on the second floor. In horror, I saw that the balcony railing was collapsing. I cried, Sonja, Sonja! My little child screamed back, 'Daddy!' I ran to her, but it was too late. The child fell and lay dead at my feet". His voice was choked with emotion as he told this story, and the court was appropriately moved. When officials checked out his story, they discovered that the only part of his story he had not made up was that Martinus was the father of a little girl. He was sentenced to serve one and a half year in jail.

Sonja's parents divorced in 1925, but in the meantime, she had gained two little brothers. Shortly after the divorce they, and the grandmother, moved from Hengelo to Arnhem. The grandmother was partially blind and barely survived on a small pension. Mother van Hesteren earned her living by playing the church organ in the Walonian Church and teaching organ and piano lessons to school aged children. She spent most of her time away from her own children.

Sonja went to the public elementary school in the Parkstraat in Arnhem. She had to look after her brothers from a very young age, clean house and take care of her difficult grandmother.

Sonja's mother would show up for her meals, and then would be off again until all hours of the night. Sonja often begged her to spend an evening with them, but usually after only half an hour, the mother would be putting her coat back on.

There was never enough money. Sonja was often teased by her schoolmates for the tattered hand-me-downs she wore, often passed down from her mother's music students. Sonja missed school often due to frequent illness, she struggled to maintain passing grades, but she did manage to graduate from the Centrale ULO School.

When she was sixteen, Sonja joined the Evangelical Catholic youth group, "Orde van de Tafelronde", headed by the Apostolical Prefect, D.L. Thomas Tollenaar[108]. Each new member took the following oath: "To be chaste, to speak the truth, to correct one's mistakes and to follow the Lord".

Sonja's mother remarried in 1938 to J.F. de Vries Broekman. Her new stepdad was an editor at the Arnhemsche Courant, a daily Arnhem newspaper during the war years. The newspaper obediently published all the 'news' it was fed by the Nazi propaganda machine.

Soon after the wedding, Sonja and her parents moved to Amsterdam.The grandmother remained in Arnhem. Sonja's two brothers were sent to a boarding school in Amsterdam on the Binnenkant. Most of the children in the school came from parents who worked and lived aboard the cargo barges that sailed the coastal and inland waters of Holland.

Sonja's new stepdad paid for a secretarial course at the Schoevers institute. In 1938, when she was seventeen, Sonja started her first job with the postal service at Fl. 54 per month; paying her mother Fl. 17.50 per month for her room rent.

Her mother inevitably fell back into spending less and less time with Sonja at home. There were frequent quarrels between the couple, and Sonja escaped by spending more time with her cousin and her cousin's husband in the Okeghemerstraat 18. This was the Haarbosch couple.

---

[108] Tollenaar was consecrated bishop, in 1951, in the Old Catholic Church of the Saint Willibrordus church in Arnhem.

Sonja's cousin listened patiently to her complaints and provided her with the companionship she was not getting at home. The Haarbosch couple were members of the NSB, the Dutch Nazi party, and this is where the first seeds for her political future were planted. It was also during this time that she decided to join the Jungsturm, the Hitler Youth.

The Wallonian Church in Arnhem asked Sonja's mother to give a two-week series of organ recitals during the summer of 1940. Her mother was in no hurry to return home from Arnhem. When she returned a month later, she brought "Uncle Lex" with her, a man she had met after he was kicked out of his house by his wife. Sonja was told that she had to give up her room, because Uncle Lex was going to pay double the rent she had been paying. The situation became even tenser when 'Uncle Lex' attempted to molest Sonja.

In 1941, Sonja applied for a clerical position with the Versluys publishing firm. Her membership in the Hitler Youth was a deciding factor and enabled her to get the new job at a salary of Fl. 70 per month. Mrs. Haarbosch found her a room with neighbors who lived in the apartment building for Fl. 16 per month. Even so, Sonja was unable to live within her income and kept borrowing money from a number of her friends. One of the expensive habits she developed was a taste for fancy chocolates. Eventually, she also lost her new job because of frequent absenteeism. When Mrs. Haarbosch found out that Sonja was falling behind on rent payments to the Willems family, she read her the riot act. She also demanded an accounting of the people she owed money. Next, she arranged, through her party contacts, to find Sonja a better paying job as Hausraterfassung with Lippman, Rosenthal & Company in the Sarphatistraat for Fl. 120 per month. Mrs. Haarbosch paid off Sonja's debts with the stipulation that she would turn over every paycheck to control her spending habits. Her new employers were known locally as the "German Robbers Bank". Their business was to uncover Jewish bank accounts and possessions, and then clean them out before their owners were sent off to the gas chambers. Not surprisingly, the men from the SD in the Euterpestraat were frequent visitors at her "bank". As a rising star in her new job, she caught the attention of the SD crew. They offered her more money, and Sonja started work as a clerk typist in February 1943. Six months later, she was promoted to the "Sonderkommando" (Special Operations) under Willy Lages, and became Emil Rühl's assistant. She had bigger ambitions besides typing, translating and taking steno dictation.

What she really wanted was to assist her bosses in carrying out their sinister schemes.

An example of these activities, above and beyond her job description, was to accompany a younger SD operative acting as his girlfriend. The couple traveled on trains and other means of public transportation pretending to be completely absorbed in one another, while listening for conversations critical of the Hitler regime. She also attempted to infiltrate the Resistance.

Sonja told of an excursion she took with SD agent, Maarten Kuiper, in October 1943. The couple went to the café "Vlaming" on the Amstelveenseweg next to Saint Agnes church. Sonja's role was to welcome Kuiper as a good friend when he entered the establishment. When she welcomed Kuiper, two men suddenly bolted from the establishment. Maarten Kuiper chased after the men into the Lomanstraat, firing shots after them, but the two men escaped.

In September of that year, Sonja was sent out with Friederich Viermann to decoy as lovers in Kenau Park in Haarlem. This ruse was an attempt to capture Truus van Lier, but Van Lier never showed up. Truus had liquidated the much feared and hated Dutch NSB police commander Kerken, on September 3rd in Utrecht. Truus van Lier was later caught in a trap set by a member of her own Communist Resistance cell (CS-6) who had recently turned informer. Irma Seelig was a German Jewess who had been arrested and worked over by Herbert Oelschlägel of the SD in Amsterdam. In this manner, she was "converted" to betray her fellow CS-6 member.

Van Lier, Reina Prinsen Geerligs and Nel Hissink-van den Brink were also in the same Resistance group. They took part in armed Resistance activities and all three were captured by the Germans and sentenced to death. They were sent to the Sachsenhausen concentration camp for their execution. Herbert Oelschlägel was Willy Lages' Wunderkind. A handsome young man, he also possessed extraordinary skills at interrogation and in breaking down his victims. He brought in hundreds of victims to the Euterpestraat and was relentless in extracting information and 'confessions'. The Resistance circulated a warning that if you were ever caught by the SD, to avoid eye contact with Oelschlägel, because he used hypnosis as an effective tool.

One of his most damaging acts to the Dutch Resistance was to recruit Miep Oranje, code name 'Edith'. After her capture, Oelschlägel convinced her to work for the SD as a double agent. She was released from Scheveningen[109] prison, and then resumed work with the top leaders of the LO-LKP (the Dutch Resistance). She had access to their administration files, secret membership information, and she even travelled with key members of the Resistance. Hundreds of 'Edith's' compatriots were arrested, and many perished due to her treason.

Helena Kuipers-Rietberg became one of her best-known victims. She was known as "Aunt Riek" and "Mother of the Dutch Resistance". Helena was one of the very first women to become active against the Nazis, and her role in fighting oppression provided an inspiration to her people to join the underground war effort.

Rennie van Ommen met her in Vught, the week before they were packed into cattle cars and sent off to Ravensbrück. Helena Kuipers-Rietberg did not survive the hell of Ravensbrück.

After a 50-year search for Miep Oranje by the Dutch justice system the most likely result is that she was liquidated by the Dutch resistance just before war's end. There were persitant rumors that she had worked as a translator for the Americans in Germany, after the war, and that she had left for the Unites States with a high-ranking U.S. military officer. Oelschlägel was liquidated by the Resistance in October 1944, but his just reward came at a high price. In retaliation for his assassination, twenty-nine Dutchmen were executed at the exact spot where Oelschlägel was slain.

Sonja was four years old when her parents separated, but the bitterness between the couple endured. When her mother found out that Sonja had visited her father in February '43, she was furious. He had remarried Alida Schalij in 1929, who was also musically talented and who taught music at the local conservatory.

Just three months later, Sonja's father passed away. The grieving widow gave Sonja her father's personal effects along with his clothes. In return, Sonja sent the bill for funeral flowers she had ordered to the widow. Alida wrote a number of letters to Mrs. Haarbosch asking for the florist bill to be refunded and requested ten guilders in repayment for money she had loaned to Sonja.

---

[109] Coincidentally known as the "Oranje (Orange) Hotel"

Sonja began a short romance with Bob Klinge after a meeting in the Spring of 1943, but the relationship ended tragically. She met Klinge in a Gemeindschaftshaus (Wehrmacht social club). Unfortunately, he died a few months into their affair, and she later learned that he had taken his own life. Sonja spent much of her time off in the Gemeinschaftshaus, "Erika", in the Van Baarlestraat. She took most of her meals there in the company of her colleagues.

The head of the secretarial pool in the Euterpestraat was a German matron, Martha Winkler. Some of the other girls who worked in the pool were Nonnie Berlee, Maria Novis, Gustie Leijtens. Lina Thonus, Wilma Christiansen and (?) Hogenstein.Thea Hoogesteijn[110]. Of these, Sonja, Nonnie Berlee, Lina Thonus and Martha Winkler were the most fanatical collaborators. Nonnie Berlee once earned a special distinction. SD agents had been watching a home near their headquarters on the Euterpestraat where they suspected that meetings were being held by a Resistance group.

When they learned that the family in question was looking for a maid, Nonnie Berlee was told to apply. She secured the position. The idea was that she would spy on the occupants and determine whether meetings were in fact taking place. One night, Nonnie gave a signal to a squad of SD agents waiting outside. They arrested thirty Resistance members that day, thanks to her collaboration.

Berlee also served as the stenographer who recorded the fourteen-day non-stop interrogations of Koen Limpeg, a captured resistance fighter. She witnessed his merciless beatings.

Koen Limpeg was executed, along with eleven of his betrayed Resistance compatriots, in the Dunes of Hoogeveen. Limpeg had taken part in the spectacular and highly successful break-in and burglary of the Amsterdam Municipal Records. The only "Freundschaftshaus" that was still open after "Mad Tuesday" was the "Lydia" house, on Roelof Hart Square. Sonja joined the mass exodus from Amsterdam on September 17 in an attempt to escape what she suspected would be her judgment day.

---

[110] According the book: "Zwijgen over de Euterpestraat" by Jan Hopman, Thea is supposed to have assisted the Resistance, as Lages' personal assistant.

She fled via Zunderen and Bentheim across the border to Nordhorn in Germany. The Wehrmacht in Nordhorn gave her an administrative job. When the Germans managed to stop the advance of Allied liberation forces and following the defeat of the Allied airborne assault at Arnhem, Sonja returned to Holland.

She showed up in Amsterdam sometime in January '45 with her brother, Hans, who was stationed in Doetinchem as a Wehrmacht soldier.

However, she must not have had much confidence in the war's outcome, because she did not go back to her old job at the SD in Amsterdam. Instead, she started a similar job with the SD office in Oldenzaal, not far from the German border.

The Dutch Resistance posted a warning, in April, detailing the potential danger Sonja van Hesteren presented to the movement. It further warned: "She poses as a medical student under the names: Hélène Desbouviers, Jacqueline Rademakers, Eefje Mandemaker, Tonnie Verheul".

Sonja packed her suitcase again when Allied Forces regained their momentum. Always the consummate actress, she became the chambermaid to Gretl Pirelli, a popular Viennese songstress, known as the "Yodel Queen". Perelli performed all over Holland, Belgium, Germany and Austria and Sonja traveled with her. In her new job, Sonja earned Fl. 250 per month, along with free room and board and even a clothing allowance.

She was with Miss Perelli in Schönberg, Austria, when the American 7th Army took Munich without a fight. General Patton's men went on to liberate Dachau on April 29.

Hitler committed suicide the next day.

The Americans arrived in Schönberg on May 5th, the date of the World War II armistice. If we are to believe Sonja, she confessed her sins to the American command in Schönberg, they promptly gave her a job. Her minimal knowledge of English was a considerable asset in those days following the fighting and it went a long way for the Americans to remain ignorant of her traitorous past. She was employed in the Office of Strategic Services, 2677th Regiment, in Innsbruck. Later on, she worked for, of all places, the De-Nazification Office of the Public Safety Special Branch in Salzburg. It was near Christmas 1945, homesickness and the fact that the first wave of retaliatory actions in Holland had subsided, when Sonja decided to take her chances and return to her homeland. She crossed the border from Germany into Holland on Christmas Eve.

She was promptly arrested by the border control.

At her trial, the prosecutor asked for the death sentence, however, she received a prison sentence of only twelve years instead. She would serve just eight years.

After she was set free, she telephoned the widow of Henk Dienske, she identified herself: "Mrs. Dienske, can I come over and have a cup of coffee with you?" This was the last thing Mrs. Dienske wanted to do, whatever Sonja's intentions might have been, and her answer was: "No, thank you very much".

One wonders if she had wanted to share with the widow who had given in to her SD boss and revealed the real name of "de Ridder" back in April 1944. This person was still alive in 1955 and well known to Mrs. Dienske.

Sonja van Hesteren died in Dordrecht on January 24, 2002. She was eighty years old.

85. Epilogue

The Mastmaker business on the Polderdijk was closed down by van der Neut at the end of 2010. The buildings are purchased by the owners of the neighboring buildings, the former sail loft of M.F. de Vries, who will be adding the buildings to their n hotel in the former sail loft. The over a century old buildings will be restored to their original style and protected as a historical monument.

A sentimental visit from the U.S. West coast to the Polderdijk in 2010

In 2010, I managed to fulfill a dream[111] of mine, which was to moor my thirty-foot sailboat in front of the mastmakers shop.

---

[111] See: www.cometosea.us web site of of Jack van Ommen with reports on "Fleetwood" 's odyssey around the world.

257

The firm of Widow S.J. de Vries still exists even though the chandlery on the Singel was closed in 2000 by its 6th generation owner, Carol de Vries. Carol still wholesales from his upstairs Singel 2-A apartment. He continues a more than two-hundred-year-old family tradition started in 1805.

Rennie Arendt-de Vries' youngest son, Gerard Arendt, died during the August 2003 heat wave. Neighbors were alerted by the smell of the decomposing remains. Apparently, no one in his family had missed him. As you might have guessed, his nephews in Düsseldorf never saw any of the heirlooms back from Berlin.

Georg Arendt in 2003

My cousin, Georg Arendt, died in 2005, while I was sailing across the Pacific. I only became aware of our German cousins' existence in 1998 and met George for the first time in 2004. That Sunday, I attended church with Georg and his wife Heidi. The name of the church was, "Versöhnungs Kirche" which means, so very appropriate for this occasion, "Church of the Reconciliation". This reunion would have been difficult closer to the end of the war. I probably would not have appreciated seeing photos of him in his Hitlerjugend uniform, and I would have had little compassion for the hardships he and his family suffered just before war's end and right after.

But time heals, and we said, what turned out to be, our last farewell, both of us having regained a family member and a dear friend.

Photo taken in 1991. At Nel Niemantsverdriet's home, Nel left Mother on right. The two remained friends until their deaths. Nel passed away in 2001.

Rennie van Ommen-de Vries died between Christmas and New Year, 1993. She was 92 years old: 1901-1993, "My Mother's Century".

Her youngest sister, Rientje van den Boogaard-de Vries, the poet who wrote the "Polderdijk" at the beginning of this book, expressed it better than all that has been written in this story when she spoke this final farewell to her oldest sister:

"Afscheid"

t Is wonderlijk stil
nu de lijn is gebroken
waar langs jouw warme
liefde ons vond.

Ontstellend, zo stil,
het gesprek plots verbroken.
Géén gedicht of verhaal
uit jouw praat-gulle mond.

We zullen je missen,
dat deel van ons leven:
jouw waardevol "Zijn"
met beperking en al.

Je speelde het klaar,
Had nog zoveel te geven,
En nu, nu je zwijgt
het leeg worden zal.

Dit weet ik beslist:
Je wordt niet vergeten.
Te warm was je hart
Te helder je geest.

Je vertrouwen op God:
ons troost wel dit weten
maar hier rest slechts
weemoed
om wat is geweest

"Farewell"

It is miraculously still
now the line is broken
from where your
warmlove flowed

Eerily, so still
your words no longer spoken.
the prose or stories
no longer told.

We will miss you,
in the way we will live:
your precious "Being"
shortcomings and all.

You achieved many goals,
yet had much more to give.
there will be an emptiness
a silence will fall.

But this I do know:
the memories will hold.
Your hart was so warm
Your spirit so keen.

Your trust in the Lord:
leaves us consoled
but sadness remains
for all that has been.

86. Acknowledgements

First of all, I wish to acknowledge the two sources I was permitted to incorporate in the war story. The Boosman family for the memoir written by their mother, Tiny Boosman; secondly Piet Gerritsen the husband of Kiky Heinsius for the report she wrote of her experience in the three concentration camps. In addition, I received details on the members of the Dienske Resistance group from Bep Hillers-Alberts, the sister in law of Nel Hillers who was mother's roommate in Dachau. The daughter of Arie Touw, Petra Touw, provided me also with information and additional names of the Dienske group. Her father was one of the six arrested at the Hillers home. Beatrice Jongkind helped me with the part of the Sonja van Hesteren indictment. Her mother, Clary Smeenk, was one of Sonja's victims.

The Lemster Historical Society (Oudheidskamer De Lemmer) and the Frisian Maritime Museum (Friese Scheepvaartmuseum) in Sneek and the web site of Roelie Spanjaard-Visser www.spanvis.nl were a valuable source for Part One of the book.

My cousin Dick de Vries wrote a complete de Vries genealogy from the 17th century onward and Carol de Vries, the 6th generation mastmaker provided records of the mastmaker's history. My German cousin Georg Arendt and his son Hubert were my sources for parts about the second Mastmaker's Daughter, *Rennie* Arendt-de Vries.

The following volunteers have helped in editing: my daughter Jeannine McDonnell and granddaughter Corrine Spencer.

Friends: Michael St. John Smith, Pete Sabin, Ron Finholm, Mick Deines, Roberta DiLallo, Maggi Michels, Dick McKenzie, Rick Munden.

If I forgot anyone, I will correct this in the next revision.

Without your help, this story would have never been made public.

Thank you all very much!

Index of Persons Named in this book
Pages have moved several pages lower through frequent revisions

87. Contents

Made in the USA
Monee, IL
24 January 2024

52274301R00155